INDIGENOUS WOMEN'S WRITING AND THE CULTURAL STUDY OF LAW

In *Indigenous Women's Writing and the Cultural Study of Law*, Cheryl Suzack explores Indigenous women's writing in the post–civil rights period through close-reading analysis of major texts by Leslie Marmon Silko, Beatrice Culleton Mosionier, Louise Erdrich, and Winona LaDuke.

Working within a transnational framework that compares multiple tribal national contexts and U.S.–Canadian settler colonialism, Suzack sheds light on how these Indigenous writers use storytelling to engage in social justice activism by contesting discriminatory tribal membership codes, critiquing the dispossession of Indigenous women from their children, challenging dehumanizing blood quantum codes, and protesting colonial forms of land dispossession. Each chapter in this volume aligns a court case with a literary text to show how literature contributes to self-determination struggles. Situated at the intersections of critical race, Indigenous feminist, and social justice theories, *Indigenous Women's Writing and the Cultural Study of Law* crafts an Indigenous-feminist literary model in order to demonstrate how Indigenous women respond to the narrow vision of law by recuperating other relationships – to themselves, the land, the community, and the settler-nation.

CHERYL SUZACK is an associate professor of English and Indigenous Studies at the University of Toronto. She is a member of the Batchewana First Nation.

Indigenous Women's Writing and the Cultural Study of Law

CHERYL SUZACK

UNIVERSITY OF TORONTO PRESS
Toronto Buffalo London

© University of Toronto Press 2017
Toronto Buffalo London
www.utppublishing.com
Printed in Canada

ISBN 978-1-4426-5067-1 (cloth)   ISBN 978-1-4426-2858-8 (paper)

♾ Printed on acid-free, 100% post-consumer recycled paper with vegetable-based inks.

___

Library and Archives Canada Cataloguing in Publication

Suzack, Cheryl, author
Indigenous women's writing and the cultural study of law / Cheryl Suzack.

Includes bibliographical references and index.
ISBN 978-1-4426-5067-1 (hardcover). – ISBN 978-1-4426-2858-8 (softcover)

1. American literature – Indian authors – History and criticism.
2. American literature – Women authors – History and criticism.
3. Indian women – Legal status, laws, etc. – United States.
4. Law and literature – United States. 5. Indians in literature.
6. Women in literature. 7. Social justice in literature. I. Title.

PS153.I52S89 2017   810.9'897   C2017-900132-9

___

This book has been published with the help of a grant from the Federation for the Humanities and Social Sciences, through the Awards to Scholarly Publications Program, using funds provided by the Social Sciences and Humanities Research Council of Canada.

University of Toronto Press acknowledges the financial assistance to its publishing program of the Canada Council for the Arts and the Ontario Arts Council, an agency of the Government of Ontario.

Canada Council
for the Arts

Conseil des Arts
du Canada

ONTARIO ARTS COUNCIL
CONSEIL DES ARTS DE L'ONTARIO
an Ontario government agency
un organisme du gouvernement de l'Ontario

Funded by the
Government
of Canada

Financé par le
gouvernement
du Canada

Canada

For Jennifer and Katherine Shaw, with love, respect, and admiration

Contents

Acknowledgments

This book had a long genesis over several years of working with people to whom I owe a debt of gratitude for their professional support, intellectual generosity, and steadfast wisdom. To Jean Barman, Shari M. Huhndorf, and Jeanne Perreault with whom I worked closely to develop the Indigenous feminist framework that this book takes up, I offer my heartfelt thanks. That they have also become friends is a testament to the collegiality and generosity of spirit with which they engage in academic work. I was fortunate to test out the law and literature methodology that this book explores during my tenure at the University of Alberta, the University of Victoria, and the University of Toronto. For generous scholarly insights and stimulating intellectual conversations and debates, I thank Taiaiake Alfred, Karyn Ball, Ed Berry, Christopher Bracken, Jeff Corntassel, Rita Kaur Dhamoon, Christopher Douglas, Mo Engel, Len Findlay, Mary Elizabeth Leighton, Nima Naghibi, Daphne Read, Stephen Ross, Stephen Slemon, Lisa Surridge, Teresa Zackodnik, Jo-Ann Wallace, and Heather Zwicker. I am especially indebted to Jo-Ann Wallace for bringing to my attention the Association for the Study of Law, Culture, and the Humanities where I found an intellectual home. I met there and formed friendships with Ben Authers, Todd Butler, Maneesha Deckha, Valerie Karno, and Andrea Stone. The ASLCH also provided me with the tremendously rewarding opportunity to work with Matthew Anderson, Linda Meyer, Rebecca Johnson, and Austin Sarat. A move to the University of Toronto allowed me to pursue comparative research in Indigenous studies with vigour and insight. I am especially indebted to Alan Bewell, Jill Carter, Brian Corman, Denise Cruz, Jeannine DeLombard, Daniel Heath Justice, Greig Henderson, Jenny Kerber, Smaro Kamboureli, Victor Li,

Robert McGill, Heather Murray, Mary Nyquist, Simon Stern, and Karina Vernon for their friendship and support.

Generous funding from the Social Sciences and Research Council of Canada and the University of Toronto made possible the time necessary for research and writing. A visiting fellowship at the McGill Institute for the Study of Canada provided the opportunity to develop my research on transitional justice. I am grateful to Ingrid Bejerman, Suzanne Morton, and Will Straw for the warmth and hospitality they shared during my time there. I owe special thanks to Christine Bold, N. Bruce Duthu, Jeannine DeLombard, Shari Huhndorf, Simon Stern, and Pauline Wakeham for their intellectual engagement with this project. My research benefitted greatly from the assistance of Julia Boyd and Caleb Holden. The University of Toronto Press provided incisive anonymous peer review feedback from three reviewers who helped me to improve the book's focus and intellectual commitments. At the Press, I have been very fortunate to work under the superb editorial guidance of Siobhan McMenemy, Suzanne Rancourt, and Mark Thompson. My thanks to the University of Oklahoma Press for permission to reprint a portion of chapter 4 from *Reasoning Together* and to the reference librarians in law at the University of Alberta and the University of Toronto for their indispensable research help.

The support of family and friends has been essential to my professional life. I offer warm thanks to Mark, Jo, and Sam Knight, Ali and Cameron McIntosh, Andrew Munro, Clare Orchard, Brenda Roszell, Susan Sheard, and Norman Shaw for their support, generosity, and good humour. I am especially indebted to Neil McIntosh and Andrea Stone for unwavering love, support, friendship, and laughter. My daughters, Jennifer and Katherine Shaw, remain the most wonderful sources of joy, love, and inspiration. This book is dedicated to them.

INDIGENOUS WOMEN'S WRITING AND
THE CULTURAL STUDY OF LAW

Indigenous Women's Writing, Storytelling, and Law

Stories of "Yellow Woman," Leslie Marmon Silko's central mythological figure, run through Silko's short fiction and poetry to portray women's spiritual power and cultural authority. This figure inspires our admiration through her escapades that depict her remarkable capacity for adventure, sexual waywardness, and diversion. While participating in the most mundane and necessary of domestic tasks – gathering water by the stream ("Storytelling" 95) or walking by the river seeking solace from family demands ("Yellow Woman" 62) – she meets the "ka'tsina spirit and they go" (56). Sometimes she returns without incident to her husband "playing with the baby" and her mother "telling my grandmother how to fix the Jello-O" (62), her only regret being that she has to return and that "old Grandpa wasn't alive to hear my story because it was the Yellow Woman stories he liked to tell best" (62). In another adventure, she does not hide her reluctance quickly enough, invoking her husband's anger after he has travelled far with ceremony and purpose to recover her ("Cottonwood *Part Two: Buffalo Story*" 72). He kills her partly because she wishes to remain with "the Buffalo People" which through her death she rejoins (76), and partly for the spiritual and physical renewal of the community that her communion brings about to sustain the village (75). Other endings are more rueful: when her husband demands of her, "You better have a damn good story / ... about where you been for the past / ten months and how you explain these / twin baby boys" ("Storytelling" 95), she does not have such a story, and accepts the consequences: "My husband / left / after he heard the story / and moved back in with his mother. / It was my fault and / I don't blame him either. / I could have told / the story / better than I did" (98).

Silko's capacity to characterize Yellow Woman's adventures as both healing and harmful, restorative yet adverse, spiritually enabling but socially confining depicts the formative ambiguities that run through Indigenous women's writing to frame Indigenous women's identities as they intersect with their representation in cultural and social texts. Although these women writers imbue their narratives with humour and dignity, they also direct our attention to the negative side of socialized gender expectations and of Indigenous women's dismissal from political agency. Whereas Yellow Woman lives on in our imaginations as an eternal figure capable of renewal through her mythic properties, Silko depicts other women who are bound by conflicting forces that confine and silence them because of their empowering gender identities. The unnamed protagonist in "Storyteller" dramatizes this dilemma.

When she is imprisoned by legal authorities for the murder of a storekeeper who killed her parents, her lawyer refuses to believe that she is capable of planning and implementing this act of revenge which is also an act of healing undertaken to cleanse the land of the stain of her parents' deaths and the land's destruction from test drilling for oil (28). He states, "'It was an accident … That's all you have to say in court. That's all. And they will let you go home. Back to your village'" (31). She refuses: "'I will not change the story, not even to escape this place and go home. I intended that he die. The story must be told as it is'" (31). The story concludes with her physical imprisonment but spiritual reclamation, and we are left to ponder the dual implications of the protagonist's plight: incarcerated in prison (17) by non-Indigenous authorities yet claimed by the village as their honoured storyteller (32).[1]

Silko's symbolic portrayal of Indigenous women's activism in its cultural, spiritual, and political dimensions articulates a key issue raised by this writing in the post–civil rights period: how to account for legal practices that have devalued Indigenous women leading to their political marginalization and cultural disposability. This issue forms the central problem examined in this book. By aligning case law and literary texts, it shows how Indigenous women writers establish an emergent Indigenous feminist critical subject with which to engage legal events. *Indigenous Women's Writing and the Cultural Study of Law* has three objectives: to analyse how law and legal practices provide an essential context for understanding literary texts by Indigenous women writers, to provide new readings of their work by examining this literature within a historically situated framework determined in part by colonial law and legislation, and to trace the formation of an Indigenous feminist subject in cultural texts by Indigenous women writers from the post–civil rights era for whom law practices were especially formative. The "post–civil rights context" is cross-hatched by two intellectual directions that arose in response to 1960s civil rights activism which prompted a shift in cultural criticism during the 1980s by drawing more explicit links between critical theory and social practice: (1) the theoretical emphasis on intersectionality as an account of subject formation that recognizes that "self-identifications do not exist in isolation [but] derive their meaning from their relationships to other categorizations" (Bedolla 236), and (2) the abandonment of political reform as a "single-issue" struggle (Hunt 535). Intersectional identity politics and social justice movements mark out the evolving critical terrain within which this project is situated and out of which I develop a reading practice that explores how literary texts contribute to the recognition of Indigenous women's social and political agency. Law shapes the experiences of Indigenous peoples to a much greater degree than it does for any other minority group in Canada or the United States, and it is especially influential in the lives of Indigenous women. My aim is to demonstrate how the social and political contexts created by legal and legislative discourses constitute an important historical ground for reading cultural texts written by Indigenous women within the post–civil rights period.

Contemporary Indigenous women's writing participates in an established tradition of using literary texts to voice social justice and gender justice concerns.[2] From participating in land claims debates to seeking redress for past historical injustices, from portraying the devastation caused by Indian residential schooling to protesting the desecration of Indigenous lands, Indigenous women's writing depicts women's contributions to a range of community justice practices. Through their focus on these events, Indigenous women writers insist that literature has a socially responsible role to play in informing how we understand and make sense of these issues; their writing illustrates why gender identity matters to how we address these concerns. *Indigenous Women's Writing and the Cultural Study of Law* emphasizes the importance of women's knowledge claims to decolonization. By drawing attention to gender justice as an issue crucial to the survival of Indigenous peoples, this book foregrounds the relationship between literary texts and social activism, asserting that the knowledge claims embedded within Indigenous women's cultural practices are essential to conceptualizing Indigenous justice, and invoking interconnections between political, social, and cultural contexts and gender that are necessary to Indigenous peoples' future well-being. Gender justice activism by Indigenous women writers is paramount to the progressive formation of an Indigenous community's political, social, and cultural justice goals and to its realization of community decolonization.

The novels examined here – *Ceremony* by Leslie Marmon Silko, *In Search of April Raintree* by Beatrice Culleton Mosionier, *The Antelope Wife* by Louise Erdrich, and *Last Standing Woman* by Winona LaDuke – illustrate a strong commitment to demonstrating how colonial law and legislation limit Indigenous women's political, cultural, and social authority. Yet, they also establish how Indigenous women's identities and cultural knowledge are foundational to social reform. Untangling the formative ambiguities that Indigenous women's writing expresses – not only by engaging discourses of colonial law and patriarchal cultural practice, but also by delineating the emergent Indigenous feminist subject this writing constructs – represent an important objective undertaken by this book. These literary texts interrupt the partial view of Indigenous women's identities that legal texts engender, even as they demonstrate the contributions that gender identity makes to community empowerment and decolonization. How to tell these stories in such a way as to make explicit their impact on Indigenous women's lives represents a key problem that this book addresses.

To do so, it participates in a broad field of study that shows how comparative work in law and literature situates colonial law and legislation as a social and political project "'subjecting human conduct to the governance of rules'" (Hunt 540, citing Fuller 96). This comparative approach emphasizes that law and humanities criticism is not about denying the rhetorical accounts of social reality that either legal or literary studies undertake given their disciplinary specificities (Thomas 535), but rather it examines their contradictory understandings about society's social justice goals in ways that show how "literary works ... imaginatively reshape and transform them" (537).[3] Brook Thomas argues for a more concrete view of literature's engagement with law by insisting that literature "supplement[s] the law by generating the addition of new evidence rather than merely persuade[s] by appealing to already existing evidence or shared values" (538). Literature's supplemental form not only contests "monological version[s] of an official story that silences other voices"; it also emphasizes alternative accounts of social reality – "untold stor[ies]" – embedded within the social field, by drawing attention to voices that are committed to social change by seeking to "resolve the contradictions produced by a society's conflicting stories about justice" (538). These voices contribute new ways of understanding "the pressing legal issues of our time" (539). Social justice theorists have seized on this conceptual opening to argue for the possibilities of law and literature studies to alter and reform the ways in which we value both disciplines, and to reimagine the urgent political claims that each is called upon to address. Shoshana Felman proposes that because "legal meaning and literary meaning necessarily inform and displace each other" (*The Juridical Unconscious* 8), their study may signal new insights about how to conceptualize justice if, by "doing justice," we recognize "that there was something in the trial that [goes] ... beyond the jurisdiction of law" (Felman 155). Gregg Crane prioritizes the ground of the social as the site from which new innovations and progressive thinking may reconfigure law and literature studies through the adoption of an interdisciplinary framework for the interpretation of texts (769). Following Thomas, Felman, and Crane, this book uses the concepts of voice, identity, gender, and experience to develop a law and literature model that builds on these insights. Analysing court cases alongside literary texts to show the omissions that law practices enter into in "generating distinctively legal truth[s]" (Hunt 514), and exploring law's "tensions, closures, and contradictions" through which legal texts participate in "wider dynamics of power and dominant interests" (514), it reads case law in two ways: first, to show how law shapes an "extra-discursive reality" (514) that contributes to the devaluing of Indigenous women; and second, to establish a context within which to demonstrate this writing's literary social justice goals. By dialectically interrelating law and literature, this book explores how Indigenous women's writing expresses the political and social interconnections between law and literature, challenging the view that these disciplines occupy separate realms of cultural reality within our social world. Alan Hunt cautions that law has turned increasingly towards culture as the grounds for settling historical and contemporary legal disputes. It has done so, he argues, because "culture, in its infinite diversity and irreducibility, ensures the plasticity and relativity of the social" (530). Because law's reach into culture allows it to achieve a flexibility and recursive set of social effects that legal decisions cannot achieve in isolation, law participates in inscribing "unacknowledged aesthetic, psychological, historical, and cultural assumptions" (Sarat and Simon 24). My book examines legal assumptions to demonstrate the gender injustice denied by Anglo-American and Canadian law. It presents a comprehensive analysis of how legal assumptions have devalued Indigenous women by making them disposable to cultural practice and political struggle, and through this devaluing denied them physical, economic, and social benefits. Its social justice project provides alternative accounts of gender empowerment through literary texts as a crucial feature of tribal sovereignty and decolonization, countering precarious claims that sovereignty is gender neutral. Aligning literary texts with the cases to which they respond renders law accountable to social outcomes, which otherwise might not happen. In so doing, the literary is established as an important ground for an Indigenous feminist social justice practice from which to draw insights about how literature envisions Indigenous women's socio-political and cultural agency.

Indigenous Women's Writing and Social Justice

In the post–civil rights period Indigenous women writers have addressed legal subjects by practising many different forms of social and political activism, and they have expressed a heightened concern for Indigenous women's rights and the issues that affect Indigenous communities. Scholars have turned their attention to demonstrating how literary texts foreground Indigenous communities' social justice goals.[4] They have argued that legal mechanisms alone, through single-axis frameworks, are insufficient for understanding the link between current Indigenous issues and their implication in the colonial past. Stephanie Irlbacher-Fox notes, "Aboriginal justice ... focus[es] on symptoms of injustice rather than on substantively addressing injustice. One result of the assumption that injustice cannot be changed is that what can and must change are Indigenous peoples themselves" (33–4). Eric Cheyfitz argues that Indigenous justice is constrained by problems of political jurisdiction and "legal ambiguit[ies]" created "by the colonial situation" (226). He states that although "the Constitution is at once 'paramount' over ... tribes [in the United States]," in practice, "[Congressional plenary power] [is] diminished within [communities] in the tribes' relations to their members" (226). The hierarchical division of powers he observes "between the tribe's internal political autonomy and its external political dependency on the federal government" (226) creates a "colonial double bind" (233): Indigenous "sovereignty" exists in Western law both as a "pre-contact" state and as a product of Western legal discourse, yet it is deployed to "harmonize" ongoing political conflicts by incorporating Indigenous matters into the ambit of Western law, obscuring as symptomatic, rather than originary, the recognition of law as a hegemonic, political discourse formed within colonial systems that serve as a barrier to alternative accounts of Indigenous political authority and cultural practice.

Indigenous women's writing unmasks these legal realities concerning historical injustice. It addresses the relationship between tribal sovereignty and colonial intrusions by highlighting alternative systems of meaning-making in the mythological stories, local activism, and political struggles that Indigenous communities enact. Distancing itself from formal legal social justice, this writing critically engages law's gendered implications by underscoring how law alters community values and knowledge systems in ways that facilitate the political disempowerment of Indigenous women. Chapter 1 explores how Leslie Marmon Silko's novel *Ceremony* engages with the issues raised by the United States Supreme Court decision in *Santa Clara Pueblo v. Martinez*, a decision that upheld the Santa Clara Pueblo's right to disentitle from tribal membership the children of Indigenous women who married non-members. Assessing the gendered and social justice implications of this result, Silko's novel situates Indigenous women's experiences as important sources of knowledge in their framing of collective consciousness, spiritual resistance, and community empowerment. Characters such as Night Swan, Ts'eh, Thelma, and Corn Woman represent the mythological gender order within the Pueblo community that empowers the community against new forms of colonial attack brought about by colonial education and the breakdown of traditional kinship practices. By depicting Indigenous women's activism and storytelling as the foundations for social continuity and community reform, Silko demonstrates her awareness that legal texts use culture in ways that borrow from and revive negative connotations of Indigenous peoples to the detriment of Indigenous women. Her novel critiques colonial law practices to show law's capacity to reconfigure the cultural and thus contain Indigenous identities by eroding tribal sovereignty and obscuring community-centred Indigenous values relating to culture, history, gender identity, and land.

According to legal scholar N. Bruce Duthu, courts also enact negative characterizations of Indigenous communities through "frontier-era notions of inter-racial relations" (Duthu, *American Indians* 23). They do so by divesting communities of their sovereign authority through "backward-looking" and "frozen in time" formulations of tribal identity as it expresses Indigenous character (24). One of the most pernicious effects of legal discourse's construction of tribal character and identity is that these interpretations allow courts to characterize and dispossess

Indigenous peoples of their lands by applying this logic in destructive ways. When tribal lands are deemed too acculturated through non-Native development, non-Native trespass, or non-Native settlement, they are held to have lost their "Indian character" and consequently to no longer represent tribal sovereignty in its enduring cultural form (43). Through these characterizations, law-makers are authorized to open up these lands to further state and municipal intrusions. Court opinions, Duthu argues, negatively "'construct' images of Indians that comport with popular conceptions ... whether those images reflect reality or not" (84). "The significant difference," he observes, "is that judicial opinions have the force of law with the potential to unleash both protective and destructive effects in the lives of individuals and communities" (84). Responding to these incursions, Silko's novel illustrates how tribal sovereignty, gender identity, and the defence of land interconnect. Her novel configures Indigenous epistemologies as enduring capacities that express through kinship relations women's knowledge and experience as central to the protection and survival of both the community and the land.

Beatrice Culleton Mosionier's novel *In Search of April Raintree* also links Indigenous dispossession to matters of identity and land. Her novel examines the negative impact of gender identity represented by law's capacity to assess women's conduct leading to harms that Indigenous women and their children suffer from. Chapter 2 explores Mosionier's engagement with women's disempowerment through the overlapping effects of government policies and laws that render Indigenous women vulnerable. Mosionier's fictional autobiography foregrounds the issues of social isolation, poverty, and harm for children who were forced to attend residential schools, complicating the issue of Indigenous women's disposability in culture and community that Silko explores in *Ceremony*. *In Search of April Raintree* demonstrates how a lack of social and political power for Indigenous women leads to situations where they must choose between competing harms, either by protecting themselves from social vulnerability or protecting their children from violations to which they are exposed. The "penalty of choices" scenarios that Mosionier's novel portrays provide a counter-narrative to the Supreme Court of Canada's reasoning in *Racine v. Woods*, a case decided in the same year that Mosionier's novel was published and with which it shares intersecting concerns regarding the state's "out-adoption" of Indigenous children, and the priority of family and cultural identity in the life of an Indigenous child. Mosionier's novel proposes, contrary to the Supreme Court's view that a child's need for cultural background and heritage abates over time, that access to community is an essential element of Indigenous identity, playing a crucial role in providing security for Indigenous women. Her novel explores the issue of women's vulnerability by depicting how two "out-adopted" Indigenous sisters struggle to find community as they fend for themselves in society following their release from adoptive care.

Both *Ceremony* and *In Search of April Raintree* demonstrate that Indigenous women's security and connection to land represents a crucial Indigenous social justice matter. They also propose that legal mechanisms alone will not achieve the restorative recognition that Indigenous women demand. Instead, these novels insist that the social outcomes imposed by legal orders further assimilative government objectives by disavowing gender inequalities inherited from the past, and by obfuscating the role of the past in contemporary struggles. By pushing the origins of these issues as gender concerns central to the colonial situation into deeper political obscurity, law determines the scope of issues that it will address. Indigenous women's writing counters this narrow view by foregrounding the existence of alternative gender orders that we can access through literary texts in order to achieve social change. This writing makes apparent a "creative dialectic" (Delgado 2415) between law and literature that highlights the reality-creating potential in the interpretation of texts, and it establishes an alternative framework for reading practices that critical race scholars argue are necessary to overcome law's hegemonic, "[un]fair," and "[un]natural" scripting of the social world that "justif[ies] the world as it is" (2413).[5]

Storytelling for Change

Legal scholar Richard Delgado draws attention to the racialized implications of legal texts and observes that stories may provide alternative accounts of reality that contribute to the struggle for "racial reform" (2415).[6] Taking up Delgado's insight and employing an Indigenous-feminist lens, I develop a reading practice that genders critical race theory and explores the ways in which Indigenous women's writing illustrates the failure of legal decisions to account for race and gender inequalities. Through side-by-side readings of legal cases and literature that this book takes up, we are able to see more clearly the central role Indigenous women writers play in social and political activism, and we see, additionally, the significant contributions that literature can make in the assessment and interpretation of law.

The task confronting the critical race scholar concerned with gender relations is to show how legal stories influence our social reality. The cases that I examine here initiate gender disparities that are detrimental to the lives of Indigenous women – patriarchal tribal disenrolment and membership practices that negatively affect Indigenous women yet are upheld by the courts in *Santa Clara Pueblo v. Martinez* (1978), state-authorized out-adoption practices that justify the removal of an Indigenous child from her mother's care despite her efforts to reassert her legal custody in *Racine v. Woods* (1983), the colonial mismanagement of tribal lands and withering away of Indigenous land bases through the imposition of blood-quantum categories that contribute to women's social disempowerment in *State of Minnesota v. Zay Zah* (1977), and the denial of legal standing to land claims that rebuild community relations through alternative forms of collective organizing in *Manypenny v. United States* (1991). Storytelling for social change in ways that make explicit the impact of legal stories on Indigenous women's lives represents a key problem that this book addresses.

To take up this concern, I develop a reading practice informed by intersectional analysis and Indigenous feminism to examine the legal and literary representation of Indigenous women's identities in social texts through a number of co-constituting factors. These factors emphasize how identity is shaped by multiple sources of meaning-making – discourses of colonialism, practices of racialization, and systems of gender relations. These concrete sources of social power require examination because they represent lived social factors that influence the stories women tell about themselves. They thus matter to our understanding of the political and cultural conditions within which Indigenous women experience their lives.[7] Since its inception, Indigenous feminism has focused on women's storytelling as sources of knowledge about women's identities and their commitments to political struggle.[8] As a field, it aspires to an intersectional framework that not only conceptualizes social justice as a goal of community empowerment, but also explains how gender relations matter to Indigenous emancipation and tribal sovereignty practice.[9] Kathryn Shanley articulates an early approach to this problematic by arguing that social parity exists between tribal sovereignty and feminism. "Just as sovereignty cannot be granted but *must* be recognized as an inherent right to self-determination," she argues, "so Indian feminism must also be recognized as powerful in its own terms, in its own right" ("Thoughts on Indian Feminism" 215). Marie Anna Jaimes Guerrero insists that the grounds of Indigenous traditions are capable of righting the imbalance between sovereignty and gender in the "gender egalitarianism practiced by many Native societies" and in the "determined role responsibilities among all members through collective cultural practices and reciprocal kinship traditions" (Guerrero, "Patriarchal Colonialism" 63).[10] Patricia Monture-Angus emphasizes the incommensurability between sovereignty and feminism as an important critical standoff to advancing these debates. She questions feminism's capacity to explain her experiences of multiple discriminations based on race and gender, and protests against feminist demands that she "artificially separate [her] gender from [her] race and culture [which] forces [her] to deny the way [she] experience[s] the world" (178). "I do not consider my position to be anti-feminist," she states, "I just do not see feminism as removed from the colonial practices of this country" (177). The rhetorical framing of these issues that situate tribal sovereignty in opposition to gender empowerment figure a discursive impasse: tribal social justice projects and gender justice projects are either understood to be at odds with each other,[11] or tribal sovereignty is presumed to be more politically important because of its prior legal standing which gender empowerment has to take into account.[12]

Rather than assuming that tribal sovereignty projects are better equipped to address the gender concerns of Indigenous women, I situate tribal sovereignty and gender empowerment as co-constituting objectives of Indigenous women's literary activism; that is, I argue in chapters 3 and 4 that Indigenous women's writing empowers gender practices at the same time that it empowers tribal sovereignty.[13] An important line of argument I develop concerns showing how Indigenous women's writing and women's legal activism depict gender injustice as an infringement of tribal sovereignty through denials of women's dignity and human identity. Dignity-violating harms represent violations of selfhood that denigrate human identity in key ways: by making it "the target of stigmatization, humiliation, and the excuse for deprivation," which conveys the sense that individuals are unworthy of "basic human respect" (Reaume, "Discrimination and Dignity" 27, 35); by classifying it according to "the use of a characteristic [that identifies individuals] as part of a group that is devalued" (35); by using it to deny "access to benefits or opportunities available to others" because of the "false view" that such individuals are "less worthy" or "less capable of taking up those opportunities" (37); and by overlooking the way its "intersecting grounds" amplify a pre-existing "historical disadvantage" and expose an individual to "greater vulnerability" through factors that inform a person's selfhood, yet about which the individual can assert no alternative social view (Fyfe 20). Indigenous women's writing dignifies women by contesting the negative gendered outcomes of law and by establishing an emergent Indigenous feminist subject founded upon the affirmation of dignity as a principle of tribal sovereignty.

This writing also shows how the denial of dignity includes withholding support for women's socio-political agency and recognition of their experiences of restriction and harm. Chapter 1 focuses on the legal activism of Ms Julia Martinez to envision tribal membership as a dignity-based relation wherein each individual is accorded status based on individual self-worth, despite the denial by the courts of Ms Martinez's activism to secure this recognition. Silko's *Ceremony* critiques this legal consequence by proposing alternative forms of tribal enrolment in the ceremonial traditions of Indigenous women. Chapter 2 explores the subaltern legal status of Indigenous women in Canada in the context of the out-adoption of Indigenous children in order to propose connections between Indigenous feminism and transitional justice feminism. These connections demonstrate how to accord Indigenous women legal status in light of the erosion of their rights through colonial practices authorized by the state. Mosionier's *In Search of April Raintree* examines the social implications of out-adopting Indigenous children by making explicit the intergenerational effects of Indian residential school for successive generations of family members affected by these state practices that lead to women's social vulnerability and harm. Chapter 3 examines the gendered dynamics of land dispossession that intensify patterns of disempowerment for women through legally imposed forms of colonial governmentality that disrespect tribal traditions in relation to land and revive colonial hierarchies of mixed-blood and full-blood status. Erdrich's *The Antelope Wife* asserts women's kinship relations as alternative sources of Indigenous inheritance to counter law's social effects which lead to women's social isolation and impoverishment. Chapter 4 explores how "feminist indigenism" restores intertribal histories through literary-creative means to provide a foundation for new forms of collective Indigenous organizing and struggle. LaDuke's *Last Standing Woman* reimagines tribal self-determination through Indigenous women's coalitions as the foundation for political activism and the reconstitution of women's social authority.

My project's comparative literary-critical centre theorizes gender identity for Indigenous women to make explicit the contributions that Indigenous women undertake on behalf of political sovereignty struggles – not only through their direct involvement in defense of their community's legal rights, as discussed in chapters 1 and 4, but also as onlookers who observed the failure of legal mechanisms to address Indigenous women's community justice concerns, the focus of chapters 2 and 3. I show how each writer engages with legal matters in ways that directly connect legal cases with literary themes to illustrate how law provides an essential context for understanding Indigenous women's concerns and for exploring this writing's contribution to a social justice project in which the assessment of tribal sovereignty and gender justice must be theorized together.

Through side-by-side analysis, each chapter accords the court case and literary text its local specificity in order to account for the issues raised by the case and to demonstrate each author's commitment to engaging legal issues through Indigenous-feminist literary critique. By emphasizing each writer's contribution to Indigenous-feminist practice and debate, this book seeks to contribute to law and literature studies and critical race scholarship. Its Indigenous-feminist reading practice illustrates how Indigenous women's identities matter to legal contexts, and how literary texts play an essential role in altering our understanding of gender justice issues. As a comparative transnational study of law and literary texts, it builds on recent work in the field of Indigenous cultural studies to further its "transnational turn." Shari Huhndorf uses this term to establish the "[c]ommon history of colonization and shared relationships to the land that provide a foundation for ... global political alliances" (*Mapping* 13).[14] A transnational law and literature critical approach focuses on the "cross-cultural politics of power" as they intersect to "constellate discourses and denote forms of recognition that create and sanction concepts" within the nation-state (Shih 17). The Indigenous women's writing studied here articulates local and national concerns to broaden these issues "beyond the tribal" (Huhndorf 13), permitting Indigenous women's voices, through literary texts, to participate in international debates and to enact forms of symbolic justice in the hopes of achieving transitional justice goals. "Transitional justice," a term coined by Ruti Teitel, establishes "a distinctive conception of justice" during times of fundamental political change ("Global" 1). It takes into account that human rights violations are gendered (Nesiah et al. 1) and that "gender-based violence" is "a common element of conflict and authoritarian regimes" (International Centre, "Gender Justice" n.p.). As a legal mechanism, it grounds its analysis in continuities between past state practices that violate citizens' rights and future-oriented objectives that reconcile "individual and collective liability" with the goal of "shaping the political identity of the liberalizing state" (Teitel, *Transitional Justice* 119). Indigenous women's writing expresses social justice goals by engaging in acts of representation and translation that emphasize the call "to be just" not by "asserting and mastering a state of affairs" (Young 5), but by establishing responsibility for unjust acts. By showing how law has devalued women, this writing "clarifies the meaning of concepts and issues, describes and explains social relations, and articulates and defends ideals and principles" (Young 5); it thus furthers Indigenous decolonization and community justice by crafting Indigenous-feminist literary models that re-articulate Indigenous women's inheritances across intergenerational and tribal lines. The four chapters that follow demonstrate these commitments. Each analyses how Indigenous women's writing explores gender injustice and theorizes how creative texts participate in Indigenous-feminist critique. Taken together, each chapter gives priority to the literary as a source for imagining social transformation and community decolonization as goals conveyed by Indigenous women through literature's empowering cultural vision.

Chapter One

Gendering the Politics of Tribal Sovereignty: *Santa Clara Pueblo v. Martinez* (1978) and *Ceremony* (1977)

Tensions between tribal sovereignty and Indigenous women's rights were brought to the foreground in 1978 through the United States Supreme Court ruling in *Santa Clara Pueblo v. Martinez*. The case concerning the tribal disenrollment of Ms Julia Martinez's mixed-race children launched vigorous debate among critical race, feminist, and legal scholars due to its polarization of gender empowerment to tribal self-determination. In this chapter, I analyse the gender politics raised by the case in order to explore the implications of this opposition for Indigenous women in critical race assessments of it. *Martinez* continues to generate questions about the relationship between gender empowerment and tribal sovereignty. These debates have two remarkably consistent yet troubling features in their characterizations and assumptions about how gender identity matters to Indigenous social, cultural, and political life: on the one hand, scholars take a narrow view of Indigenous women's identities by privileging an unconscious heterosexism that reorders and thus contains women's rights within the domestic sphere, largely configured through the cultural; on the other hand, they participate in privileging sovereignty over gender through an "[un]critical localism" (Dirlik 22) that situates tribal sovereignty as the end-point to liberation struggles. Without questioning the "fundamental occlusions" (Butler, "Is Kinship" 17) to Indigenous women's identities authorized by these claims, and by overlooking the implications of gender struggles in inequalities and oppressions inherited from the colonial past, supporters of *Martinez*'s outcome take for granted that sovereignty may be conceived of as gender-blind and gender identity may remain culturally and politically neutral. Julia Martinez's cause troubles both of these assumptions.

Taking critical distance from her community's enforcement of its gender discriminatory membership rules, Ms Martinez envisioned a different understanding of tribal identity as a capacity that could empower members to value and enact respectful tribal status and social relations. Conforming neither to prior practices that had been altered by imposed colonial legal orders nor to an acceptance of the status quo as sufficient to reflect and articulate her community's well-being, Ms Martinez sought to envision tribal identity through a demeanor of self-respect that accorded Indigenous peoples recognition of their inherent self-worth. Her legal activism to change the Pueblo's membership ordinance pursued two goals: (1) to end the discriminatory provisions that used sexist criteria to determine membership and thus fostered disrespect towards Pueblo women and their children; and (2) to propose a vision of tribal sovereignty as an expression of tribal identity that defined membership as a capacity represented by a person's aspirational self-hood. In committing to these principles, Ms Martinez's legal activism articulated tribal sovereignty in relation to gender identity through its associations with a dignity-based claim. My objective in this chapter is to show how Ms Martinez's suit expressed this goal. I begin by highlighting the terms of self-determination and gender empowerment that were central to Ms Martinez's legal action on behalf of herself and other Pueblo women similarly situated. Next, I consider Ms Martinez's suit in the context of critical race assessments of it to demonstrate its arguments for a dignity-based claim. Third, I explore how these debates concerning gender identity and tribal sovereignty inform Leslie Marmon Silko's *Ceremony*, a novel that writes back to the case by showing how Indigenous women are essential to community decolonization because their knowledge and experiences provide insights about how to protect Indigenous peoples from evolving forms of colonial attack. As the case makes apparent, one of the Pueblo tribe's strongest legal claims for excluding Ms Martinez's children from tribal membership asserted that their inclusion would constitute a fundamental threat to the tribe's distinct nationhood and culture. Silko's novel challenges this view by illustrating how community regeneration and land renewal require the collective struggle of all community members. Her novel contests women's social and political marginalization by depicting women's contributions to tribal decolonization, the restoration of community, and the protection of land, elements of tribal identity that were made precarious by the *Martinez* ruling.

Santa Clara Pueblo v. Martinez

Santa Clara Pueblo v. Martinez, the 1978 United States Supreme Court decision that established the sovereign immunity of Indian tribes from civil actions under Title 1 of the Indian Civil Rights Act, remains a crucial case in debates concerning the relationship between tribal sovereignty – in this case, an Indigenous nation asserting a right to determine its citizenship – and the equal rights claims of Indigenous women. The case and lower-court decisions convey the decades-long struggle of Ms Julia Martinez, a female member of the Santa Clara Pueblo, who petitioned to have her children enrolled as members of the Pueblo despite their mixed-race parentage, which disqualified them from membership under the Tribe's 1939 Ordinance.[1] Ms Martinez claimed that the Ordinance that denied tribal membership to the children of female tribal members who married outside the tribe, while extending membership to the children of male members who married outside the tribe, discriminated against her on the basis of sex and inheritance, violating the equal rights provision of Title 1 of the Indian Civil Rights Act, which states that "an Indian tribe, in exercising its powers of self-government, cannot deny to any persons within its jurisdiction the equal protection of its laws" ("Summary" 436 U.S. 49, 98 S. Ct. 1670, 56 L. Ed. 2d 106 (U.S. N.M. May 15, 1978) (NO. 76-682). Ms Martinez brought suit against the tribe and one of its officials in the United States District Court for the District of New Mexico on behalf of herself, her daughter, Audrey, and all other women similarly situated. She sought an injunction against the tribe's enforcement of its membership provisions which denied her children political rights to vote and hold office; land use rights, including the right to hunt and fish, and the use of irrigation water; and residency rights which, in the event of her death, prevented her children and husband from continuing to live at the Pueblo, unless they resided with other family members (402 F. Supp. 5, 14).[2] Ms Martinez asserted that the "operation of the Ordinance rendering her children non-members denie[d] her the equal protection of the laws and deprive[d] her of property without due process of law" (402 F. Supp. 9).

The United States District Court disallowed Ms Martinez's claim of sex discrimination[3] by finding that the tribal ordinance did not violate the equal protection provisions of the Indian Civil Rights Act because it relied on membership criteria that had been "traditionally employed by the tribe in considering membership questions" (402 F. Supp. 2). The court also asserted its "jurisdiction to decide intertribal controversies affecting matters of tribal self-government and sovereignty" ("Summary"). On appeal, however, the United States Court of Appeals, Tenth Circuit, reversed the lower court's decision, finding instead that "the tribe was not justified in deviating from the Fourteenth Amendment standard" when it argued that "tribal, cultural and ethnic survival would suffer from full-scale enforcement of the Indian Civil Rights Act's equal protection guarantee" (540 F.2d 1039 [1976] 1039). In reversing, it also "remanded [the case] for further proceedings" (1048).[4]

When the case appeared before the United States Supreme Court two years later, Ms Martinez's claim of sex discrimination in the denial of tribal membership to her children became the two threshold issues of whether the "[Indian Civil Rights] Act may be interpreted to impliedly authorize ... actions, against a tribe or its officers, in the federal courts" (436 US 49, 56 L Ed 2d 106, 98 S.Ct., 111), and whether or not "a federal court may [decide] on the validity of an Indian tribe's ordinance denying membership to the children of ... female tribal members" (98 S. Ct., 110). The Supreme Court found for the petitioners, Santa Clara Pueblo, on both counts. It argued that not only was Congress "committed to the goal of tribal self-determination," and thus the Indian Civil Rights Act "manifest[ed] a congressional purpose to protect tribal sovereignty from undue interference," but also that in matters arising in a civil context that "depend on questions of tribal tradition and custom ... tribal [courts] [are] in a better position to evaluate [these actions]," which are immune from review by federal courts (98 S. Ct., 110). On this reasoning, the Supreme Court reversed the ruling by the Court of Appeals, and in so doing, exhausted all legal remedies permitting Ms Martinez to confer tribal membership on her children.[5]

By all accounts of the Supreme Court's decision, the *Martinez* ruling represents a "hard case"[6] for disentangling the gender conduct of Indigenous women from its implication in "traditional values" that are held to "promote the cultural survival of the tribe" (Brief for Petitioners, WL 189105 32). As court records indicate, Julia Martinez embodied the ideal feminine-cultural standpoint of Indigenous womanhood affirmed by the Santa Clara Pueblo: she had lived at the Pueblo all her life except for a brief absence to further her education; she spoke her traditional language; she was raised in the Santa Claran culture; she participated in religious ceremonies; and she emotionally identified as a Santa Claran woman (402 F.Supp. 14). Following her marriage to Myles Martinez, she and her husband lived continuously at the Pueblo and raised their eight living children there, all of whom spoke the Tewa language, were allowed to practise their traditional religion, and were culturally considered to be Santa Claran. What Ms Martinez lacked, according to the cultural and political conventions asserted by her tribe through law, was the appropriate gender identity for conferring sovereign status and tribal recognition on her children because such rights were held by the tribe to be patriarchal in origin and practice.[7]

I begin this chapter with the legal story that emerges in the *Martinez* case because the story it tells seems so obviously one of injustice. I am not alone in holding this view. Critical race and feminist scholars demonstrate a strong preoccupation with attempting to think through why the Supreme Court reached its decision to refuse membership to Ms Martinez's children.[8] Their arguments indicate the case's wider implications as a legal story that not only concerns gender disempowerment, but also reflects political value systems, Indigenous self-determination, and legal justice, and what these terms mean for Indigenous women in social discourses. In what follows, I explore these debates by arguing that Ms Martinez's struggle for tribal recognition articulated an emerging dignity-based consciousness, one that accorded Indigenous women personhood status in their own right as individuals bearing self-worth, self-hood, and inherent dignity. Far from opposing tribal sovereignty to gender identity, as the courts claimed, Ms Martinez sought to show how the "definition of legal personhood," a definition that Judith Butler argues is "rigorously circumscribed by cultural norms that are indissociable from their material effects" ("Merely Cultural" 41), harmed Indigenous women by withholding from them access to social power. Her legal activism attempted to show that tribal identities and gender meanings are not "merely cultural" ("Merely Cultural" 42)[9] in their deployment of tradition and identity, but rather political and social in establishing the cultural attitudes that inform the sexual and political economy within which Indigenous women are situated and through which they are permitted or denied access to tribal tradition and cultural authority. These effects are not accidental or unintended consequences of how law influences social discourses. Rather, they are constitutive of how legal culture, gender identity, and political discourses work together to facilitate Indigenous women's disempowerment and cultural erasure through the intersections of law and social discourses that characterize the colonial frameworks imposed on Indigenous cultures and that situate Indigenous women in politically confining ways.

I focus on the scholarly arguments that support the court's reasoning because they demonstrate how Indigenous women's political confinement and disposability are two social effects that follow from the *Martinez* case. These arguments achieve this result by limiting Indigenous women's gender identities in two ways: first, by sustaining through their analyses the "patriarchal"[10] reasoning established by the Pueblo in the case which held that kinship through membership represented the "mechanism of social ... psychological and cultural self-definition ... that makes its members unique ... and distinguishes a Santa Clara Indian from everyone else in the United States" (402 F. Supp. 15); and second, by confining Indigenous women's identities to their reproductive roles as a form of domestic labour in the transmission of culture. In conjunction with the intervenant factums, these arguments establish how gender configurations enact authority to disenfranchise Indigenous women and their children. They are important to the development of an Indigenous-feminist critical practice concerned with membership exclusions because they show how these disentitlements lead to other forms of social vulnerability and dispossession. They also illustrate why law practices matter for Indigenous women. Because this case materializes the issue of gender discrimination and political vulnerability through the assessment of the political status of Indian tribes, it shows how gender disempowerment is built into legal mechanisms. Indigenous communities know all too well the power of the state to deny "legal and economic entitlements" (Butler, "Merely Cultural" 41) by politically regulating Indian tribes.[11] My objective is to show why gender identity also matters to these acts of dispossession.

In the discussion that follows, my arguments proceed in two ways: first, I explore the implications of gender identity as necessarily hetero-normative in critical race and feminist assessments of the *Martinez* case; second, I show how Silko's novel *Ceremony* writes back to its reasoning by challenging conventional representations of Pueblo women that emphasize kinship as the source and meaning of Pueblo identity. Silko's community, the Laguna Pueblo, intervened in the case before it reached the United States Supreme Court by filing a brief, together with eight other Pueblos, supporting Santa Clara's refusal to grant membership to Ms Martinez's children. They argued collectively that the membership ordinances of their individual communities "prohibit[] women members who marry non-members from residing on the reservations, a prohibition that does not apply to male members who marry non-members," and asserted that the membership practices "[are] a codification of long-existing traditional rules, based on religion, land-holdings and tradition" (1976 WL 181159, 4). Laguna

Pueblo foregrounded its membership provisions as enacting specific requirements relating to the date of birth, blood quantum, and marital status of parents (1976 WL 181159, 3–4), and they emphasized the significance of "a traditional background in connection with each of the membership standards prescribed in their respective constitutions" (4). They also included a section of their constitution that disenfranchises "[t]he illegitimate child of a Laguna father and a non-Laguna mother," arguing that this exclusion is based on the assumption that "[the child] will most likely not have any contact with the Pueblo because such a child would, in most cases, be living off the reservation" (17). As they remarked in their brief, "The problem [of illegitimacy] was acute in 1958 and still is, because … a large number of Laguna men have served in the Armed Forces of the United States, in World War II, the Korean conflict, the Vietnam Conflict and … [they] have fathered children by women who are non-Lagunas" (17).

Silko's *Ceremony* was published in 1977, one year before the Supreme Court handed down the *Martinez* decision and one year after the Pueblo of Laguna acted as a party to the case. The novel's central themes explore the problem of community integration for a returning Second World War veteran of mixed-raced inheritance as he struggles to overcome his sense of social fragmentation, family loss, and community dislocation. Tayo's story is widely regarded by critics as describing the "mixed-blood's" quest (Owens, "The Very Essence" 91) for community integration. His attempts to understand his mixed-race inheritance and to recover a place for himself in the community are struggles that occur against the background of his quest to heal the community from an influx of external forces: a drought which is caused by his participation in the war, an apathy that he cannot overcome due to his failed attempts to save his cousin, Rocky, after he is wounded in battle, and a spiritual and material blight within the community caused by his cursing of the rain. Tayo's personal quest and individual development form the central plot to Silko's novel, which weaves together mythic, historical, and contemporary events to depict colonialism's sweeping alterations in the life of the community and in the lives of its most vulnerable members, women and children. Resisting the violence of his companions who are veterans is also bound up with the rite of passage Tayo must undertake to acquire the traditional knowledge necessary for healing the land. Silko shows how Tayo's struggle is not only a quest for understanding to restore harmony to the community and end the drought. It is also a story about women and their experiences of exile that he must reconcile to himself if he is to empower a vision that will reinstate balance to the community's gender order and bring about his own self-knowledge and individual empowerment.

Women are central figures in Silko's novel acting in ways that facilitate multiple forms of cultural and individual liberation. Their experiences contextualize the insights that Tayo requires in order to understand the interrelationships between healing, redemption, sacrifice, and land. These women include his mother, Laura, whose loss haunts him due to his incomplete understanding of her death as bound up in some essential way with her act of saving his life; his aunt, Thelma, whose antagonism towards him is ambiguous because she displays anger and resentment in private ways that cause him great suffering while also taking a central role in restoring his physical health when he returns from the war; and Night Swan, his uncle Josiah's lover, whom critics argue "awakens Tayo to sexual maturity" (Swan 318), yet whose self-less acts of acceptance he betrays – first, by bringing about her exile from the community at Cubero when his uncle dies, and second, by breaking his promise to stay with Josiah and help with the farm, when he chooses to follow Rocky to war, an act which results in Josiah's death. Women's stories represent sources of kinship and intergenerational knowledge that Tayo must accept to complete his quest, right the imbalance, and restore the community by sharing his experiences with the old men of the kiva. Women's experiences thus provide an essential storytelling context to Tayo's quest narrative. On the one hand, their narratives depict an alternative historical-community structure and mythic consciousness that explains the origins of social transformation in women's epistemologies and healing capacities; on the other, they show how women suffer from community ostracization and fear because they have the courage to take risks and bring into being transformative skills by behaving in ways that express their gender non-conformity, enacting power that exceeds the authority of men. These figures include Helen Jean, whose story explains Laura's past and whose personal vulnerability reflects Laura's plight when she ventures away from the community, finds herself living in poverty, and becomes susceptible to sexual violence and exploitation by men; Betonie's great-grandmother, a captive Mexican woman who is representative of social transformation and empowering spiritual capacities, yet who thwarts the gender conventions upheld by both men and women, engendering suspicion, antipathy, and awe due to her unorthodox behaviour; and Ts'eh, a healing spiritual figure and Tayo's lover, who guides Tayo from the spiritual realm, permitting him to escape from his vindictive war companions and enabling him to act in ways that restore his confidence and spiritual abilities but who also consciously eludes his confining domesticating desire in order to maintain her independence and authority. Silko shows how Tayo must reconcile women's experiences with his healing capacities to rebalance the beliefs in fraternity that he has accepted. By framing women's knowledge and spiritual understanding as legacies integral to Tayo's quest, Silko introduces women's gender nonconformity and illicit behaviour to rewrite the prescriptive and narrow view of gender identity launched by the *Martinez* case. In Silko's view, women's practices represent spiritual and cultural centres in their secular, sacred, timeless, and historical meanings that empower different understandings of tribal agency. These kinds of knowledge are essential to a community's decolonizing quest because they represent sources of tribal sovereignty that exist beyond colonial legal paradigms, calling into question legally determined definitions of sovereignty as pseudosovereignty, because it reconstitutes tribal sovereignty in Anglo-American terms.

Silko's non-fiction writing also demonstrates an awareness of how legal contexts disrupt the intertribal transmission of knowledge and the storytelling traditions that represent sources of collective memory and sovereignty in the defence of the land.[12] In "Land and Literature from a Pueblo Indian Perspective," she recalls the Felipe case, a legal event that concerned the arrest and incarceration of three Acoma Pueblo men for the murder of a New Mexico state trooper. In Silko's version of the story, the event represents "traditional knowledge" because the meaning it has for the community exceeds the meaning it has in legal contexts. She writes:

> I had been away from Laguna Pueblo for a couple of years ... and I was wondering how the telling was continuing, because Laguna Pueblo, as the anthropologists have said, is one of the more acculturated pueblos. So I walked into this high school English class and there they were sitting, these very beautiful Laguna and Acoma kids ... I was almost afraid, but I had to ask – I had with me a book of short fiction ... And there is one particular story in the book about the killing of a state policeman in New Mexico by three Acoma Pueblo men ... I looked at the class and I said, "How many of you heard this story before you read it in the book?" And I was prepared to hear this crushing truth that indeed the anthropologists were right about the old traditions dying out. But it was amazing, you know, almost all but one or two students raised their hands. (68)[13]

Stories that demonstrate this gap – the gap between what institutions assert is the meaning of stories and what communities claim as knowledge in these texts – articulate Silko's view that traditional knowledge and sovereignty intersect in the storytelling traditions of the people as these capacities inspire transformative behaviour for the community and empower new meanings and sources of cultural resistance. The juxtaposition of competing authoritative accounts that enter into creative and contestatory dialogue with each other distil the forms of storytelling innovation that Silko's writing practices and the objectives for which she uses stories to convey the evolving importance of community knowledge to decolonizing frameworks.

Silko's advocacy on behalf of a community's storytelling traditions represents an important creative intervention that contrasts with the authoritative accounts used in the *Martinez* case. Court records demonstrate how community knowledge was introduced by anthropologists who served as expert witnesses to disadvantage Indigenous women in two ways: first by supporting the tribe's view that patriarchal gender practices represented crucial aspects of Pueblo sovereignty,[14] thus undermining prior community-centred traditional Pueblo membership codes that did not rely on gender discrimination for their membership criteria, and second, by calling into question Ms Martinez's authoritative voice as a community member who understood, firsthand, the meaning and experience of the Pueblo's injustice towards women.[15] Silko's novel engages this obfuscation and silencing by asserting that a community must turn to its own traditions, members, and creative storytelling sources for practices that not only empower its self-governance and gender justice objectives but also to counter outsider authorities.

Storytelling about Indigenous Women in *Martinez*

Because the patriarchal origin and effects of the ordinance were never in question nor denied by the Pueblo, scholars have struggled to reconcile the gender discrimination authorized by its passage with the authority of Indigenous governments to undertake exclusionary practices that are discriminatory in effect, yet justified on the grounds of furthering tradition and tribal sovereignty.[16] *Martinez's* advocates grapple with these tensions, showing a concern for the "linked fates" (Bedolla 241) of communities disentitled by law but upholding the terms set by legal reasoning in opposing tribal sovereignty to gender justice and equality.

They also demonstrate the need for a critical language to address this opposition.[17]

Scholars writing about the case further the institutionalization of colonial law in relation to Indigenous peoples by defending the ordinance's discriminatory underpinnings. They protect law's authority by expanding the legal terrain within which tribal practices are accorded meaning, thus providing law with a stable understanding of tribal gender identity through which to justify law's regulatory reach. They also sustain law's unity practices by relying on expert accounts to link Santa Clara Pueblo's patriarchal gender order to the gender systems of other tribal communities by upholding a tribe's right to defend its traditions and local practices, thus furthering law's capacity to analogically know tribes by permitting one tribe's particular attribute to stand in for the universality of all tribal cultures.[18] These arguments achieve two important symbolic and material effects that occlude the rights of women: (1) they mask the political content of the ideological struggle taking place in relation to the Pueblo's gender practices, which depend on the subordination of women justified as a form of traditional tribal sovereign practice;[19] and (2) they omit recognition that Ms Martinez's actions represent a form of tribal sovereignty in their own right, as an aspirational mode of gender empowerment and identity formation addressed to remedying the gender injustice that women, such as herself and others, experienced and observed. Ms Martinez advocated not only for herself and her children, citing the "extremely grave" circumstances her children faced in being denied membership, conditions that included being "forced to leave their lifelong home" should their mother predecease them, and the refusal of emergency medical treatment by the Indian Health Service which relied on tribal recognition for access to its services (1977 WL 189106 18, 5), a situation that prompted the National Tribal Chairman's Association, which opposed the suit, to note her "anguish" (1977 WL 189110 8). Ms Martinez also supported women who were "missing" from the Pueblo for marrying non-members, women "[who] had been subjected to severe discrimination and mistreatment" over a 30-year period, suffering what she characterized as "indignities" towards them in their treatment by the Pueblo (1977 WL 189106, 27).

Indigenous scholars exacerbate these gender injustice issues in their support of the *Martinez* ruling by arguing for its legal status as a defence of a tribe's sovereign practices. Gloria Valencia-Weber and Christine P. Zuni take issue with scholars who challenge the Pueblo's right to enact gender discrimination. They observe that "the gender equality viewpoint fails to recognize both the indigenous peoples' view of male/female relationships as complementary," a relation informed by indigenous peoples' abilities to "conserve and innovate in order to promote tribal interests and continuity" (134). Angela R. Riley defends the Pueblo's right to its decision-making autonomy by stating that "some tribes maintain roles for men and women that are complementary and equal, but nevertheless fixed and immutable" (843). Robert A. Williams expands the understanding of gender relations across wider political practices within which women had power to "remove the male chiefs," were accorded "property interests," and "held the power to initiate or call off war" (1034). Although these approaches are best characterized as furthering an "intra-tribal perspective" that Williams proposes for "understand[ing] an Indian cultural context according to its own terms" (1023), they take for granted that tribal culture requires an "organic" mode in relation to its traditions in order to safeguard and secure its political authority. They do so by valorizing culture as a site of social stability in which unfair gender practices and exclusions are necessarily legitimated (Das 123). Two essential problems follow from these assessments that undermine the human capacity that culture is meant to express: culture is narrowed to a prescriptive mode that "freeze[s]" and "fix[es]" tradition in a static sense; and culture becomes "lifeless" to the extent that "the individual [is kept] within such tight bonds that the capacity to experiment with one's self – which is equally a mark of one's humanity – comes to be severely at risk" (Das 123). The "double life of culture" that accords it relational value for "its potential to give radical recognition to the humanity of its subjects," as well as its capacity to express "passions" and "interests" (123), is withheld from Indigenous communities through the "exclusion of alternatives" that consolidate culture in its current form (123). Such exclusions are discounted as representing the "outside" of culture, or requiring "domestication" by it, so that what is obscured from view is culture as a site of liberation, as a form of human interaction that provides opportunities to conceptualize "ideal[s] of empowerment" that free it from "unnecessarily confining premises" (Das 123, citing R.M. Unger 339–40).

In "Indian feminist" (Skenandore 354) assessments of *Martinez*, scholars omit this crucial understanding in striving to reconcile the interpretation of tribal traditions asserted by the Pueblo with gender identity as a source of authority for Indigenous women. They argue that Indigenous women *desire* tribal national autonomy at the expense of their gender rights, consequently enacting defence-of-culture arguments that "sacrifice women" by discounting non-conforming practices of gender consciousness, experience, and identity. Francine Skenandore asserts that "Indian feminists have captured the seemingly accepted belief among most Indian women, and in particular those women who have been raised in and near tribal communities, that tribal sovereignty underlies most ideas of feminism because an Indian woman's identity is inextricably connected to the existence of her tribe. As a consequence, 'Indian feminists have rejected the Western feminist approach to gender equality by retaining the cultural framework and a commitment to the tribal nation's autonomy'" (354). Valencia-Weber observes, "Indian feminist writing reminds us that the creation stories of many indigenous peoples start with a feminine force with power to manifest itself in male form ... The law discourse can only benefit from indigenous women who value tribal sovereignty and women who understand the complementary roles customary in many tribes" (54). Riley proposes that "Indian tribes embody the most basic cultural unit in the human experience: they are, in many respects, families. Tribes are bound by bloodlines, clan affiliations, and kinship, with ancestry or descent often constituting the dominant factor in determining tribal membership. Family structure is a defining characteristic of tribal life ... For an Indian who lives, socializes, exercises, and worships on a reservation, there is no other government that has a larger role in her day to day life than her tribe" (831, 834).

These assessments are important in masking the gender discrimination raised by the *Martinez* case because they circumscribe the gender identities and feminist politics that Indigenous women are permitted to imagine for themselves in several key ways: they reduce Indigenous women's gender identity to a reproductive relationship based on kinship, family, culture, and nation; they reinscribe Indigenous women's rights within a cultural framework superceded by tribal sovereignty; they relegate Indigenous female identity to the mythology of a historical past; and they disavow Indigenous feminist politics through an uncritical affirmation of tribal processes as liberating political struggle. In so doing, they participate in a broader social disavowal of Indigenous women's gender rights, subjectivity, and cultural aspirations, a disavowal that Melissa S. Wright theorizes as "the story of female disposability" (27), story that "cloak[s] political situations with narratives of human essence and naturalized tautologies" (3) by emphasizing a woman's reproductive capacity in order to justify the conditions of her exploitation (7). These theories defending Indigenous women's cultural authority require a foundational concept of gender identity that does not restrain the humanity of women, either through uncritical assumptions about normative gender expectations or beliefs that tribal sovereignty will of its own accord facilitate gender rights.[20] Such a theory emerges in the language of human dignity made apparent by Ms Martinez's membership entitlement claim.

Ms Martinez's cause reflected her view that the Pueblo's treatment of women constituted an unbearability[21] engendering profound consequences for women and children that altered their life circumstances, conditions that imparted a burden of responsibility to her as she tried to make her protest known. Ms Martinez first attempted to have her daughter recognized as a member in 1946, shortly after she was born, undertaking efforts that were described by the district court as "vigorous and constant" (402 F. Supp. 5, 11).[22] She committed several years of her life to working on behalf of herself, her children, and other women similarly situated to bring attention to their treatment. As the court record notes,

> [She] ... met with her representative to the Council, to request that he present the request that Audrey be enrolled ... When her representative refused to bring the matter up in Council, she obtained special permission from the Governor to address the Council herself. She and other women in her situation ... formed a committee which as a group petitioned representatives and, with special permission, the Council. [Acting] individually and with the committee, [she] succeeded in having a special meeting of the entire Pueblo convened to discuss the situation. [She], and with the committee of similarly situated women, attended meetings with various BIA officials, and with the All-Pueblo Agency in Albuquerque. She and her husband Myles attempted to have him naturalized as a member of the Pueblo, in which case their children would have automatically been recognized as members [She] ... met with her State Representative concerning the recognition of her children as members of Santa Clara. [She] attended hearings held by the Subcommittee on Constitutional Rights of the United States Senate Committee on the Judiciary, where she sought the help of then Senator Sam Erwin, Jr. ... Finally, in 1971, [she and her daughter] sought legal advice ... only after attempts by their lawyer to gain recognition for Audrey had failed. (F. Supp. 5, 7)

To recognize the political value of Ms Martinez's activism, one need not oppose tribal sovereignty to gender empowerment as debates and subsequent hearings of the case have done,[23] but rather deploy a critical language that accords meaning to Ms Martinez's struggle as expressing a form of Indigenous-feminist tribal sovereignty in its own right, a form of activism that also sought to demonstrate the invisibly gendered work of law. Because tribal sovereignty and gender empowerment represent two of the most powerful political movements for Indigenous peoples in the post–civil rights era, reconciling their goals represents an urgent, politically important, and mutually empowering task. I turn next to showing how Ms Martinez's activism articulated a dignity-based framework before turning to my discussion of the case and its meanings in Silko's novel, *Ceremony*. By applying the methods of an intersectional analysis to "open ... up alternative ways of constituting subjectivity and social relations" (Dhamoon, *Identity/Difference* 61; "Consideration" 241) through a law and literature comparison, I illustrate how an Indigenous-feminist reading practice advances both tribal sovereignty and gender justice aims.

Martinez in the Context of a Dignity-Based Claim

Because Julia Martinez contended that the sex and inheritance discrimination authorized by the ordinance served no purpose in "preserving Santa Clara culture," since the rules excluding "female-line children" and admitting "male-line children" were applied "without regard to religious or cultural affinity of the Pueblo" (1977 WL 189106, 20), she questioned the cultural conventions and patriarchal logic through which the ordinance was held to accord membership its value and to further the social relations of the tribe. On the one hand, her legal action challenged the tribe's failure to protect the status of her human dignity and aspirational selfhood as empowering characteristics of her gender subjectivity that were meaningful to its tribal community vision; on the other, it disputed the Pueblo's self-conception in undermining the goals of self-respect and personal dignity through the ordinance that used sexist criteria to express tribal sovereignty relations which her action called into question.[24] By claiming that the ordinance's rules exposed Indigenous women to individual and social violations, Martinez's cause made visible two important insights about how race and gender intersect at the level of government legislation: (1) by illustrating how gender identity serves as a proxy for other types of disadvantages intensified at the macro-level of policy supported by the state and upheld through colonial law; and (2) by providing a portrait for how gender identity characterizes the value-coding of Indigenous women as expendable in relations governing the social circulation of membership criteria established and promoted by the tribe.[25] Her challenge thus drew attention to the collective and individual effects of gender discrimination that the ordinance authorized as enacting violations to Indigenous women's selfhood through dignity-violating harms.[26] These harms infringe selfhood and denigrate identity in several important ways.

Ms Martinez argued that denying Indigenous women the right to develop a positive self-identity in their community of "upbringing,"[27] and preventing them from forming attachments to this community that express their selfhood in socially meaningful ways, cause them to suffer injustices that deprive them of their basic self-worth. The harms she made visible were not "subjective," individual rights violations attributable to an infringement of the goals of choice or autonomy,[28] but rather principled objections to the material, social, and political effects that indignity in the form of the Pueblo's conduct towards her, and social vulnerability through its withholding of rights and material necessities from herself and other women similarly situated, exposed women to. In the colonial-legal context, these disadvantages are amplified by demeaning social attitudes that prevent Indigenous women from enacting alternative sources of gender relations within their home communities, and by the law's willingness to allow the stereotypical gender assumptions grounding such legislation to stand.

"Choice" arguments as a substitute for women's agency were important factors in the case, presented as negative characterizations of Ms Martinez's decision knowingly to marry outside the tribe. In their brief to the Supreme Court, Santa Clara Pueblo stated, "Mrs. Julia Martinez was fully aware of the consequences if she married a non-Santa Clara male. She was told by her uncle that if she married a nonmember of Santa Clara Pueblo her children could not be enrolled" (Brief for Petitioners 1977 WL 189105, 6). This argument appears to rely on the fact that Ms Martinez should have consented to the implications of the ordinance since she knew about its practical effects for her children, rather than follow other practices or values that were important to her. Knowledge and consent, here, are doubly invidious in their gender connotations of obedience and restraint, not only for confining women in terms of their life choices by limiting their access to the social field in the formation of "intimate relationships of great personal significance to them, emotionally, socially, and economically" (Reaume, "Discrimination" 20), but also in displacing an understanding of the gender violence that their consent-through-knowledge implies, which suggests that should women suffer as a consequence of their behaviour, their knowing will weigh against them as complicity with their victimization for so acting and for not abiding by the social rules in place.

To argue that the Pueblo's conduct and the Supreme Court's ruling disadvantaged Indigenous women by stigmatizing them as disposable in the formation of cultural values, and by fostering stereotypical beliefs that undermined their gender subjectivity, is to foreground the feminist insight that "gender norms ... [are] the product of society rather than the expression of an 'authentic' identity" (Reaume, "Comparing" 561). This fact, as feminist legal scholars point out, poses challenges for feminist theory in so far as it shifts attention from individual identity as a source of voice and experience for "achieving change" to an analysis of the "particular social forms that constitute the forms of life that can be successfully led in ... society" (561). On the one hand, such a shift prioritizes social relations as the basis of oppression by redirecting attention from the "attitudes of victims" to the "cessation of the abusive conduct" (561); on the other hand, it requires an account that makes visible the attributes of Indigenous women *as women* that such devaluing calls into question (560). To sidestep either commitment is to ignore how gender is implicated in power relations of penalty, privilege, and choice that the post–civil rights context has instituted. It is also to discount the key insight raised by critical race scholars that the dynamics of gender discrimination require "a multidimensional analysis of how power operates and its effects on different levels of political life" (Dhamoon, "Consideration" 233). These insights further the gender empowerment commitments that Indigenous feminists have called for in turning to intersectional frameworks that prioritize gender analysis not only to show "how gender norms and expectations cabin and confine women," but also to convey "how difficult it can be to shake off their constraining effects" (Reaume, "Comparing" 560).

Relying on legal narratives alone to alter social practices of devaluation and discrimination that have eroded Indigenous women's social status will be inadequate, however, as the *Martinez* case makes apparent, because law has played a key role in diminishing Indigenous women's status within their communities,[29] and because law practices committed to gender equity misrepresent Indigenous women by defaulting in their reasoning to cultural expectations and beliefs that have been entrenched through the status quo.[30] Alternative sources of knowledge about Indigenous women's gender roles are necessary to further the insights advanced by anti-discrimination scholars that "the social meaning of imposed inferiority is not easily eradicated ... the fact of having been associated with a wide array of negative meanings in the past makes the group more vulnerable to continued devaluation" (Reaume, "Discrimination" 40–1). The "cultural study of law" (Kahn 6) that creative writers such as Silko practise permits alternative views of Indigenous culture to emerge and different understandings of gender relations to be made socially meaningful. These engagements show how Indigenous women writers challenge the prevailing norms about Indigenous women that law and social discourses enact, while also taking critical distance from them in order to affirm how gender identity can be, paradoxically, the vehicle through which Indigenous women experience gender oppression and the social identity that makes them crucial to a community's self-recovery and renewal.

"Trapped in One of the Oldest Ways": Leslie Marmon Silko's *Ceremony*

Indigenous women's disposability and the cultural narratives that are deployed as its justification represent a crucial feature of the gender-decolonizing framework that Silko's novel *Ceremony* takes up in its focus on the intersections between gender relations that empower women, on the one hand, and confining social codes and cultural expectations that oppress them, on the other hand. *Ceremony*'s vision disperses these relations across the mythic, social, and individual connections that encompass the community's world view as it confronts changes to its organizing social structures and formative cultural practices through the imposition of "outsider" colonial-knowledge systems. In keeping with her aesthetic vision that when disharmony arises in human social relations, the land is made vulnerable, Silko characterizes the crisis in the form of a drought.[31] The drought occurs through the simplest of misunderstandings, as a dispute between women: "Corn Woman" becomes angry with her sister "Reed Woman" because while "[she] worked hard all day / sweating in the sun," Reed Woman "spent all day long / sitting in the river / splashing down / the summer rain." When Corn Woman scolds her sister for "bathing all day long," Reed Woman leaves, taking away the rain that sustains the people so that "Everything dried up / all the plants / the corn / the beans / they all dried up," resulting in a famine that afflicts both the people and the animals so that all within their care are "thirsty" and "starving" (13–14). The sisters' spiritual dispute leads to uncertainty and discord among the people, who mirror the conflict by acting in ways that meddle with magic, ignore the ceremonies, and dishonour their ties to "the mother" (48, 54). In order to end the conflict and dispel the drought, everyone within the spiritual community must act together to restore the "balance of the world" that "had been disturbed" by the sister's disagreement and the community's lack of respect for "the mother," which results in "droughts and hard days to come" as "the holy men at Laguna and Acoma warned" (186). Righting the balance entails not only that the spiritual community renew relations with the mother, but also that it create "something new" – "a big green fly" – to accompany "Hummingbird" to petition the mother and "see / what she wants" (82), to act as a messenger to aid in "purify[ing] the town" (255), and to help "set [things] straight again" (256).

By highlighting relations between women as the origin and form of harms warned against by the elders that, when disrupted, threaten the community's survival, Silko shows how women's relations organize the community's governing spiritual order and how gender dynamics provide a language of power and knowledge through which the community conceptualizes its spiritual practices. These practices are made normative and conventional through everyday habits, and they enable the community to enact social relations that are socially, politically, and culturally meaningful to itself. Countering the effects of the drought at the mythic level thus requires members to undertake a set of incremental acts of consultation not only to understand why "the mother" is angry with them (54), and why they must offer gifts of reparation to "purify" the town (105), but also to learn from the conflict by "stay[ing] out of trouble" and remembering that "It isn't very easy to fix up things again" (256).

If family discord at the mythic level inspires community relations that rebuild its social bonds and create new forms of culturally redemptive acts that accord respect to women, Silko depicts secular relations within the community that are far more conflicted. Because the novel configures the everyday world as intersected by spiritual events but not bound by them, Silko's mythic world is both relational, as the principle source for conceptualizing how gender relations matter symbolically, and autonomous, in guiding how gender relations should be accorded their value, but not determining how these values are put into everyday practice. The relational-autonomous gender order that the novel sets up expresses the complexity of gender relations in two central ways that highlight the importance of women: first, as a mirror for the mythic dispute between Reed Woman and Corn Woman in the family dynamics that develop between Tayo's mother, Laura, and her sister, Thelma, through the breakdown of their personal relations which leads to Laura's ostracization, banishment, and death; and second, as an accretive tension that exists among women and through which new knowledge enters the community in accordance with women's capacities to act in socially transformative ways. Silko constructs the people's gender order to materially intersect with and guide its spiritual order. If instability or disharmony occurs in one realm, vulnerability and loss for women occur in the other. Social instability, spiritual disrespect, and community disharmony invariably provoke conflicts in the community's gender relations, which result in the cultural, social, and sexual exploitation of women. Stories of gender vulnerability and women's cultural disempowerment thus contextualize Tayo's quest to restore community stability. They convey how women's losses affect community relations over time and call attention, through the novel's omniscient narrative perspective, to the importance of women's capacities and experiences that are absent from but necessary to its renewal. The material consequences of law are thus directly embedded within Silko's narrative. *Ceremony* demonstrates how the legally enforced social disposability of Indigenous women produces dire consequences for the entire community. Thus, both genders must bear the burden of healing from these damages.

Through a series of flashbacks, Silko portrays how Tayo's family resides at the centre of community knowledge and spiritual practices not only due to the status they are accorded by the village, but also because of prior acts that accumulate over time and make them vulnerable to both secular and sacred attacks. These acts originate from new forms of colonial invasion that target the community's most vulnerable members represented by women and children. Silko's omniscient narrator describes how colonialism works through educational institutions to disrupt its knowledge systems and to interfere with its ability to commune together through the ceremonies. Because Silko constructs the spiritual life of the people as centred in the family home, changes to its governing system are most visible in the lives of women. Like the medicine man, Betonie, who mirrors Thelma's healing capacities in the spiritual realm, and to whom Tayo is sent to be healed when Western medicine and Old Man Ku'oosh cannot restore him (38),

Thelma's powers reside in "Keeping track of things" (121), in under-standing the village through its "lineage, clan, and family name," and in maintaining a capacity to "know everything about anyone" (223). In a long passage that focuses on Thelma's redemptive characteristics and spiritual properties – powers which are not only recognized by the peo-ple because she represents their connection to the spiritual world, but also constrained and misdirected by them when their authority fails to guide her about how to act to save her sister, Laura – the passage describes how changes in women's behaviour undermine the people's will by fragmenting the bonds that unite its collective consciousness. These changes destroy its traditional knowledge about how to respond appropriately to empower women, as Silko's narrator explains:

> An old sensitivity had descended in her, surviving thousands of years from the oldest times, when the people shared a single clan name and they told each other who they were; they recounted the actions and words each of their clan had taken, and would take; from before they were born and long after they died, the people shared the same consciousness ... But the fifth world had become entangled with European names ... words were not necessary, but the messages the people felt were confused now ... When Little Sister had started drinking wine and riding in cars with white men and Mexicans, the people could not define their feeling about her ... The older sister had to act; she had to act for the people, to get this young girl back ... So Auntie had tried desperately to reconcile the family with the people; the old instinct had always been to gather the feelings and opinions that were scattered through the village, to gather them like wil-low twigs and tie them into a single prayer bundle that would bring peace to all of them. But now the feelings were twisted, tangled roots, and all the names for the source of this growth were buried under English words, out of reach. And there would be no peace and the people would have no rest until the entanglement had been unwound to the source. (68–9)

The consequences of Thelma's failure to save Laura resonate through-out the community, undermining and distorting its communal vision. Mirroring the spiritual disharmony between Reed Woman and Corn Woman to which Reed Woman responds by going away, Laura also leaves the people in ways that amplify her loss as it contributes to kin-ship disharmony and family distress. Because the earthly offering of a "single prayer bundle" will not be adequate to cover the harm brought about by Laura's absence in its spiritual and cultural dimensions, something new must be proposed as a token of redemption and respect to take her place. When Laura leaves for the final time, she offers her son Tayo who remains with the community and initiates anew the right of passage that restores its spiritual order.[32] Thelma understands and Tayo acknowledges that it was always to be this way, that he would remain behind to reconcile and atone for his mother's loss. Thelma explains about Tayo to old Grandma and Josiah when Tayo shares the news that he and Rocky enlisted: "Rocky is different ... but this one, he's supposed to stay here" (73). Because Tayo is lured from his family commitments by the promise of fraternity with his "brother" Rocky (65), he sets in motion the events that recapitulate his mother's loss with new tragic consequences for the people: Josiah dies as he struggles alone to recover the cattle that were stolen from the family (124), Night Swan is banished from Cubero (104) where she was protected by Josiah's love because the women and men of the town feared her (87), and the spiritual bond of Josiah's unconditional love for Tayo that restores the people's kinship relations withers away, despite its source in Josiah's unquestioned acceptance of Tayo, and despite its overcoming Thelma's fear for what the people would say, and the people's censure towards the family and Laura, a fear which they express through their desire to "run" her "off the reservation for good" (34). Since the people's anger "focused on the girl and her family, [even though] knowing from many years of this conflict that the anger could not be contained by a single person or family, but that it must leak out and soak into the ground under the entire village" (69), their antagonism not only harms the family but also taints the village and corrupts the land, causing discord in the people's spiritual, physical, and emotional well-being. Tayo's search for individual healing and redemption is also a quest to remedy the intergenerational harms represented by the community's prior injustice in their behaviour towards his family, and a journey undertaken to become worthy to inherit his role as a successor to the healing and redemption that are offered by and owed to women.

An important aspect of his task in seeking redemption for the community is to come to terms with the "shame" that he feels towards his mother, a feeling associated with women's sexually promiscuous behaviour and symbolically represented by his "Mexican eyes" (99). These feelings of shame are accorded secular, spiritual, and cultural connotations as "old feelings" that justify Indigenous peoples defeat in "anger and frustration" and "blame ... for losing the land the white people took" (43). This anger abets their acceptance of colonialism as the way things are, feelings which Betonie teaches Tayo to guard against (127) as the meaning behind the fraternity and ceremonial bond he establishes with Emo and his former war comrades (43). Shame also figures as "a private understanding" that Tayo shares with his aunt Thelma, which he associates in his grief-stricken state with her decision to keep and care for him because "he was all she had left," as a consequence of his mother's death and as a duty to him that he perceives as "concealing the shame of her younger sister" (29). Tayo's understanding of shame as bound up in his mother's promiscuity and his lack of self-worth represent aspects of his selfhood that he must overcome because they signify elements of his identity that he wishes to deny (99).

In other ways, Tayo's bond with his aunt expresses a recognition of how she is trapped by family obligations and kinship demands that tie her powers to the people and misshape her selfhood by mirroring his own sense of being confined and frustrated by family and community judgment. Focused through Tayo's point of view, a key passage establishes how Thelma's family acknowledges but ignores her suffering. Silko's omniscient narrator describes this experience of confinement as an understanding that they share, establishing Silko's vision of complementarity in gender relations through Tayo's perception and subjectivity, which align with those of his female family members:

> Tayo and Auntie understood each other very well. Years later Tayo wondered if anyone, even old Grandma or Josiah, ever understood her as well as he did. He learned to listen to the undertones of her voice. Robert and Josiah evaded her; they were deaf to those undertones. In her blindness and old age, old Grandma stubbornly ignored her and heard only what she wanted to hear. Rocky had his own way, with his after-school sports and his girl friends. Only Tayo could hear it, like fingernails scratching against bare rock, her terror at being trapped in one of the oldest ways. (67)

Thelma's method of escape from "being trapped in one of the oldest ways" by community obligations and family duties that confine and oppress her is to take up an exhausting vigilance in regard to the people's moral will. Although she "fiercely protect[s] [her family] from the gossip in the village" (30), she is also forced to answer to the priest when he calls her aside after mass (88), to ask her to take and conceal the photograph that Tayo keeps of his mother for fear that visitors might see it (71), and to suffer in silence with tears and frustration in being surrounded by a family that disregards the community's authority (88).

When she voices her resentment towards "Young people who don't understand how important it is. To be able to walk through the village without worrying or wondering what the people are whispering about you" (89), her criticism and vulnerability fall on deaf ears, and she is forced to recognize her powerlessness to change their behaviour. She reacts to their indifference by constructing a domestic solitude within the home where she cares for her mother, old Grandma, whose powers are past and who sits by the stove gossiping about former times that involve "the people who were talking about their family" (89).[33] Although she protects Tayo during his illness by advising old Grandma and Robert not to mention Rocky or Josiah when his sickness and crying "overwhelmed them" (31), she cannot escape from the community's censure by retreating from them, as the medicine-man Betonie does, when he relocates into the hills above Gallup in order to enact and evolve the ceremonies (123). By drawing a comparison between Thelma and Betonie in this way, Silko depicts how gender complementarity exceeds its meaning as egalitarian in theory by illustrating its differences for women and men in social practice. Gender complementarity, as noted earlier, was a key argument used by supporters of the *Martinez* decision to protect from further scrutiny the patriarchal implications of the Santa Clara tribe's membership ordinance that disentitled Ms Martinez's children. Its meaning in literary practice highlights how its penalties as a response to violence occur through the gendered effects of legal disposal and social discrimination that cross-hatch. As a consequence of her spiritual and domestic isolation and feelings of shame, Thelma shuns community with other women, denying their capacities to aid her and stifling her ability to understand the sources of their physical and spiritual empowerment and aspects of their confinement that they share with her own.

In a key moment of intimacy with Tayo, she discloses her ambivalence and incredulity about an incident that occurred before he was born, when her sister returned home at dawn, walking, naked and alone, from under the cottonwood tree. She observes:

"One morning, before you were born, I got up to go outside, right before sunrise. I knew she had been out all night because I never heard her come in. Anyway, I thought I would walk down toward the river. I just had a feeling, you know. I stood on that sandrock, above the big curve in the river, and there she was, coming down the trail on the other side." She looked at him closely. "I'm only telling you this because she was your mother, and you have to understand." She cleared her throat. "Right as the sun came up, she walked under that big cottonwood tree, and I could see her clearly; she had no clothes on. Nothing. She was completely naked except for her high-heel shoes. She dropped her purse under that tree. Later on some kids found it there and brought it back. It was empty except for a lipstick." (70)

As an account of kinship accord, Thelma's disclosure bears witness to the mystery surrounding Laura's behaviour and her struggle to understand her sister's transformative capacities and death.[34] Thelma's isolation also stymies her understanding of other women, such as Night Swan, whom she condemns for her immodesty and Mexican inheritance (76), distancing herself from behaviours that she perceives as enabling the people to laugh at or mock the family, and assuming a stance of shame towards women's sexual identities that contrast with her own (77). By casting Thelma in this truncated role, Silko characterizes the wider consequences of Laura's loss as enacting "twisting ... tangling" implications for her sister that mirror the community's inability to evolve its understanding of women's sexual identities. Tayo's emerging sense of duty and responsibility are bound up in altering this view. Because the meaning of Laura's death is bequeathed to him as part of his inheritance, his quest involves recovering women's stories and experiences in order to understand Laura's spiritual and physical legacy. By sharing this knowledge before the old men in the kiva, Tayo's story guides the people for future struggles to prevent the repetition of their injustice and suspicion towards women. Because Laura dies doubly dehumanized as disposable by both the community, which should protect her, and the ambiguous gendered/raced violence, which murders her, we never know the details of what her death signifies nor the degree to which both law and community have stripped her dignity. Tayo reasserts this dignity by redefining her being within the wounding community consciousness with which Thelma must contend, thus enacting a dignity-based reparation.

Silko's gender-decolonizing vision is consequently complex in its portrayal of women's identities as both facilitating and confining, and in her critique of rigid traditionalism. By referring back to the issues of gender disrespect and legally enforced discriminatory membership codes upheld by the *Martinez* case, Silko's novel focuses on the dynamics of women's social relations to show how women must be accorded recognition and dignity in their personhood if they are to act in ways that support the community through their knowledge and life experiences, and if the community is to evolve and change in order to counter new forms of colonial invasion and attack that target vulnerable members. The novel foregrounds women's agency through tradition in the associations that link their spiritual abilities to the abstract, mythic world represented by Reed Woman and Corn Woman as they bring renewal to the people. At the same time, it demonstrates that women's authority evolves from multiple sites of social interaction and cultural struggle to convey patterns of social intervention and cultural inheritance that are necessary for "completing the ceremony" and restoring the land since a "cure would be found only in something great and inclusive of everything" (126).

Thus, women figure as inheritors of Laura's spiritual legacy in ways that contest the patrilineality of Pueblo cultural transmission asserted by the Santa Clara Pueblo in the *Martinez* case. They also mirror Laura's experiences and enact aspects of her life story to provide alternative cultural narratives that are essential to the broad goals of community decolonization that are conveyed as missing about her past. Night Swan, Helen Jean, and Ts'eh demonstrate that a community that claims its authority over tradition and culture by policing women's sexual identities and cultural behaviour participates in undermining its own political authority and decolonizing vision. These women are also portrayed as socially vulnerable when they lack knowledge about other women's life stories, when they seek autonomy and gender empowerment in their own right by acting independently of a community's will, and when they challenge the people by disobeying their cultural conventions. Silko raises these gender dynamics to demonstrate that women's identities represent the strategic grounds through which colonialism and patriarchy work together to suppress social change. Her purpose is to illustrate how these restrictions have wider implications not only as injustice towards women but also as harms to the people and the land.

As a figure of creative-artistic vision, Night Swan's autonomy expresses a charismatic physical force that is both sought after and feared by the communities she encounters. Driven from small town to small town in pursuit of communion with the dance, her performances inspire an "ecstasy that illuminate[s] the dead tissues ... and hollow[s] of [her audience's] spirit" (85), inciting awe through her ability to uncover desires that have been hidden, and enabling sexual transcendence that takes the form of "wings that could fly" and "escape the gravity of the Church, the town ... mother[s] and [wives]" (85). In her youth and wilfulness, and lacking associations with other women, she mistakes the "feeling" she has for the spiritual world's creative force for the passion she shares with men. Silko's omniscient narrator observes the violent consequences that follow for her from this misunderstanding:

> If she had not been so young, she would have realized that he was nothing, that the power she was feeling had always been growing inside her, growing, pushing to the surface, only its season coinciding with her new lover. But she was young and she had never felt the power of the dance so strongly before, and she wanted to keep it; she wanted it with a great ferocity which she mistook for passion for this man ... She could have accepted it if he had told her that her light brown body no longer excited him. She would have sensed it herself and told him to go. But he was quitting because his desire for her had uncovered something which had been hiding inside him, something with wings that could fly, escape the gravity of the Church, the town, his mother, his wife. So he wanted to kill it: to crush the skull into the feathers and snap the bones of the wings. (83–4)

When she scorns her lover for ending their affair, he threatens to "run [her] out of town" through his authority as "somebody" that people listen to (85), accusing her of being a "Whore! Witch!" (85), for tempting him from his wife and church and for luring him from his proper behaviour (85). He dies tragically in a strange, unnatural event before he can act on his intention, and Night Swan leaves, but not before sensing a change in the land's well-being brought about by his abusive behaviour towards her, which also exemplifies an attack against the land, one that takes the form of a drought "drying out the land" and threatening to dissolve the "feeling" and "living" spirit that inspire her dance, spiritual awareness, and creativity (87). When she retreats to Cubero to live in the shadow of "Tse-pi'na, the woman veiled in clouds," dancing, now, only for her granddaughters (87), she removes her mythic power from the world and limits her capacity to bring about social transformation and community change. In so doing, her conduct makes other women vulnerable because they lack access to her experiences to enhance their achievement of autonomy, creativity, and self-worth.[35]

The negative consequences for women of Night Swan's retreat are also replicated in the story that Betonie tells of his grandmother and her relations with his wives who seek to limit her spiritual properties and the people's ability to evolve. Despite her role as a healer and inheritor of "Root Woman['s]" knowledge (151),[36] and a figure who empowers Betonie to change the peoples' ceremonies because things that do not "shift and grow are dead" (126), Betonie's grandmother elicits "fear" as an "alien thing," whom his grandfather's other wives disdain because he shows favouritism towards her by "sleep[ing] with her every night" and by "disgrace[ing]" them (147, 149). To protect her from their jealousy and from the "old men" who captured her and would have "kill[ed] her as soon as they found somebody who knew how it should be done" (148), he takes her into the mountains where they live in isolation and where he shares "his ceremonies …the chants and the stories they grew from" that she came for (150). Their spiritual retreat brings about ambiguous results for the people: although the rituals evolve to incorporate new elements so that "growth keeps the ceremonies strong," their seclusion engenders the people's "mistrust," which alters their faith in the traditions and in their capacity to grow (126). As a consequence, Betonie lives alone to protect his healing powers but warns Tayo about withdrawing from the world: "That's what the witchery is counting on; that we will cling to the ceremonies as the way they were, and then their power will triumph, and the people will be no more" (126).

Prophetically, Helen Jean's story demonstrates the intergenerational gap that exists when women and their stories are removed from the community by showing the social vulnerability and violence that women are subjected to because of their exclusion. Like Laura, Tayo's mother, whom she bears an uncanny resemblance to in the signs of her youthful self-consciousness – a "tooled leather purse with … rose designs … and little brass tubes of lipstick" (159) – Helen Jean is embarrassed by the old peoples' beliefs and strict traditionalism which conflict with her understanding of the world. When she is confronted by the "old Utes [who] said it was a lie; there were no such things" as "elevators," "tall buildings," and "juke boxes that could play a hundred different songs" (163), her uncertainty about their denial forces her to seek out like-minded individuals who affirm her sense of self-worth. She finds community with other young women who have left the reservation in search of work, after her job at the missionary school ends, but she cannot make ends meet when she is employed as a cleaning woman rather than as a secretary, and her roommates "tire of helping her out" (162). She is forced to quit when her boss begins sexually harassing her, "wait[ing] for her now" while she changed her clothes in the "toilet stall" (162–3). In her insecurity and lack of hope, she turns to sex work and consorting with Indigenous men who have returned from the war, believing their stories because "[t]hey had ribbons and medals they carried in their wallets; and if the U.S. Government decorated them, they must be okay" (163). The naivety of her point of view, and her affinity for "a feeling" that reflects "Ceremonial time," recall the reservation and the sisters that she misses to contrast with her experiences of physical, verbal, and sexual abuse in the towns that she travels through, and of hiding in bathrooms until the men she meets fall asleep and she can escape (162, 161, 165). She fears Tayo because he watches her constantly and is too quiet (155), reminding her of the "Pawnees" that she met from Oklahoma who took turns "holding and hitting her" because they thought "she was trying to split them up" (161). She leaves Tayo and his friends by soliciting the interests of a Mexican man in a bar whom she takes to be the lesser of two evils, promising herself to no longer "wast[e] her time there, in the middle of nowhere, some place worse than the reservation she had left" (166). Her story resonates with Tayo's mother through a memory of childhood hopelessness from Tayo's past when he lived in shelters outside of Gallup among other children that "women were ashamed to send home for their families to raise" (108). Through Helen Jean's story, Silko imparts her recognition that women's lives reflect the "social dynamics" of systematized disadvantage that "reinforce exclusion without being directly tied to the initial contexts of discrimination" (Reaume, "Discrimination and Dignity" 50). Her narrative also recalls the communities of women who were "missing" from the Pueblo for marrying non-members, women "[who] had been subjected to severe discrimination and mistreatment" over a thirty-year period, suffering what Ms Martinez characterized as "indignities" towards them in their treatment by the Pueblo (1977 WL 189106, 27), as noted above.

Silko resolves the tensions between women's cultural and social disempowerment and the land's renewal by foregrounding the interventions of women. Tayo's agency draws from his mixed-race inheritances through Indigenous and Mexican ancestry symbolized by his "green eyes" (119), in what may be a pointed revisioning of *Martinez*. Here, a mixed-race young adult's spiritual and political agency becomes a unique force for community healing rather than the grounds for economic and social disenfranchisement. Tayo is susceptible to violence and despair as traditions that also contextualize these lineages represented by the women's stories that are aligned with his quest.[37] On the occasions when he is tempted to give up the search for Josiah's cattle, his will is restored by Ts'eh. Ts'eh is portrayed as a beautiful young woman who intervenes from the spiritual world to offer Tayo physical, emotional, and spiritual regeneration. She is associated with both natural and mythic elements that convey her role in Betonie's healing ceremony through the constellations that adorn her blanket and the night sky above her cabin (177–8). However, she acts autonomously of Tayo's desire and domestic containment of her, resisting both his search for her and his unspoken entreaties that she not leave him (234). Her spiritual aid empowers him to envision an emerging story of love and renewal through memory and storytelling that assist him in overcoming the ritualistic lure of his war comrades' violence (231). Yet, owing to her associations with the willow tree (176, 221), she also recalls the physical and creative powers of Night Swan (82) and Laura (70) in their natural and mythic capacities. By gathering the "roots and leaves from many different plants" (222), and tying together the "short willow twigs into bundles" (229) in his presence, she enacts a ceremony of redemption at the spiritual level that is undertaken for women and men, a ceremony that replicates and completes the unifying task of rescuing Laura left incomplete and undone by Thelma's incapacity. In so doing, Ts'eh embodies the link between women's spiritual and secular relations to recall not only their source in traditions represented by the mythic stories of Reed Woman and Corn Woman, but also the central place of these relations in ending the drought and protecting the land in regard for the multilayered and secular causes that lead to its violation. For this reason, the people must enact new ceremonies and cultural practices as a collective in order to restore women's status, and as a duty to the past, to the protection of the land, and to the women whose suffering was an unacknowledged part of its knowledge, struggle, and protection.

Silko's vision of decolonization in relation to colonial law and patriarchal culture is thus complex: on the one hand, it envisions women as essential to community empowerment and land protection as actors who articulate tribal sovereignty; on the other, it confers the task of renewal and creativity on the people in order to imagine new relations beyond colonial legal frameworks and rigid traditionalism so as to empower decolonization without the suffering of women and their children. Silko's view of the people's readiness for this task is ambiguous. Because Ts'eh remains in the spiritual world, Silko implies that the community is not yet prepared to accept women's cultural power and social authority but must work towards their reconciliation by untangling community practices from their "tangled, twisted roots" (69) in colonial law and patriarchal uses of tradition.

Envisioning a Tribally Situated Feminist Consciousness

Silko's novel articulates the need for the recognition of women's roles as they empower a community to act in ways that accord social justice to Indigenous women. *Ceremony* restores dignity by showing how stories represent new sources of creativity to counter gender injustice. As a contribution to Indigenous-feminist practice, her novel also addresses the dignity that Ms Martinez sought from her Pueblo and through courts of law. By undertaking the creative task of imagining stories that empower and respect women's selfhood, Silko claims for literary practices the authority to recognize dignity in personhood. She does so by openly addressing the injustice of the Santa Clara Pueblo's discrimination towards women in such a way as to take seriously Denise Reaume's insight that although "Legislators may not have been consciously aware of the stereotypical assumptions grounding their conduct in enacting legislation to begin with ... once these assumptions are brought to the surface through litigation, the issue becomes what message is sent by continuing to enforce such legislation" ("Discrimination and Dignity" 38). The political necessity of conceptualizing conditions and practices for Indigenous women's empowerment not only through the formation of political consciousness but also through the recognition of Indigenous women writers as both activists and translocal actors emerges powerfully in stories that these writers tell about the gender politics of Indigenous communities. Such stories resonate with those represented by law stories, such as Ms Martinez's, in her efforts to secure tribal membership for her children because they show the failure of tribal practices to value women's gender knowledge and their capacities. Silko's novel, written on the cusp of the *Martinez* ruling, undertakes a gender-decolonizing framework to propose that this political necessity has not yet been realized. Her recognition is apt given that Indigenous-feminist projects continue to be dismissed for their seeming opposition to tribal sovereignty. Jo Carrillo argues, for example, in "Tribal Governance/Gender," that "American feminists used *Santa Clara* as a foil to argue the plausibility of a universal patriarchal oppression of a universal female culture. Even those who distanced themselves from the premise of a universal female "culture" still used the case to argue that issues like these needed to be viewed in context. None of these feminists spoke with Julia Martinez, the woman who brought the lawsuit against her tribal government; they simply supported or condemned her action. But as Ms Martinez's own attorney noted, "'Julia was *not* suing her tribe for feminist reasons. She was participating in her tribal government in the ways that were available to her'" ("Tribal Governance/Gender" 208).

To argue that Martinez sought *solely* to situate her political rights within the sovereignty rights of her community would be to overlook her tireless efforts to change the membership ordinance that disentitled her children and other women similarly situated. Such a claim is a call for political quietism, rendering Indigenous women's concerns as necessarily subsidiary to a social and political order that confines their roles to a historical past or to normative community expectations, for the changes to the membership ordinance that Ms Martinez sought to challenge emerged out of the contradictions inherited from the colonial past which proposed to eliminate tribal sovereignty through imposed forms of colonial government authority. For Indigenous feminists *not* to support her cause through creative and critical means is to become complicit in the colonial process that she fought so courageously to change. Silko proposes a different path to gender empowerment, through stories that depend on valuing Indigenous women's capacities in the formation of struggles that serve both to reimagine their experiences and knowledge in socially meaningful ways, stories that open up a path to the pasts of missing women, and stories that situate gender identity as facilitating community revival as an important yet unrealized goal that serves both the recovery and redemptive ends of tribal liberation.

Chapter Two

The Legal Silencing of Indigenous Women: *Racine v. Woods* (1983) and *In Search of April Raintree* (1983)

Silko's portrayal of Indigenous women, "trapped in one of the oldest ways," by cultural roles and domestic obligations that involve aspects of self-sacrifice in the care or interests of their children demonstrates how gender identity intersects with law to signify its discriminatory effects and to highlight urgent social justice issues that matter to Indigenous women. Silko shares with other creative writers and social activists a concern for treating law "as a cultural reality" by scrutinizing its "signs," "symbols," and metaphors of self-expression (Sarat & Simon 13) to show how law's authority "lives [on] in our imaginations" (13), influencing our "modes of thought" and "determining conduct" (15). The recognition of law's material and socially symbolic power makes its interdisciplinary analysis essential to interrupting its culturally and politically confining reach. Analysing its patterns of exclusion, confinement, and erasure, this book's cultural analysis of law framework demonstrates how law partakes of a twofold method of representation: by proxying Indigenous women in order to fold them into its mechanisms of authority and by portraying them in order to determine their conduct. Through dialectically interrelating law and literature, this approach highlights the relationship between legal texts and literary narratives to make apparent the wider critical terrain within which law practices circulate to enact disparities for Indigenous women, deploying literature as a source of cultural authority with which to interrupt and contest these enactments. Literary texts question legal appropriations by articulating the gender injustice that follows from legal reasoning as it forecloses on Indigenous women's capacities to achieve their full social and political wellbeing and potential. An Indigenous-feminist lens theorizes these disparities to make apparent gender injustice by tracking law's implication in the social and political struggles that Indigenous women confront, and by illustrating the consequences that they endure when they fail to conform to gender behaviours that are defined and imposed by colonial-legal orders and enforced by Indigenous communities.

Storytelling represents an important source for establishing these disparities. Like Silko, storytellers such as Thomas King also engage legal events. King's coming of age novel, *Medicine River*, demonstrates how Indigenous women suffer from economic and social deprivation for not complying with Indigenous community value systems, for failing to conform to colonial laws and legislation, or for being legally prevented from returning to their reservation homes. King's portrayal of these discriminatory conditions is both poignant and direct: Will's mother, Rose, loses her job at The Bay after she steals dress shirts for her sons to wear so that they may pose for a family photograph to honour the death of their non-Indigenous father, a man whose abandonment forces his wife and children into abject poverty and cultural and social isolation as a consequence of Rose's "marrying out" (Kirby 77), that is, of her having married a non-Indigenous man.[1]

Eden Robinson also depicts penalty-of-choices circumstances in which Indigenous women must decide among competing harms in order to secure safety for themselves or their children. Robinson's engagement with this issue is even more politically uncompromising in showing how gender injustice is connected to wider patterns of social discrimination that Indigenous women suffer from as a result of intrusive colonial laws or exploitative social practices. In *Monkey Beach*, when LisaMarie's grandmother, Ma-ma-oo, is subject to spousal assault, she reacts by sending two of her children to residential school in order to protect them from her husband's abuse. Ma-ma-oo spares her children by removing them from the family home but only by making them vulnerable to other forms of physical and cultural harm. She is thus subject to two forms of oppression that are socially created: domestic assault by her husband that law enforcement officials do not act on and alienation from her children who fail to understand why she sent them to residential school.[2]

Because these writers depict gender violence and social discrimination as intersecting harms, they show how the "political unconscious"[3] of literary texts enables recognition of the ways that race and gender identities intersect in colonially created legal contexts to withhold protection of Indigenous women's legal, cultural, and political rights.

As they demonstrate, colonial laws enacted through the discriminatory provisions of the Indian Act, and patriarchal violence within Indigenous communities interact through different levels of the social formation to create the interlocking conditions that lead to Indigenous women's social, cultural, and political disempowerment. Frederic Jameson theorizes these overlapping constraints as "practices of expressive causality" in which "similar processes are observed in two distinct regions of social life" (41). Creative writers such as Silko, Robinson, and King highlight these causal connections in law and social discourses in order to show their integrated effects. Their writing illustrates how gender violence is politically organized, as one set of exploitative conditions sutures violence against Indigenous women into another level of the social formation, making Indigenous women vulnerable in overlapping and systemic ways; at the same time, their writing calls attention to these issues in order to bring wider awareness to them while also fostering public debate about how gender injustice matters as an urgent social concern.

In this chapter, I explore how Beatrice Culleton Mosionier's fictional autobiography, *In Search of April Raintree*, contributes to these debates. Mosionier's portrayal of systemic injustice towards Indigenous women connects the issue of Indigenous women's vulnerability to social outcomes that follow from legal assessments of their conduct. I align *In Search of April Raintree* with the Supreme Court of Canada's ruling in *Racine v. Woods* to demonstrate Mosionier's construction of a law-and-literature dialectic of representation that situates gender injustice as one of the "human consequences of legal actions" (Brooks 350). I compare the court case and the novel in two ways: first, I situate the text in the field of transitional justice feminism to analyse how it contributes to debates concerning Indigenous women's lack of access to justice resources; second, I explore how Mosionier's novel addresses a key tension in transitional justice literature concerning criminal prosecutions and the social consequences of trials, by asking: to what extent can Indigenous women turn to law to fulfil their expectations of justice when law and its social consequences have been the source of their disentitlement and oppression? I take up this question by exploring the novel's engagement with the Supreme Court of Canada's "best interests of the child" legal standard that was established in *Racine v. Woods*, a case decided in the same year that Mosionier's novel was published.

Structural parallels exist between the *Racine* case and *In Search of April Raintree* that connect the "hard facts of law" with the "imaginary facts of literature" (Felman, "Forms" 740). The case arose in Brandon, Manitoba, appearing before the Court of Queen's Bench in 1982, the Manitoba Court of Appeal in Winnipeg later that same year, and the Supreme Court of Canada in 1983. As a child-custody matter involving a First Nations mother and Metis adoptive parents, the case generated widespread media attention at each level of the court system.[4] Both the case and the novel raise questions concerning how the state justifies "out-adoption" practices affecting Indigenous children, and both explore an important issue regarding the relationship between parental bonding and a child's need for culture and heritage over time. The texts differ in so far as the Supreme Court's reasoning resolves the question of how culture relates to identity through abstract means, first, by theoretically separating a child from its culture of origin, and second, by situating the child as an autonomous actor whose needs may be conceptualized through the "best interests of the child" legal standard, a principle of assessment that remains in effect today.

Mosionier's novel addresses the social implications of the Supreme Court's reasoning by foregrounding the essential role that family plays in forming a child's sense of personal security and cultural identity. Conveyed through the first-person account of an Indigenous woman who grows to adulthood in non-Indigenous foster care, *In Search of April Raintree* depicts identity and culture as interconnected factors. The novel tells the life story of April Raintree, a woman of Indigenous – Ojibway and Metis – ancestry living in Winnipeg, Manitoba, who is placed in adoptive custody at an early age with her younger sister, Cheryl. April's narrative describes how both sisters are taken from their family home due to parental neglect and alcohol abuse, and how both girls are raised by adoptive families without access to knowledge about their Indigenous ancestry, with only intermittent contact from their parents and each other, and with only a passing concern by child welfare authorities for their desire to remain together as siblings. Centred through April's personal account, the novel foregrounds her memories of the girls' experiences of removal and foster care, emphasizing the disconcerting effects of several legal scenarios that they are confronted with: their confusing and alienating treatment by child welfare actors, their ongoing uncertainty and anxiety about why they are not permitted to see their parents, and their unsuccessful attempts to find their parents and restore the elements of their missing pasts. As the principal narrator of the story, April's perspective highlights her quest to find meaning in these events, as they depict the breakdown of her family relations, her concern to remain intimately connected with her sister, and her struggle to overcome her sister's traumatic loss through suicide. In her search for meaning from her past in order to move forward with her life in the future – one of the principle goals of legal judgment and resolution (Felman, "Forms" 738) – April's quest for "symbolic understanding" (738) demonstrates Mosionier's recognition of the unfinished work of legal justice. Mosionier's novel calls into question law's privileging of justice in the form of "truth," "finality," and the "force of resolution" (738) by contrasting the principled objectivity of law with the immediacy of personal experience. Through this juxtaposition, her text makes apparent aspects of gender violence that law discounts and omissions within legal reasoning that engender discriminatory social consequences for Indigenous women that the novel portrays through April's voice and experience.

This chapter begins by analysing *Racine v. Woods* to demonstrate how Indigenous women's conduct emerges as a central factor in the case. Next, I situate the ruling in the context of other cases concerning Indigenous women's status and their rights in order to establish a "cross-legal structure" (Felman, "Forms" 745) within which *Racine* participates. Third, I show how Mosionier's novel intervenes in these cases by using storytelling to act as a bridge between legal texts and literary practices by highlighting how law creates the conditions of social segregation that lead to Indigenous women's disempowerment. I conclude by analysing the theme of learned powerlessness that *In Search of April Raintree* portrays to contest the erosion of Indigenous women's rights through the state's regulation of their identities. One of the novel's most important contributions to debates concerning justice for Indigenous women in liberal-democratic states that have not undergone regime change but adopted transitional justice measures is the connection it establishes between the out-adoption of Indigenous children and unresolved legacies of dispossession enacted by Canada's Indian residential school system. Mosionier's novel foregrounds these colonial practices as central in creating the discriminatory conditions that both sisters, as foster children, confront in their quests to overcome their social isolation as a consequence of their out-adopted status.

Indigenous Women's Rights and *Racine v. Woods* (1983)

When the Supreme Court of Canada handed down its decision in *Racine v. Woods* in the fall of 1983, it brought to an end the five-year struggle by

Ms Linda Jean Woods to recover custody of her seven-year old daughter. Ms Woods, a member of the Long Plain First Nation, appeared before the Supreme Court as a respondent in an appeal brought by Mr Allan Norman Racine and Mrs Sandra Christine Racine, a married couple and members of the Metis Federation, who were awarded custody of Ms Woods's daughter by the Trial Division Court of Manitoba after they filed an application for adoption under s. 103(2) of the Child Welfare Act (S.M. 1974, c. 30; *Woods v. Racine and Racine* 1982 para. 62, para. 1).[5] Ms Woods appealed the decision of the Trial Court that dismissed her custody application and granted Mr and Mrs Racine's adoption order (*Woods v. Racine and Racine* para. 20). When the Manitoba Court of Appeal upheld Ms Woods's appeal, by overturning the adoption order, by pronouncing her daughter a ward of the Court of Appeal, by granting custody of her child to Mr and Mrs Racine, and by permitting Ms Woods to apply for access and custody (*Racine v. Woods* 177–8), both parties appealed to the Supreme Court: Ms Woods, on the grounds that the appellate court erred in not restoring legal custody to her when it set aside the adoption order granted to Mr and Mrs Racine; and Mr and Mrs Racine, by arguing that the appellate court erred in overturning the trial judge's decision of a "*de facto* adoption" based on "evidence of a forcible refusal to give up custody in a situation in which the proposed adopting parents themselves concede[d] they had no legal right" (*Woods v. Racine and Racine* para. 148). The appellate court characterized Mr and Mrs Racine's refusal to return the child to her mother in 1978 as a form of "illegal assertion of title" (*Racine v. Woods* 183) that permitted them to "embark ... on a three-year waiting period to simplify the legal procedures to be followed in adopting (the girl)" (*Racine v. Woods* 184).[6] The key issues that came before the Supreme Court concerned two questions: (1) what were Ms Woods's intentions when, with her consent, she relinquished custody of her daughter to Mr and Mrs Racine in May 1978, giving the child into their care (*Racine v. Woods* 175), and thus facilitating their legal action in October 1978 of filing a "Notice of Receiving a Child for Private Adoption" (*Racine v. Woods*, header); and (2) what was in the "child's best interests" in an "interracial context" (*Racine v. Woods* 174) in which conflicting expert testimony at the trial and appellate level characterized the removal of the child from Sandra Racine's care as "tantamount to frank emotional abuse" (*Woods v. Racine and Racine* para. 150), on the one hand, yet questioned the long-term effects and "finality of an adoption order" that severed contact "both from her natural mother and from her Indian heritage and culture" (*Racine v. Woods* 186; see also *Woods v. Racine and Racine* para. 98), on the other hand.[7]

The Supreme Court found in favour of Mr and Mrs Racine by upholding their appeal, dismissing Ms Woods's cross-appeal, and reinstating the "Order of Adoption made by the trial judge" (*Racine v. Woods* 189). Using strong language to express the Court's concurrence with the view held by Justice Hall from the Court of Appeal who argued that "this child should not be allowed to become a battleground" (187), Justice Wilson stated: "In my view, when the test to be met is the best interests of the child, the significance of cultural background and heritage as opposed to bonding abates over time. The closer the bond that develops with the prospective adoptive parents the less important the racial element becomes ... While the Court can feel great compassion for the respondent, and respect for her determined efforts to overcome her adversities, it has an obligation to ensure that any order it makes will promote the best interests of her child. This and this alone is our task" (187–8). In so deciding that the child's best interests lay in granting her custody to Mr and Mrs Racine, the Court settled with "finality" an adoption order that severed all legal ties between Ms Woods and her daughter (186).

Racine v. Woods represents a crucial case in Canadian jurisprudence. It serves as the legal test that determined the principle by which courts in custody disputes "no longer treat ... children as the property of those who gave them birth" but instead assess "what is in [the child's] best interests" (*Racine v. Woods* 174). Feminist legal scholar Marlee Kline argues that the case and its formulation of the "best interests" standard mark a turning point in family law practice that has had a devastating impact on Indigenous communities through the Court's ideological coding of Indigenous peoples in legal discourse. According to Kline, the case not only ushered in a view of the child "as an individual abstracted out of her community and cultural contexts," but also "helped to justify her separation from it" ("Child Welfare Law" 390, 396). By providing an "interpretive legal framework" that makes the removal of Indigenous children from their families "appear[] natural, necessary, and legitimate," Kline contends, the case "minimize[s] and even negate[s] ... the relevance and importance of maintaining a child's First Nations identity and culture" (393).[8]

As a record of the legal system's "structural capacity to deliver 'justice'" (Franke 815), the case also stages a key problem in transitional justice literature: how to account for the "causal" ways in which social institutions, such as law, practice or create conditions of gender vulnerability that beset women. Alison Jaggar poses the problem as one that concerns reconciling an institutional commitment to social justice with women's ongoing experiences of gender disempowerment that are socially created and that pre-exist their current conditions (47). Institutions, such as law, she notes, which characterize women in autonomous ways as actors capable of "inexplicable coincidences," "bad choices," or "false consciousness," impede the "[d]etermination [of] causation" in understanding women's social vulnerability because the question of gender inequality as a pre-existing social condition is poorly understood (37). According to Jaggar, not only do women suffer from inadequate access to resources, their deprivation is amplified when subsequent injustices occur, permitting institutions to characterize their vulnerability to social disadvantage as the outcome of their "natural victim" status or "need [for] special protection," gendered characterizations that are not representative of how institutions erode a woman's agency or will, but rather are indicative of the failure to understand that "gendered vulnerabilities" are "socially created" and inhibit "women's autonomy and agency" (47).

That Ms Woods appeared before the Supreme Court as a person impeded by "inexplicable coincidences," "bad choices," and "false consciousness" in such a way that disparaged her autonomy and agency and discounted aspects of interlocking social conditions that contributed to her personal vulnerability emerges in the Supreme Court's account of her behaviour. In reviewing the Trial Judge's decision to award custody to Mr and Mrs Racine in light of Ms Woods's conduct to recover her daughter outside of legal means, Justice Wilson described Ms Woods's actions as "unfortunate" when, by "taking matters into her own hands," she attempted to "abduct [her daughter] first from her school and then from the Racine home" (177); as "manifest[ing] an incredible indifference" towards her daughter when Ms Woods arranged for the media to be present at her first "exercise of access" (177), an act that drew special criticism from the Trial Judge who questioned Ms Woods's behaviour as exhibiting "concern for the child as a person or as a political issue" (179); and as irresponsible, when she filed a "*habeas corpus* application" to recover her daughter in 1982 rather than in 1978, prompting Justice Wilson to remark that "Mrs. Woods had a responsibility when her rights were challenged to pursue them in the court if necessary and not to wait until her child was bonded to the Racines with all the problems for the child that the disruption of that bond was likely to create" (184).[9] The Supreme Court distanced itself from the Trial Judge's finding of "abandonment" (184) as a cause for upholding the adoption order, but singled out for further comment the appropriate form of "parental tie" the Court "has to be concerned about," as one that represents "a meaningful and positive force in the life of the child and not in the life of the parent" (185). It also noted the higher standards of conduct that the "legislature" had empowered the Court to impose when it stated, "In giving the court power to dispense with the consent of the parent on a *de facto* adoption the legislature has recognized an aspect of the human condition – that our own self-interest sometimes clouds our perception of what is best for those for whom we are responsible" (185).[10]

The Supreme Court's characterization of Ms Woods's behaviour shows how conduct by Indigenous women informs a court's legal outcome, determining their access to and attainment of justice. Because legal processes reflect practices of colonial judicial bias, legal reasoning draws on evaluative structures that impose constraints on Indigenous peoples' rights as a consequence of the law's recourse to a "cultural framework" (Povinelli 580) that dictates which judicial resources they have access to. These frameworks subject Indigenous peoples to a predominance of "colonial perspectives" that shape a judicial common sense and construct a "devaluative ideology of Indianness" through which their rights are granted or withheld (Kline, "Colour" 452, 455).[11] Kline argues, in relation to the *Racine* case, that it authorizes the cultural view that it is *not* in the "best interests" of Indigenous children to have a "political First Nations mother" because of the potential detrimental impact such a person might have on a child. She states, "Linda Woods not only failed to conform to the dominant conception of a good mother, but also that of a "good Indian," one who "is defined in terms of white values and culture and in terms of docile and apolitical behavior'" ("Child Welfare Law" 409, citations omitted).

As a narrative concerning Indigenous women's conduct, the *Racine* case establishes a legal and social context for the issue of Indigenous women's access to justice that *In Search of April Raintree* explores. Because the case institutes and recalls legal outcomes that have wider political consequences for Indigenous women, it not only inscribes in legal discourse a "politically interested figuration" (Spivak, "Imperialism" 225) of Indigenous women's selfhood; it also shows the struggle taking place in cultural discourses over the power to define Indigenous women's rights and their attainment of state mechanisms to protect their interests. By troping Indigenous women's behaviour as "like" and "unlike" an implied legal standard, the case makes apparent how courts erode Indigenous women's justice initiatives by undermining or misrepresenting their collective historical identities and legal claims. It does so by enacting what Shoshana Felman describes as a "cross-legal" structure that "recapitulates the memory, the themes, the legal questions, and the arguments" of other cases ("Forms" 745). Indigenous women's identity forms the grounds for this comparative repetition and assessment. Despite arising as a dispute concerning custody of a child, *Racine* repeats the structural analogues of earlier cases involving the rights claims to culture and identity launched by Indigenous women. Two former cases demonstrate the "historical duality," "cumulative legal meaning," and "traumatic" constraints (Felman, "Forms" 747, 746) of prior decisions: *Attorney General of Canada v. Lavell – Isaac v. Bedard* S.C.R. (1974), and *Sandra Lovelace v. Canada*, Communication No. R.6/24, U.N. Doc. Supp. No. 40 (A/36/40) at 166 (1981).

The *Lavell – Bedard* Supreme Court case concerned Jeannette Lavell and Yvonne Bedard's challenge to a decision by the Attorney General of Canada that disentitled them from their Indian status as a result of their marriages to non-Indian men. Ms Lavell and Ms Bedard claimed that section 12(1)(b) of the Indian Act discriminated against them on the basis of sex because "in defining Indian status so as to exclude women of Indian birth who ... married non-Indians," the legislation sanctioned a different result for Indian women in comparison with Indian men who were not subject to the membership exclusions, thereby "abrogating, abridging, [and] infringing the rights of such women to equality before the law" (1350). The Supreme Court of Canada disagreed. It held that "equality before the law," within the meaning of the Canadian Bill of Rights, meant "equality of treatment in the enforcement and application of the laws of Canada before the law enforcement authorities and the ordinary courts of the land" (1373). Because section 12(1)(b) applied equally to all Indian women as a class who married non-Indian men, no inequality existed among Indian women in the application and enforcement of the legislation. The Supreme Court's ruling reinstated the Attorney General's decision and affirmed the Canadian government's authority to enact law that discriminated on the basis of sex in establishing the qualifications and entitlement of persons "to status as Indians and to the use and benefit of Crown 'lands reserved for Indians'" (1359). Ms Lavell and Ms Bedard lost their Indian status, were barred from returning to their reserve communities following the dissolution of their marriages, prevented from accessing and using reserve lands, and prohibited from transmitting their Indian status and cultural identity to their children, who were also disentitled from residing with their Indigenous communities on reserve lands. As a consequence of the Supreme Court's ruling, Indigenous women who sought protection from state discrimination in maintaining their Indian status were forced to appeal to external legal sources in order to remedy the government's unequal treatment of them. In October 1977, Sandra Lovelace, a Maliseet woman from the Tobique Indian Reserve in New Brunswick, appealed her disentitlement from Indian status to the United Nations Human Rights Committee under the International Covenant on Civil and Political Rights, to which Canada was a signatory.[12]

Contending that Canada was in violation of articles 23, 26, and 27, which protect the rights of the family, the right to equal protection before the law without discrimination, and the rights of minorities to the enjoyment of their culture, religion, and language, Ms Lovelace asserted that the legislation which requires an "Indian woman ... to refrain from marrying the spouse of her choice in order to retain rights under the Indian Act for herself and her children ... violates the duty of the state to protect the family unit" (2). Ms Lovelace argued that although the legislation intended the "laudable" goal of protecting "the Indian minority and its reservation lands from outsiders" (3), the method of protection was achieved in a "discriminatory manner" that "the government must revise" (Communication dated 29 December 1977, 3–4). The Committee upheld Ms Lovelace's complaint. It found that Canada had violated article 27 in preventing Ms Lovelace from residing on the Tobique Reserve and in denying her access to "her native culture and language" because "there is no place outside the Tobique Reserve where such a community exits" (Communication dated 17 August 1981, 9). In finding Canada had been negligent in its obligations to protect the rights of minorities to "enjoy their ... culture and use their own language in community with other members" (9), the Committee also held that denying Ms Lovelace the right to live on the Tobique Reserve did not appear "reasonable" or "necessary to preserve the identity of the tribe" (Communication No. R.6/24 10).

The *Lavell – Bedard* and *Lovelace* cases are important indicators of state barriers that prevent Indigenous women's access to and attainment of their legal rights. They are significant because they establish a culture of legal uncertainty that contextualizes the gender issues raised by the *Racine* case to highlight how political inequality is built into Canada's treatment of Indigenous women. Questions about Indigenous women's access to justice and the equity of their legal representation inform the social terrain that Mosionier's novel constructs. Focused through April's first-person account, it depicts Indigenous women's political and social vulnerability by conveying the stark immediacy and sense of violation that April experiences as she navigates the criminal court system. Recounting the traumatic events of a vicious rape and the subsequent trial, April's narrative reveals her bewildered sense of injury and growing doubt that the crown attorney will be able to convince the jury that her attacker is guilty "because of what he had done" and not because she "was such a pitiful creature" (168). Describing her "unreasonable fear" that the investigating police might turn on her, the indifference of doctors who "chide" her for removing urine residue from her mouth as destruction of evidence (134), and the futility of her efforts to wash herself clean of the rapists' "dirty, stinking bodies" (136), April voices despair that the legal system can provide justice for her. "What would I and other 'squaws' get out of my going to court?" (139) she asks, deploying against herself the language of hatred[13] used during the sexual assault to describe her feelings of powerlessness as her testimony recalling the event is translated into legal norms and outcomes that are governed by the court's rules of procedures.

Informed by the crown attorney that she could "testify only to what was directly known," she worries that the instructions controlling "hearsay evidence" will impede her ability to convey what happened or that the defence counsel will misconstrue her statements (149). At the hearing, she falters repeatedly under cross-examination, minimizing "the dirty details" that "overwhelm [her]" as she struggles to "describe the act itself," even as she is unnerved by courtroom "eyes" that appear to be "burning into [her]" (150). She admits to grasping why the defence attorney must defend his client, but finds his persistent scrutinizing of her testimony upsetting to the point of feeling "morally wrong[ed]" (150). She reacts by breaking down in the bathroom, vomiting and crying for having realized "why some women choose not to seek justice in the courtrooms" (151, 150). During the trial, her feelings of disempowerment are realized when the opposing counsel's lawyer informs the jury that his client had been drinking heavily; believed that April was a "prostitute," consenting "by her own silence to have sexual intercourse"; and "object[ing] because "she had not received compensation for her services" (169). As she sits in the courtroom fuming to herself – "That man, the accused, that bastard, Donnelly, had raped me ... He deserved to be found guilty and nothing else" – she is beset by worry that "there was a possibility that the jurists would find him innocent" (169). The judge's jury instructions also cause her consternation and distress as his summary of the evidence and explanation of how the charges relate to the facts "strain ... [her] patience [in having] to listen to him" (170). The guilty verdict is both anti-climactic and a relief as court procedures force her to the uncomfortable realization that "Justice, to a certain point, had been done" (170). When her feelings of violation remain with her following the trial, she attempts to find a source for her victimization, initially, by blaming her sister who was the intended target for the brutal attack (166), and subsequently, through anger at the dismissal of how she feels – "dirty and rotten and used" – convinced by her treatment that she'll "never be the same again" (172). Rebuked for not moving on or permitting herself "to heal," she asks, "How was I supposed to just 'let go'[?] ... It simply wasn't possible" (172–3).

April's sexual assault trial forms the centerpiece in Mosionier's novel. It not only recalls prior incidents of injustice April experiences as an out-adopted child through interactions with social institutions that organize, regulate, and scrutinize her life; it also foregrounds how a criminal trial and its disciplinary procedures establish "authoritative determinations of legalized events," by narrowing victim accounts to fit a systematic approach that "shape[s] cultural ideas of justice, truth, and responsibility that law has been integral to constructing" (Authers 2–3). Scholars of transitional justice argue that women experience gender injustice and ongoing perceptions of violation when they testify as victims in criminal cases. They note that those who give evidence suffer revictimization because their accounts of sexual violence seem "less important than the larger picture which their testimony helps [to] establish," and because legal outcomes "translate [their] suffering into the language of law and rights ... [to] satisfy the interests of legal authorities more than those who are called to narrate their pain" (Franke 816, 821). "To bear witness," they argue, is to pose one's self and one's memories "in a way that allows them to be harvested by judicial actors in the service of larger [justice] goals" (821). "Healing the witness," they contend, "is not and cannot be the court's concern" (821).

By showing how April struggles to resist the appropriation and containment of her experience of violation through a court system that rearticulates and thereby alters her account, Mosionier deploys the literary to demonstrate the structural displacement of April's voice and to challenge authoritative accounts of legal events. She does so not only by illuminating how legal discourses proxy women's testimonies, but also by demonstrating how the objective aims of legal discourse depend on displacing law's predication in multivocality.[14] By aligning April's treatment with the experiences of Indigenous women who have been objectified, silenced, or displaced by law practices that systematically set aside their suffering – cases such as *Racine, Lavell – Bedard*, and *Lovelace* – Mosionier uses April's narrative and her experience to restore recognition of gender disparities built into legal mechanisms as they erode Indigenous women's rights. April's cry of despair expressing her humiliation and mistreatment at the hands of legal actors thus recalls earlier episodes in her life when women were subjected to legal scrutiny and their rights denied, as when her mother was deprived of her newborn daughter, Anna, at the same time as April and Cheryl were taken into custody by child welfare authorities. Her uncertainty about how her sister is involved as the target for the vicious attack, and her worry that her assailant will be absolved of his crime because her sister was working as a "prostitute" at the time, focus attention on the silent figure of the Indigenous woman that Cheryl's presence in the courtroom represents, a figure who is depicted negatively by legal discourses that subject her actions to legal scrutiny in order to apportion blame, yet whose presence, paradoxically, displaces recognition of prior legal mechanisms that are responsible for her vulnerability which assessments of her conduct obscure. April's refusal to resign herself to her exploitative treatment by legal actors demonstrates how the interests of law and the interests of justice are at odds with each other, carrying a burden of self-disclosure and sacrifice for Indigenous women that seeking legal remedies through the courts requires of them. In thus depicting the multilayered and incremental ways in which legal processes achieve wide-ranging, gender-discriminatory effects for April and other Indigenous women with whom she is associated, Mosionier uses storytelling to act as a bridge between cases that withhold the state's protection of Indigenous women's collective rights, and cases that depict acts of violence against them as individuals. Her novel attests to the importance of decolonizing law mechanisms in countries, such as Canada, which have not undergone regime transition in their relations with Indigenous peoples and in which courts of law continue to function as intermediaries carrying out the government's illiberal, assimilative, and discriminatory ends.

Transitional Justice, Indigenous Women, and Literature

By illustrating how Indigenous women are subjected to gender violence not only as deliberate targets, but also as members of communities weakened by colonial policies that historically eroded their political rights, Mosionier's novel raises an important insight for transitional justice feminism – that violence against Indigenous women is neither random nor isolated but rather a direct result of prior state and colonial legal policies that make Indigenous women susceptible to violation. Although transitional justice paradigms recognize the gender disparities built into legal frameworks, they do not analyse the gendered dimensions of colonial-law mechanisms in non-transition countries to the same extent.[15] Transitional justice scholars argue that women are excluded, silenced, or exploited by law mechanisms in several important ways: they are "absent" from "formal negotiations" even when their absence does not "equate with" a lack of "demands for accountability" (Bell and O'Rourke 25; Otto 50–1); they are subject to prior forms of "gendered, social patterns of suffering" in times of transition despite disclosing that "patterns of inequality" are linked to gender-exploitative practices that preceded conflicts (Ni Aoláin and Rooney 347); they are singled out to account for experiences of "extraordinary violence" in ways that discount their experiences of "ordinary" violence in the form of "poverty, "racism," or "crime" (Nagy 284; Nesiah et al. 7); they are silenced by "local attitudes" that "tend to overshadow legal rights" when they are "referred back to communities by formal authorities, who consider such cases to be 'private matters'" (Chopra and Isser 343); and they are subject to "alienating" (Franke 818) forms of witness-testifying on behalf of themselves or other women (Nagy 286).

For women in Western-style democracies, these erasures are compounded by their location in states that are not subject to the same human-rights scrutiny as countries rebuilding from systemic war or political and civil strife, countries such as Canada. *In Search of April Raintree* participates in transitional justice debates by portraying how law provokes adverse social conditions for Indigenous women. The task of showing how and why legal mechanisms in liberal-democratic countries committed to ending gender discrepancies, achieving social reparations, and fostering future social justice goals fail to achieve gender justice for Indigenous women thus represents a key concern for liberal-democratic countries as they undertake transitional justice in their relations with Indigenous peoples, a duty to which literary texts in their cultural analysis of law engagements contribute. Literary texts do so by showing how colonial policies continue to influence the lives of women, how prior court decisions matter for Indigenous peoples, and how transitional justice may be applied to achieve more equitable gender relations.

Indigenous women's justice objectives intersect with transitional justice's global framework in three ways that replicate women's exclusions in other countries that have adopted these legal measures: (1) their concerns about ongoing gender disparities are omitted from government recognition in so far as they are permitted to participate in state processes solely as "survivors" of violence, rather than as citizens expressing wider patterns of social vulnerability that exist due to state policies, such as "the residential school system and present child welfare policies" (Jung, "Transitional Justice" 3) that impact directly on Indigenous women; (2) they engage in "sharing circles" about residential school experiences on behalf of themselves and other family members, expressing "feeling ashamed and silenced" (Angel 207), yet they are not permitted to connect this experience to forms of domestic and social violence that they disproportionately suffer from (Amnesty International, Canada 1; Kuokkanen 227); (3) the legal system in Canada, like other countries engaged in transitional justice, relies on courts of law to ground, assess, and display publicly the achievement of a political transition to reparatory justice through measures that (a) revive the state's accountability (Teitel, "Global" 2), (b) "promot[e] cultures of justice" (James 25), and (c) facilitate "reconciliation" among members of society (Jung, "Canada and the Legacy" 242). Courts of law, however, are not scrutinized for their capacity to achieve or facilitate these changes. As Nitya Iyer explains, the law's systematic approach to equality impedes recognition of pre-existing "relations of inequality" that organize the social field and that "require ... those injured ... to caricature both themselves and their experiences ... in order to succeed with a legal claim" (181). To address legal disparities that confront Indigenous women, transitional justice feminism requires different sites of analysis for conceptualizing how colonial laws organize the social field in ways that amplify Indigenous women's vulnerability in non-transitional societies and different sources of representation for understanding their deprivations. Mosionier's novel intervenes in these debates by shifting the grounds on which legal events are understood to the symbolic capacities of the literary text in order to foreground issues of legal representation and gender disparities that Indigenous women confront due to Canada's colonial past. Her novel consequently establishes the literary as an important cultural site that bears witness to the legally unrepresentable.

Memory, Agency, and a Body in Pain: *In Search of April Raintree*

The absence of Indigenous women's rights and positive conceptions of their identities inform the social terrain that Mosionier's novel constructs to show how habits of learned powerlessness shape April's identity as she strives to negotiate the agency she is permitted by legal institutions that supervise and control her life. As a narrative that conveys her search for meaning, selfhood, and personal understanding, April's quest depicts the classic struggle of the powerless that Iris Marion Young describes as "those who lack authority or power ... [those who] are situated so that they must take orders and rarely have the right to give them" (56). Mosionier uses a first-person narrative style to bring us into direct contact with April's experiences of subjection as she recalls how her life has been altered by state actors who disrupt her family ties and erode her self-confidence and security. The novel highlights how these changes occur after she is apprehended as a child and placed in adoptive care. Despite the intervention by child welfare authorities that remove her from the substance abuse and neglect of her family home, her transfer to an orphanage fails to inspire safety and stability. Instead, April recounts how her treatment represents a continuation of the deprivations that she and her sister suffered within their family home. One of the lasting effects of their removal is that April learns to perceive her safety as bound up in important ways with either losing or being forced to relinquish responsibility for her sister.

Mosionier crafts April's testimonial narrative to dramatize the wide-ranging effects of this lesson, expanding its scope through her point of view to link her story to experiences of loss suffered by other Indigenous women with whom she is connected. Describing the activities of her early life before she is out-adopted, she recalls the intimacy she shared with her sister through rituals that included "tend[ing] to Cheryl's needs," "dress[ing] her in clean clothes," and walking with her to the park (16). These practices inspire feelings of confidence and security, engendering her sense of family connections and pride. In contrast, when she is placed in the orphanage, and separated from Cheryl, April's self-assurance and demeanour change. Through narrative

shifts that foreground her feelings of vulnerability as she is objectified by strangers who undress, bathe her, and check her hair for bugs
(19), her memories emphasize confrontations with adults who compel
her to obey their instructions and comply with their demands. Incidents of demeaning treatment occur alongside episodes that include
"scolding," to learn not to gulp her food "like a little animal"; bullying,
to avoid conflicts with other children when they insist that she hand
over toys; and self-questioning, to determine if her behaviour is "bad
or good" (20). As she develops habits of self-effacement by anticipating what "different nuns wanted" in order to avoid punishment, she
begins to understand herself as vulnerable through social dynamics
based in fear: "I feared being ridiculed in front of the other children;
I feared getting the strap; I feared even a harsh word" (20). When she
attempts to leave the orphanage to rejoin her father, a nun apprehends,
straps, and interrogates her, demanding to know what she "intend[ed]
on doing" (21). Sick and in despair over the loss of her parents, she is
stricken by a fever and hospitalized, overcome by nightmares in which
her desire to run away and be reunited with them is foiled by an invis-
ible white presence that threatens to engulf her. When she recovers and
is returned to the orphanage, she discovers that the girls are not to be
taken home, that they are to be separated from each other, and that
Cheryl has already been placed with a foster family. Recalling how,
before her illness, Cheryl "groped her way to my bed and crawled in
with me," April observes, "That was the last night we'd share the same
bed, or be really close, for a long time" (19).

April's lessons in dependence and self-restraint are formative for her.
Reflecting on the removal several years later, as a young woman in her
twenties, she struggles to grasp why her parents permitted the girls
to be taken, blaming them for the punishment she experiences in the
orphanage. Declaring her mother's actions inadequate in protecting
them – "My mother should have fought with her life to keep us with
her" (18) – she fails to understand how her race and gender subjectivity
intersect with a lack of political power and social agency. Although she
admits to not comprehending her mother's role, and likens her confusion to "grown-up things" she could not fathom, she remains upset by
the removal as an incident that "didn't make any sense" (18). Mosionier shows how her uncertainty in understanding her family loss aligns
with the erosion of her self-esteem that the disciplinary effects of the
orphanage inspire. As April's narrative evolves, it conveys her search to
develop a positive sense of herself and to fulfil her need for meaningful

social connections to replace intimate practices associated with her family that her experience at the orphanage taught her to reject. A tragic consequence of April's search for social acceptance and community is that it parallels her mother's quest. As she develops habits to distance herself from her Indigenous inheritance and gender identity that she believes to be high-risk, she enacts a *residential school sensibility* brought about by her institutionalization, undertaking practices of self-protection that lead to her social isolation and gender conformity in ways that replicate her mother's behaviour to demonstrate how both women are deprived of positive conceptions of their identities and how both lack a sense of their rights.

April's placement with a non-Indigenous foster family where she is subjected to physical and verbal abuse underscores how the novel connects the out-adoption of Indigenous children to Indian residential school legacies, gender vulnerability, and demeaning treatment authorized by the state. When she is taunted by the DeRosier children with whom she boards for having "drunkards" for parents" (51), for being identifiable as a "stupid … half-breed … and Indian" (45), and for dressing like "Gramma Squaw" (67), she experiences indignities to her personhood that diminish her race, gender, and collective self in ways that illuminate how she is discriminated against because of her association with a group that is devalued by society. When they circulate rumors that she engages in promiscuous behaviour by consorting with the foster boys who live in their home and flirting with their father (73), her reprimand by the guidance counsellor likening her "foster girl" status to a "psychological need to be loved" (75) highlights the counsellor's acceptance of her sexually harassing treatment, displacing recognition of the state's role in positioning her as defenceless and in exposing her to the children's malicious attacks. Helpless to defend herself against the rumours, she responds with despair, voicing a desire "to die, crawl away into some hole, and never be seen again" (73). Her feelings of desolation emanate not only from the falseness of their accusations, but also from the counsellor's warning that recalls earlier episodes of dismissal that she and her sister experienced when they fled from the DeRosier home and were threatened with "reform school" if they did not behave (61). April equates the guidance counsellor's disparagement of her "foster girl" status with her case worker's rebuke that she and her sister are enacting "'native girl' syndrome": by "fighting … running away … [and telling] lies" (62); by acting out their susceptibility for "get[ting] pregnant," losing "jobs," and "start[ing]

with alcohol and drugs"; by "get[ting] into shoplifting and prostitution," and "liv[ing] with men who abuse [them]"; and ultimately
"end[ing] up like [their] parents, living off [of] society" (62). The cata-
logue of negative consequences that the caseworker expounds illustrates how April's personhood is disposed of in language that builds on
her prior conditioning to code her conduct in ways that disparage her
race and gender selfhood.[16] Despite her sister's encouragement that she
seek out positive role models for herself in stories of Metis resistance
from the past that her sister embraces to "earn their respect" because
of her "difference" (70), she dismisses this idea as a contrived form
of empowerment, seeing instead the children of Indigenous ancestry
in her classroom who remain silent, disregarded, and alone "because
they knew their places" (43). As her sense of "[h]elpless fury" in being
ordered about by the DeRosier children forces her to the realization
that she cannot act because she is "unsure of … [her] rights," given her
dependent status (40), she becomes increasingly indecisive about how
to protect both herself and her sister, whose mistreatment she perceives
as "unjust" because Cheryl is "the more innocent" (63). Contemplat-
ing stealing money to run away, and questioning what "native girls
do" in these circumstances that most likely lead them to "skid row"
in search of "freedom and peace," she is confronted by the isolation
of her social position in being "forced to go out into the world, unpre-
pared and alone … [w]ith only Grade Ten and no money," despite the
"good intentions" that she has about leading a meaningful life (79). The
accumulated effects of her exploitative treatment force her to the recognition of her situation of powerlessness and marginalization. A letter
that she writes for a school assignment expressing a Christmas wish
for "somebody to listen to me and to believe in me" (76) engineers her
removal from the DeRosier home and her placement in a girls' academy, where she establishes friendships with the other young women by
denying all aspects of her Indigenous ancestry, including information
about her sister and parents, whose absence she explains by claiming
that they are dead (82).

The novel shows how April's body and voice signify complicated
metaphors that convey her susceptibility to race and gender discrimination that inhibits her ability to act. It does so not only to illustrate April's
vulnerability to social confinement but also to challenge the law's reliance on speaking as social agency and the corollary assumption that
knowing one's rights will permit a person to act. These presumptions
arose in the *Racine* case to provide the legal grounds through which the

Supreme Court refused Ms Woods's custody of her daughter when she failed to behave in accordance with the Supreme Court's understanding of her rights. April's efforts to overcome her powerless status invoke these expectations to illustrate their limits in judicial reasoning. If before her removal from the DeRosier home, she questions the exploitative conditions that she finds herself within, then after her relocation to the girls' academy she abandons all resistance to the social restrictions that society places on her. Despite her earlier conviction that she and Cheryl are mistreated by her adoptive family, she distances herself from her sister by espousing a goal to "live as a white person" (50), negotiating the social violence that has been directed against her and her lack of personal security by choosing to "pass" into white society and by submitting to behaviour that the orphanage and child welfare agencies espouse. As a consequence of her internalization of race and gender stereotypes that the state's control of her life subjects her to, she navigates her time at St Bernadette's Academy by recapitulating her demeanour from the orphanage when she "had known nuns" (62) and knew how to behave. Through her encounters with other young women, she classifies them in two ways: "Good in that native girls I saw were beautiful and sure of themselves ... Bad in that they went shoplifting, drank liquor ... and had easy sexual relationships" (86). Because she is taught to fear social and sexual experimentation by "Ms. Semple's speech on the syndrome," she withdraws from their company, justifying her decision on the grounds that "I enjoyed the good things they offered but stayed away from the bad" (86). When she experiences racial slurs, sexual advances, and indifferent service during outings to restaurants with her sister and Cheryl's friend, Nancy, a woman whom April regards as a "wilted flower" due to the sexual and physical exploitation she suffers at the hands of her father (98), she discontinues her association with them, abandoning her desire to celebrate her work successes, and withdrawing into seclusion out of a need for self-protection caused by her "embarrass[ment] to be seen with natives," and surprise that her sister falls silent in response to the public attacks as she "had always been sharp-tongued" (98). In avoiding the companionship and influence of other women, April puts into practice a lesson that she learns in school about the dangers of "being judged by the company you keep" (75). To overcome her loneliness, she engages in "daydreams" of surrounding herself with "lots of friends," "giving lavish parties," and "shopping for just the right thing" (91), fantasies of fulfilment that she associates with the affluence of "white" society.

As she publicly foregoes associations with her more visibly "Native" sister, privately, she embarks on a search to locate her parents. When she meets an elderly Indigenous woman with whom they might have been connected, she perceives in her stature the negative images about Indigenous peoples that she has been forced to internalize. For April, the woman's home represents "a horrible place," covered with "flies" and "germs" and an imaginary "smell" that she is afraid will consume her. She recoils from her physical appearance, finding her "stocking-less" feet grotesque, her legs "lumpy with varicose veins or some other disease," and her heels "dried and scaly" (90). As her thoughts turn towards escape, she recalls: "Suddenly, it was very important to me that those flies not touch me, and I waved them away" (90). When she leaves shortly thereafter to return home, she engages in the first of several acts of ritual bathing "to wash[] off all those germs I'd probably picked up" (91). Choosing to discontinue her search by outwardly disposing of the papers she has gathered so that they are "out of sight and out of mind" (91), she inwardly reconciles herself to her parents' loss and her self-imposed isolation. In so doing, she enacts a form of her mother's "normal remoteness" (12) that she recalls with anxiety and desperation from her childhood (12), when her mother withdrew from her presence for no apparent reason. Mosionier demonstrates through April's seclusion and her practice of ritual bathing parallels with her mother's behaviour when she would cook, clean, do laundry, and sew, activities that reflected how she was "raised in a residential school and then worked as a housekeeper for the priest in her hometown" (12–13). Through this repetition in manner and behaviour, the novel establishes an intergenerational link between Indian residential schooling and the out-adoption of Indigenous children in habits of social isolation that proscribe the formation of community and that prevent the transmission of positive conceptions of women's identities and knowledge about their empowerment and rights. That April justifies discontinuing the search because it would be too painful for herself and her sister illuminates how the novel portrays social segregation and self-protection as consequences of the intersections between out-adoption, a lack of community, and loss of family in the residential schooling sensibility that April is forced to take up.

The complexity of Mosionier's text, in deploying a first-person narrative account to show how April undergoes social conditioning to dispense with elements of her Indigenous ancestry, gender identity, and family's past, arises not only in its invitation to readers to see the violence against her body that her voice obscures, but also in its insistence that we resist the mediation of her verbal strategies as they ideologically code her voice to demonstrate speaking-as-agency. Mosionier's novel draws attention to verbalization as "self-agency" (Scarry 47) in order to construct April's memories as signposts for a "body in pain." As she is made over to assume a structural position of powerlessness in society, her voice serves, in complicated ways, as both a source of violation to express how social institutions "unmake" her world, and as the ground that stabilizes the "verbal strategies" that compel her to use language-as-agency through which her experiences may be shared and enter the world (Scarry 13). Mosionier crafts April's narrative to grapple with the paradox of representation that Elaine Scarry theorizes as "the body in pain": a body situated as a subject to provide an origin for language as the "verbal sign" that coaxes pain into visibility, by providing pain with a source in the body's referential status and stability; and the body as the agent of the voice that conveys "human speech" through the inherently unstable signifier of language as the body's intermediary that makes possible a relationship between the subject and verbalization (61). April's memories articulate a position of "unthinkable isolation" (50) by alternating between depicting her body as "the locus of pain" and her voice as the "locus of power" to show how the "felt-attributes" of pain may "be appropriated away from the body" (13) through narrative "self-extension" to become the means by which April's story enters the world (33).[17] Because the act of expressing pain represents the first step in "the collective task of diminishing [it]" (9), Mosionier's text deploys April's voice not only to highlight the social discrimination and gender violence that she suffers from, but also to engage speaking on behalf of Indigenous women with whom she is associated who cannot speak for themselves. April's narrative thus incorporates aspects of her sister's experiences and her mother's story in order to challenge the state's right "to give or withhold voice" and to situate literature as a site for overcoming the injustice of "restorative forgetting" (Booth 778).

Within transitional justice, the state's duty to victims through memory, justice, and amnesty towards the past represents a complex obligation, hampered, in many ways, by the state's determination of what is best for society to remember in carrying out its democratic aims and what is best to forget. As W. James Booth explains, although forgetting permits the state to "move on" from the past by displacing its "evils ... [into] the shadows of civic forgetting" (778), remembering keeps existent acts of injustice that have "weakened the already weak hold of justice in the world" (779). Since amnesty provokes forgetting for the sake "of a future in common," victims are abandoned as "the past is moved beyond the reach of justice" (778). By incorporating the stories of April's family and her losses into the novel form, Mosionier's text enacts a form of what Booth defines as "memory-justice" (779), a method of remembrance that "keep[s] ... the past present" and "recognize[s] the dignity of ... victims" by "keeping faith with ... [them]" (780). The novel achieves this goal by "insisting on the restoration of justice in the world against the oblivion of forgetting," and by "restoring integrity to a community [that has] gone astray from justice ... and from its own core values" (780).[18] Mosionier crafts April's memories to serve this complex function: to restore presence against loss to the women in her family by "witness[ing] [to] the fact of their existence and fate" (Booth 782). Because Canada, as a colonial nation, has "no past democratic and law-governed regime to serve as the focal point of a restorative narrative" (780), its objective to establish just relations with Indigenous peoples requires literature by Indigenous women to provide a source for directing attention to the state's failures to address and lay bare the injustices of its colonial practices and to recognize that gender injustice from the past has a continuing effect in the present that must be understood in order to achieve a justice-oriented future.[19]

Mosionier's use of narrative devices in the form of personal letters, diaries, and memories serve the function of keeping the "past present" through the voices of victims represented by the life stories of April and her sister.[20] These devices not only provide a deus ex machina plot function by permitting April to remain informed about her sister's life even after they have been separated. They also enable insight into how Cheryl's experience of out-adoption differs from April's, by highlighting April's search into her past as a quest to recover knowledge and understanding about the events that lead to the loss of her sister to suicide. Mosionier's novel shows how their separate experiences of foster care are instrumental to this disruption, in the feelings of shame and betrayal that each expresses for their relationship. In contrast to April's social isolation, Cheryl develops an idealized image of Indigenous identity that becomes foundational to her by overlooking its social and historical distortions.[21] Raised in a foster home that nurtures her sense of self and promotes her attachment to romantic "Indian" otherness, her letters to April indicate how she equates the dominant conception of Indigenous peoples with a glorified notion of their historical past. She acts out in school and antagonizes her family and friends

(43, 105). She suffers from racial discrimination, embarrassment, and shame when her boyfriend abandons her on the street so that they are not seen together in public (94). She searches for her parents only to realize that the sickness they suffer from that prompted the girls' removal is alcoholism rather than tuberculosis (109). Unable to bear the disillusionment of her family history, she spirals into despair and economic destitution that leads to prostitution and alcoholism when she fails to reconcile her vision of an idealized racial status with the grim reality of social exploitation that she sees in her father and the community she associates with. She reflects in her journal on the causes of their deprivation, and her uncertainty about how to account for it: "They are losers. But there is a reason why they are the way they are. Everything they once had has been taken from them. And the white bureaucracy has helped create the image of parasitic natives. But sometimes I do wonder if these people don't accept defeat too easily, like a dog with his tail between his legs, on his back, his throat forever exposed" (196). Mosionier illuminates how Cheryl separates from a raced underclass her personal sense of helplessness and the political causes of exploitation in order to prioritize the claim that Indigenous people can and must transcend the conditions that cause their suffering and alienation. In so doing, she exposes the ideological false-consciousness of stark individualism and attributions of agency, promulgated through legal reasoning, which suggest that Indigenous peoples can side-step the constraints of materiality and the power of social and political structures through the project of "self-reliant, self-making" (Code 183).

In contrast to her sister's efforts to remain connected to an Indigenous community, April internalizes the values of rugged individualism and individual autonomy that she is forced by her working class status and social isolation to take up as she attempts to pass into "white society" (50), amplifying the social distance and growing conflict between the girls. Mosionier shows how April's embrace of these values depends on a process of social "[o]thering" (Spivak, "Three Women's Texts" 254) to which she is subjected. When she learns that her marriage is founded on her racist manipulation by her husband, Bob Radcliffe, and his mother (115–16), she confronts two courses of action that force her to choose between leaving her husband on the grounds of his racism or leaving him because of his infidelity. In choosing to identify with an idealized image of herself as a "married woman," April forgoes the terrain of racial exploitation and leaves unexamined questions of her implication in racist and sexist discourses. Mosionier problematizes the issue of racism with the issue of infidelity in order to examine difficult questions regarding the ethics of financial compensation: would April have been justified in leaving her husband and accepting a settlement had she been subjected to anything short of infidelity? Would her acceptance of a settlement, had her husband not been unfaithful, suggest that money can compensate for the absence of rights? By complicating the issue of racism with the issue of social reparation, Mosionier raises one of the most difficult issues in transitional justice literature: the status of financial compensation.

As one measure within reparative justice, financial compensation speaks to a capacity to "reorder[] ... material and symbolic resources based upon a particular account of culpability, desert, accountability, injury, and fairness" (Franke 814). Resources to be redistributed may include "money," "land," or "shame" (814). As a form of "moral reparation" that compensates victims in symbolic ways by "restor[ing] their reputation and equal status in the public eye" (Teitel, *Transitional Justice* 126–7), financial compensation also "redraw[s] the borders of political community" in ways that shift attention from "victims' harms to state's wrongdoing" (127). If the reparation is "not linked to prosecutions" or public "truth-telling" (Jung, "Canada" 233), then the financial compensation bears the stigma of "blood money," as an "attempt to buy the silence or acquiescence of victims" (233). By depicting April failing to make public her racist mistreatment, Mosionier questions financial compensation as a form of reparation, anticipating through her representation of this issue Canada's positioning of itself within transitional justice paradigms. April's moral elation upon realizing that she will receive a very large settlement underscores her earlier exclamation that she "wouldn't want the seed of [Mother Radcliff's] son passed on to [her] children" (127). When she confesses, shortly thereafter, to a fear of producing brown-skinned babies and to a self-consciousness about Cheryl, she diverts what had been a sense of outrage into a sense of shame – and seems, at this moment, to stop herself from judging lest she herself be judged. The dismissal of race consciousness that Mosionier engineers on April's part discloses that the underlying assumption to the principle of financial compensation cannot be separated from its implication in appearances of self-interest. Mosionier emphasizes this point in the tragic and final confrontation between the sisters when Cheryl accuses April of "prostituting [herself] when she took Bob's money" (179). The settlement money that April receives is thus multi-stigmatized: by her complicity with her mistreatment, by her recognition that she has colluded with racist discourses through her expressed feelings of "racial shame" that are redirected towards her sister, and by her knowledge that Indigenous land dispossession facilitated her ex-husband's wealth and her divorce settlement since she met Bob Radcliffe when he travelled to Winnipeg in order to purchase property to expand his business (99). The novel provides a symbolic account of the intersections between land loss and Indigenous peoples' removal to establish continuities between historical injustices and their ongoing implication in contemporary forms of Indigenous peoples' dispossession through residential school and out-adoption, complicating the question of financial compensation with its implication in the loss of Indigenous lands and the assimilation of Indigenous communities.

What interrupts the progressivist logic in the development of each sister's belief in her autonomy is a brutal sexual assault in which one sister is mistaken for the other. Mosionier's construction of a rape scene in which the rapists justify their actions on the grounds that their victim was both "Native" and a "prostitute" (165) emphasizes the politically interested figuration of Indigenous womanhood that the court deploys in order to depict the dependence of the "imperial self" on the interpellation and subjugation of the "Native woman as other" (Spivak, "Three Women's Texts" 807). April's rapist, Oliver Donnelly, claims that "the girl never said anything so I figured it would be all right to have sex with her" (167), demonstrating his manipulation of social discourses governing "silence" and "consent."[22] Through Donnelly's lie, Mosionier exposes the intersecting power relations of the dominant society in the course of which the agency of Indigenous women is simultaneously affirmed and denied, thus, in turn, demonstrating the extent to which the dominant ideology is responsible for – and depends on – processes of social "othering." Donnelly's conviction rests on the fact that April is not a sex trade worker with the implication that had he assaulted Cheryl – or April, had she been a "prostitute" – he would not have been convicted. Mosionier's crafting of the court's skewed sense of legal justice illustrates how Donnelly is punished not for sexual assault but for mistaking a morally pure, middle-class woman for an Indigenous woman who is not.

When she seeks solace for the sense of abjection she experiences due to the court's characterization of her as "a pitiful creature" (168), she confronts and accuses her sister, redirecting her sense of outrage and shame by attacking someone who is as equally vulnerable to sexual violence as she is herself. April blames Cheryl's conduct for her violation, recovering her anger and self-respect by insisting that she "paid" (171) for Cheryl's misjudgment in engaging in sex-trade work. The moral bankruptcy of the position that April holds tragically expresses her isolation due to her loss of family and community: not only does she blame other women for gender violence that is socially sanctioned and male derived, but she also dismisses as "ordinary" the physical violence that Cheryl suffers from her common-law spouse (132). The irony of her indignation is further exposed by the twist of fate that Mosionier constructs when April is hospitalized following the sexual assault in the same institution where she discovered her sister after returning to Winnipeg following her divorce. When she enters Cheryl's hospital room she is shocked to see her sister physically beaten and dramatically altered in appearance. She states, "At first, I wasn't sure it was Cheryl. I mean, I knew it was Cheryl but it didn't look like Cheryl. Her beautiful, strong face was now puffy and bruised, and her cheeks were hollow. She had lost so much weight. Under the fluorescent lights, her skin was yellowish" (121). Rather than inquire into Cheryl's altered state, she distances herself from her and learns of her destitution and sex trade work by reading her diaries. She confronts Cheryl's desolation that leads to her suicide when she throws herself off the Louise Bridge, whereby she repeats their mother's despairing act upon realizing that her children will never be returned to her (189).

Despite April's stated conviction that the deaths of her sister and mother instil a political transformation on her part that will lead to Indigenous activism (207), little evidence of this potential is realized by the novel. Instead, its circular structure suggests the opposite, in so far as April's narrative begins and ends with her consciousness of being overtaken by memories that she cannot forget and fails to understand the meaning of. She writes, "Memories. Some memories are elusive, fleeting, like a butterfly that touches down and is free until it is caught. Others are haunting. You'd never forget them, but they won't be forgotten. And some are always there. No matter where you are, they are there, too. I always felt most of my memories were better avoided, but now I think it's best to go back in my life before I go forward. Last month, April 18th, I celebrated my twenty-fourth birthday. That's still young but I feel so old" (11). Narrating on behalf of herself and other Indigenous women, April's voice shuttles between autonomy and integration, alienation and assimilation, "white" and "'Native' other." Mosionier thus signals her recognition of feminist criticism's willed desire to write an "autobiography of the West" as the "fight for individualism" (Spivak,"Imperialism" 226) in which literary texts "model" and engender our desire for social change without our recognizing that the "other must always be consolidated by way of consolidating the self" (229). To counter our abstention from recognizing our implication in desiring the literary text to model social and political transformation, Mosionier practises a mode of storytelling that "aggressively bears witness to the displacement of testimony into places, times, concepts and encounters that have not been institutionally authorized as sites of testimonial emergence" (Cubilie and Good 11). By storytelling on behalf of Indigenous women her novel calls for a form of literary justice that mirrors yet inflects with new meaning the silences, omissions, and practices of erasure that social and legal institutions subject Indigenous women to. Aligning Mosionier's novel with the *Racine* case indicates why Mosionier takes up this position. When the Supreme Court of Canada decided to withhold restoring custody of Ms Woods's daughter to her, it omitted the Court of Appeal's overview of the multiple attempts and desperate measures that Ms Woods undertook to protect and to recover her daughter. She placed her daughter with the Children's Aid Society in 1977 when she was six weeks old and "consented to a one-year guardianship order" because she sought to shield her daughter from her husband's "aversion ... for her" (*Woods v. Racine and Racine* para. 27). She attempted to recover her daughter in 1980 by appealing for help to "child care agencies, legal aid lawyers and the police" (*Woods v. Racine and Racine* para. 142), in an effort that was described by the Trial Judge as a "half-baked stab at breaking the abandonment" (para. 142). She engaged in frequent and wide-ranging requests for help that are recorded in the Court of Appeal case, which states:

> She approached a worker of the Dakota-Ojibway Child and Family Service which was in its formative stages on the Long Plains reserve. She spoke to a Mel Courchene of that agency; he promised to help her get a lawyer but this help never materialized. She then approached George Beaulieu, a child care worker, who requested the Children's Aid Society of Western Manitoba for help but was unable to obtain it. [She] went with Mr. Beaulieu to Deloraine in an attempt to recover her child but the trip was unsuccessful; it was suggested in the evidence that Mr. Beaulieu ran short of money and gasoline and they had to turn back ... [T]hey approached the R.C.M.P. at Boissevain but were refused any assistance. (para. 142)

Transitional justice feminists urge attention to women's voices as they express "losses that cannot be spoken ... debts that cannot be repaid" and "subject[s] who will not speak [their] suffering in the time and place and languages offered to [them] by the mechanisms of transitional justice feminism" (Orford 882, 883). Mosionier's novel contributes to transitional justice an Indigenous-feminist representation that strives to articulate Indigenous women's injustice by representing women as they are silently positioned within the social text, asking what justice obligations are owed to them when legal mechanisms fail and social institutions exacerbate their vulnerability. By leaving this questioned unanswered, *In Search of April Raintree* asserts that the quest for Indigenous women's social justice in Western contexts has yet to be achieved while at the same time calling for the formation of a community of women who may struggle together for this cause.

Chapter Three

Colonial Governmentality and Gender Violence: *State of Minnesota v. Zay Zah* (1977) and *The Antelope Wife* (1998)

Louise Erdrich's literary and social justice activism brought the issue of violence against Indigenous women to national awareness through the publication in the *New York Times* of her op-ed piece, "Rape on the Reservation." Descrying the opinions of two Republican delegates who spoke out in favour of "legitimate rape" and "God-approved conceptions during rape," Erdrich's article rebuked the misogyny of the Republican Party, observing the growing numbers of Indigenous women affected by sexual violence as survivors, family members, allies, and friends. Urging support for the Violence Against Women Act, which recognizes crimes such as "rape, domestic abuse, and stalking as matters of human rights" that disproportionately affect women, Erdrich argued for the jurisdiction of tribal courts as the authorities best able to "apprehend, charge, and try rapists – regardless of race" (Erdrich, "Rape" n.p.). Her words represented a direct appeal to the United States Congress and Justice Department to rethink the United States Supreme Court's reasoning in *Oliphant v. Suquamish Indian Tribe* (1978). The decision that rescinds the authority of tribal nations to prosecute non-Indian offenders on tribal lands has had dire consequences for Indigenous communities.[1] Neither able to try non-Indian offenders in tribal courts nor to pursue them beyond tribal boundaries, *Oliphant* exacerbates the desperate situation of Indigenous women who are the victims of domestic assault and sexual violence by subjecting them to the alienating entanglement of competing legal jurisdictions and delays in investigating crimes, delays that heighten their suffering due to the requirement that the appropriate authority be established before investigations are pursued. Amnesty International's *Maze of Injustice* (2007) report condemns the United States for its "deeply entrenched marginalization" of Indigenous peoples as part of "a long history of systemic and pervasive abuse and persecution" manifested in its indifference to the plight of Indigenous women who are "2.5 times more likely than U.S. women in general to be sexually assaulted" (2). The issues of sexual violence, tribal jurisdiction, and access to justice for Indigenous women are central to Erdrich's literary account of an Ojibway family's breakdown in the aftermath of the brutal crime of sexual assault in *The Round House* (2012). The novel, which won the National Book Award, affirmed Erdrich's status as an important voice in debates concerning Indigenous justice, sexual violence, and the politics of representation in depicting legal events.

Erdrich's use of fiction to ask what justice means for Indigenous peoples reflects how her storytelling activism recognizes the failures of federal Indian law to carry out in just and responsible ways its obligations to tribal communities. Following in the footsteps of legal scholars who note the judiciary's capricious disregard for Indigenous peoples, Erdrich's novel *The Round House* highlights the injustice of the federal government's indifference to the recognition of tribal authority by showing its devastating impact on women, their families, and the wider communities with whom they are associated.[2] When the protagonist's mother, Geraldine, is sexually assaulted by a non-Indian man who not only studies the law to determine how jurisdiction applies in order to evade tribal authority, but also executes the rape on territory where "three classes of land meet" to delay prosecution of his crime (*The Round House* 160), Joe urges his mother to lie and claim that she is certain the violence occurred on tribal lands in order to permit his father, a tribal judge, to pursue the known offender (260). Erdrich characterizes Joe's commitment to justice as akin to "retribution" rather than to "a just condition" (Booth 779) to demonstrate the erosion of the inherent dignity of tribal peoples as they struggle to build a platform of "impeccable decisions" (Erdrich, "Rape" n.p.) against the ineffectiveness of "scattershot" law practised by U.S. Federal and Supreme Courts (Erdrich, *The Round House* 229). At a pivotal moment, when Joe is condemning his father for enforcing tribal law in the face of minor infractions concerning "drunks and hot dog thieves" (228–9), his father obliges Joe to observe a "rotting casserole" to convey the racist logic and decaying "mess" that federal Indian law doctrine has bequeathed to tribal peoples in order to counter his son's dismissal of a duty to justice as he demands to know why his father "bothers" to act with integrity and uphold the law. Joe's father demonstrates how the crumbling edifice represents an apt metaphor of colonial law's legacy for tribal courts. Not only are they required to make certain that their decisions are "crafted keenly" (229) to "build a solid base for ... sovereignty" (229); they must also negotiate around "unsavory cases," "extra incidental wording," and "medieval doctrine" put in place to facilitate the loss of "Indian land," "[s]peculators ... acquiring rights on treaty-held Indian land and on land still owned and occupied by Indians," and "opinion[s] ... that strip away all Indian title to all lands viewed as ... 'discovered' ... by Europeans" (228). As Joe's father nudges the rotting mess to demonstrate how one movement could cause a chain reaction that collapses the entire structure, he highlights the underlying message of Erdrich's text which illuminates the failure of government and law makers to recognize the inherent dignity of tribal nations, and to accord them "basic human respect" (Reaume, "Discrimination" 27) by protecting their lands and peoples from outright "dispossession" (Erdrich, *The Round House* 229).

The decaying edifice of federal Indian law that Erdrich's novel constructs provides an apt image to symbolize the capricious and unsystematic methods that have abetted federal Indian law as it enacts the colonial dispossession of tribal communities. American Indian legal scholar Charles F. Wilkinson observes that American Indian law evolved according to a "checkerboard jurisdiction" that was "clumsy and without consolidating doctrine," due to the erosion of Indigenous lands and tribal peoples' sovereign status in the determination of tribal, federal, and state boundaries (9). Wilkinson notes that until Felix S. Cohen's famous pronouncement of the "doctrine of tribal sovereignty" – "tribes initially possessed complete sovereignty, they lost some of those powers to a more powerful nation, and they retain all powers not lost" (58; see also Cohen 122–3) – the administration of tribes existed in a state of "disarray" that worked against centralizing case law and building "predictable doctrine" (9). Wilkinson argues that federal Indian law's disorder amplifies issues of scale and duress with consequences that are both doctrinal and real-world in their effects for Indigenous peoples: what is the connection between issues of "hunting and fishing litigation" in their "grand scale" and "whether a two-year-old Pueblo child will be allowed to retain her culture and traditions or be assimilated into the majority society[?]" he asks (9). Answering this question in the context of contesting the "scattering forces" (10) that federal Indian law enacts in order to provide an understanding of how tribal traditions, the retention of culture and identity, and protecting the land are co-implicated with each other represents precisely the task taken up by Indigenous women's writing. In this chapter, I explore how Erdrich's novel *The Antelope Wife* intervenes in a land claim dispute to offer an alternative story of origins that recasts the narrative established by the Minnesota Supreme Court in its adjudication of this complex issue.

Erdrich's novel addresses the uncertainty and "scattering forces" engendered by legal rulings through its engagement with the legal outcome achieved by the White Earth land claim settlement. As a legal event that involved title to more than 4,000 acres of land held by Indigenous and non-Indigenous community members, the White Earth land claim illustrates how legal conflict and resolution require not only the invention of origins that establish "a system of rules to be observed," but also the creation of "[legal] worlds in which we live" (Cover, "Foreword: Nomos and Narrative" 5). These worlds, as Robert Cover explains, are brought into being through the "force" of law and narrative (10). Their creation depends on what Cover describes as law's recourse to the "prescription" in law of an "origin" and an "experience" that is "embodied in the legal text" (5). The legal outcome enacted by the *Zay Zah* case demonstrates this genesis. It invokes prior acts and agreements between the United States government and the Chippewa of Minnesota to resolve a land dispute, illustrating how the Court's reasoning enters into "interpretive commitments" (7) to remain faithful to the colonial objectives of earlier legal decisions. In transcending the differences in historical events, the Court's reasoning engages in the construction of "myths" that "establish paradigms for behavior" by "culling" (9) meaningful narratives from law's colonial past in order to dispose and regulate tribal identity. This disposal occurs through the revival of U.S. racialized blood-quantum categories, categories that determine anew the relations between Indigenous peoples and land and that facilitate dispossession (9). Erdrich's novel challenges law's creation of this legal world by contesting the origin story that the *Zay Zah* case constructs. The story her novel tells provides an alternative account of the legal-colonial encounter by articulating Indigenous women's inheritances across intergenerational and tribal lines in order to critique the blood-quantum categories enacted and made normative by the *Zay Zah* case and to show how the patriarchal norms it establishes in law engender violence against Indigenous women.

Blood Quantum and *State of Minnesota v. Zay Zah*

On 21 October 1977, George Aubid appeared as a defendant before the Supreme Court of Minnesota in an action to quiet title to real estate property located within the original boundaries of the White Earth Reservation in the State of Minnesota.[3] Aubid, a "mixed–blood" Chippewa Indian and the sole surviving heir of Zay Zah (also known as Charles Aubid), contested the sale of his grandfather's allotment to Eugene and Laurie Stevens, a married couple of non-Indian descent who purchased the property from Clearwater County after title to the land became vested in the State of Minnesota for non-payment of taxes. Both parties agreed that the land, allotted to Zay Zah in 1927 under the terms of the 1889 Nelson Act, had been improperly assessed taxes by the auditor for Clearwater County for the year 1931.[4] They conceded that Zay Zah was, for the purposes of the allotment roll, "an adult mixed blood Indian" (*State of Minnesota v. Zay Zah* 583) who "did not at any time during his lifetime apply for a patent in fee simple" (582) for his allotment, and that according to the terms of the trust patent issued by the United States, the land was to be held in trust "for a period of twenty-five years ... for the sole use and benefit of said Indian" (582).[5] Mr Aubid and Mr and Mrs Stevens disagreed, however, as to whether or not the auditor had rightly assessed property taxes for the year 1954, which, when unpaid, enabled the county to execute a tax certificate of forfeiture, "certifying that the time for redemption of said real estate had expired, and that absolute title to said real estate thereby vested in the State of Minnesota" (582). The conveyance of the property to Mr and Mrs Stevens by the Commissioner of Taxation in May 1973 thus became the source of contention between Zay Zah's hereditary heir, George Aubid, and Mr and Mrs Stevens, who were joined in suit with Clearwater County and the State of Minnesota as indispensable parties to the case.

Basing their appeal on a legislative act of 1906, known as the Clapp Amendment,[6] Mr and Mrs Stevens argued that Zay Zah's trust status as a "mixed-blood Indian" had been altered significantly by the terms of the Clapp Amendment, which, they alleged, removed "all restrictions as to the sale, incumbrance [*sic*], or taxation for allotments . . . held by adult mixed-blood Indians" (584). The removal of the land's trust status thereby enabled taxation of Zay Zah's allotment, which was subject to taxation at the end of the 25-year trust period as stipulated in the trust patent. Mr Aubid disagreed.

He contended that the "trust status" of the allotment did not attach to Indian identity as appellants claimed, but rather, was in itself "a constitutionally protected vested property right" which consequently "prevent[ed] taxation, not only during the 25-year period, but also thereafter by reason of indefinite extension of the 'trust status' by the Wheeler-Howard Act of 1934" (583). Although Mr and Mrs Stevens maintained that the Wheeler-Howard Act was inapplicable by reason of the Clapp Amendment's alteration of Zay Zah's legal status as a mixed-blood Indian,[7] the Supreme Court of Minnesota upheld Mr Aubid's claim. Noting the contradictory logic implied by the appellants' argument that the Clapp Amendment converted title to the land from a "trust" relationship vested in the federal government to a "fee simple" relationship vested in the individual allottee, the court held that since both parties agreed that Zay Zah's land was appropriately tax exempt during the initial 25-year period as stipulated in the trust patent, the land could not then be considered taxable under the same patent because the "vested right to be free from state taxation had to derive from somewhere, and the only possible source was the trust patent itself" (584). The court retained intact the trusteeship agreement between Zay Zah and the United States and endorsed the decision by the District Court for Clearwater County which ordered that the tax certificate of forfeiture that had enabled Mr and Mrs Stevens to purchase the property from Clearwater County be cancelled. It affirmed that equitable title to the land under the trust patent remained in Zay Zah and passed to his sole heir, George Aubid, Sr. Fee title to the land remained in the United States until such time as the holder of the trust patent, George Aubid, Sr, applied for and obtained a patent in fee simple.

The *Zay Zah* decision, in the archive of Indigenous land claims cases in the United States, represents an important turning point in land disputes. It not only highlights the failure of the federal government to safeguard Indigenous peoples' land rights through its fiduciary responsibility to them, but also demonstrates the judiciary's inability to determine a "consistent Federal policy" with regard to Congress's intent towards American Indian peoples in matters concerning their land protection.[8] As a consequence of these failures, the case brought into dispute thousands of acres of land in the State of Minnesota.[9]

This chapter introduces the *Zay Zah* case in order to situate it as an account of "colonial governmentality" (Scott, *Refashioning Futures* 36) in the formation of modern tribal identity. Colonial governmentality represents a mode of governing through subject-constitution that shapes the subject of power, "not *in spite of* but *through* the construction of the space of free social exchange, and through construction of a subjectivity normatively experienced as the source of free will, and rational, autonomous agency" (Scott, *Refashioning Futures* 36).[10] Mr Aubid's legal action, in restoring his grandfather's allotment to tax-exempt status by deploying the language of blood-quantum status through legal discourse, demonstrates these subject-constituting effects. On the one hand, the case shows how Mr Aubid's successful claim revived asymmetrically organized race relations in the form of blood-quantum categories that had been used historically to disenfranchise Indigenous peoples from their lands through imposed policies of colonial management;[11] on the other hand, it illuminates how law deploys racial categories to permit its reach into the wider social field while granting racialized terms new meanings, thus grounding contemporary identity in social relations that obfuscate how these terms originated in prior practices of Indigenous land dispossession from the past.[12] Both processes show how colonial-legal texts participate in generating new forms of legal representation through which symbolic and historical practices construct the grounds of subjectivity in relation to social reality in a manner that is made "real," at the same time as these texts displace prior forms of knowledge and social practice.

In this chapter, I explore how Erdrich's *The Antelope Wife* provides an alternative understanding of these origins. In 1988, Erdrich and her former husband, Michael Dorris, travelled to the White Earth Indian Reservation to view first-hand the conflict over land ownership and dispossession that polarized the community across tribal, racial, and class lines (Dorris and Erdrich, "Who Owns the Land?"). Centred on the community's "acrimonious conflict over land ownership" concretized anew by the *Zay Zah* case, their article highlights the causal legal history of White Earth as a series of legislative acts "so outrageous" in their "land-grab" objectives that no one could dispute the illegality and injustice of land theft that the Chippewa community claimed, even as answers to the issue of land ownership remained frustrated by ongoing political tensions and social inequalities experienced by both communities, Indigenous and non-Indigenous, alike.[13] Participating at a meeting of the United Township Association, they observed, "[i]t turn[ed] out that nearly everyone in the room is related by blood, marriage, godparentage or long friendship to members of the White Earth Chippewa band" (n.p.). The authors' public, even-handed depiction of both sides of the dispute – that of "local non-Indian" land owners who were unable "to sell, trade or use the land for collateral until the issue was settled in Washington" and that of "Anishinabe Akeeng," the grass-roots organization that included Winona LaDuke and tribal members who opposed the White Earth Land Settlement Act for pre-empting alternative dispute resolution processes – prompted a response by attorneys representing the "Indians of White Earth" in their challenge to the "constitutionality of the White Earth Land Settlement Act" (Ratner and Perkins n.p.).

Attorneys Michael Ratner and Mahlon Perkins responded to Dorris and Erdrich's *New York Times Magazine* article by arguing that, contrary to Dorris and Erdrich's view that the "'state [of Minnesota] is liberal, sensitive'" and "that there are no 'evil geniuses'" (n.p.), the government's misconduct towards the Chippewa of White Earth was directly attributable to the collusion between federal, state, and county governments who continued to own "240,000 acres of land on the White Earth Reservation," of which only "10,000 acres" were returned by the State of Minnesota "under duress" (n.p). They took to task Dorris and Erdrich for their failure to note the "injustice of the compensation given to the Indians for land not returned," for their omission "regarding the Congressionally imposed statute of limitations" that restricted Chippewa members to "only six months to sue for return of their land," and for disregarding Congress's intent to act unfairly towards the Chippewa community because "the Indians were too poor and too unaware of their rights to sue to regain their land" (n.p.). Ratner and Perkins defended their account of the conflict at White Earth, citing the legacy of government and legal injustice levelled by Dorris and Erdrich's characterization of the conflict in community-based terms, and they objected to Dorris and Erdrich's version of events as not only one-sided in its failure to note the federal government as the culpable agent responsible to protect "the Indians' best interests" (n.p.), but also as quite simply incorrect.[14]

The public debate that arose between Ratner/Perkins and Dorris/Erdrich provides an entry point to my discussion of Erdrich's novel because their disagreement illustrates, in a paradoxical way, how land claims issues are implicated in questions concerning the politics of legal representation and the justice objectives made possible through competing accounts that govern the representation of social reality. This tension, between legal and humanistic narratives as alternative sources of decision-making authority and social power, is central to the field of law and literature. As Brook Thomas explains, law and literature's "revival,"[15] as a field of study, and its constitution, as a disciplinary domain, depend on "how seriously" it engages debates concerning the "crisis of representation and representativeness" (510, 513). This crisis is especially pronounced in attempts to resolve how law and literature intersect to inform each other's justice-seeking objectives. If "[w]e can read a legal text *as if* it were literature, but doing so deprives it of its legal function" (533), Thomas argues, and if "deny[ing] literature ... [its] privileged status ... leaves us with one less institutional space from which to criticize ... the historically specific rhetorical constructions of the *doxa*," (535), then on what basis, Thomas asks, does one decide that "another ground would be more just"? (517). Put another way, if Dorris and Erdrich's community-focused account of the conflict does not achieve legal "representativeness" because it privileges the resolution of social conflict rather than the objective of legal culpability, then what role does literature play in resolving social conflicts without abandoning literary justice objectives?

As I will demonstrate, literary texts enact justice-seeking objectives by telling stories to make explicit the limits of legal reasoning and to demonstrate the impact of settler-colonial dispossession on Indigenous communities by depicting accounts that open up a horizon for understanding injustice in other ways. For Indigenous women, the "pressing issues of our time" concern their landless status, gender vulnerability, and lack of connections across tribal lines.[16] Representing these concerns through Indigenous women's literary activism contributes new ways of thinking through social conflicts, a critical task made more urgent by unsuccessful legal attempts to resolve acts of historical injustice solely through legal means. As I illustrate in chapter 4, the legal suit brought by Ratner and Perkins in conjunction with Anishinaabe Akeeng failed in its challenge to the constitutionality of the White Earth Land Settlement Act (WELSA). By participating in this action, community members forfeited all legal means for recovering disputed lands outside of the terms established by WELSA. Erdrich's novel is important when considering this failure because it shows the gender-injustice of such defeats as they affect Indigenous women, thus filling a "justice gap" (Bell and O'Rouke 36) in Indigenous literary studies, and by theorizing the specificity of land claims issues and land rights to Indigenous women, a view which is seldom accorded its singular status in law, as I argued in chapter 1. Erdrich's text focuses on the socio-economic plight of Indigenous women to show how their landless status informs their socio-economic vulnerability and lack of rights, a situation not adequately understood in legal contexts. In this chapter I ask how literary texts advance our understanding of colonial-legal gender injustice in ways not accounted for by legal narratives.

This question is central to postcolonial-feminist research. In her important reading of the postcolonial critic's task in seeking to establish a relationship between literature and the colonial-legal archive, Gayatri Spivak cautions against using the historical past to restore the lost agency of a resistant "sovereign subject" that has been disrupted by "the planned epistemic violence of the imperialist project" ("The Rani of Sirmur" 250–1). Spivak argues that such a project risks its own act of colonial violence by dissimulating the desire of the critic for a sovereign self in two ways: (1) through a recuperation that omits recognition of the power relations that separate these disciplinary fields through a "traffic in telescoped symbols" (250) that erases their political and disciplinary specificity; and (2) by inscribing a subject that masquerades as a "willed (auto)biography of the West" that levels the differences between the historical past and ongoing colonialism in the present, losing sight of how social relations are historically embedded and how hierarchical arrangements are organized and may change. The political project of Indigenous-feminist literary analysis and settler-colonial critique thus loses two of its most powerful forms of intervention – (1) an understanding of how to conceptualize power relations in order to bring about social change, and (2) an account of how to theorize current social disparities and violence against Indigenous women in ways that retain a socio-political subject as their object of analysis.

Indigenous feminist criticism has struggled to bring about both of these political objectives. It is especially fraught by problems of how to theorize gender relations in the administration of colonial governmentality, a struggle which comprises an intractable problem for its political project because practices of governmentality erase gender specificity, on the one hand, and prioritize normative colonial accounts of gender identity, on the other hand. As Caroline Desbiens explains, "[t]he separation and privileging of gender over race – or race over gender – helps to maintain the processes of separation and exclusion that are constantly at work within the nation ... the task of bringing them back within the same sphere, and subsequently tracing how they are enacted through state governmentality, is ... a difficult one" (362). Despite this dilemma of social visibility yet theoretical/political erasure, Desbiens proposes that researchers "write historical geography backwards," to account for "stages of de-settlement that made possible the re-settlement of the landscape by non-Aboriginal actors" and to undertake new forms of analysis in order to re-envision how Indigenous "institutions and bonds of sociability were derived from the relationship to land" (366). Desbiens's crucial insight, that "a key aspect of colonialism" was to "systematically... separate bodies from land" (366), provides Indigenous feminist criticism with a mode of analysis that prioritizes gender relations while also making explicit the loss of Indigenous women's knowledge practices and their relationships to land over time. As Desbiens explains,

> If this weakening of cultural patterns is effected most directly by removing populations from their ancestral territories, it also proceeds through re-education into a white cosmology where the relationship to the land is configured differently. The loss of traditional knowledge about how to survive on the land – or the lack of access altogether to that knowledge through traditional Aboriginal education – effectively finalizes this separation of body from land. (366)

The *Zay Zah* case and its supporting legislation make apparent how a long history of colonial occupation deployed blood-quantum categories for the primary purpose at White Earth of "separate[ing] [Indigenous] bodies from land." It also foregrounds the ways in which colonial practices erase gender relations and Indigenous women's knowledge practices. At White Earth, as Melissa Meyer notes, treaties literally "papered over" complex social and political arrangements among the Anishinaabe community with "some treaties establish[ing] 'bands' and 'nations' whose entire legitimacy rested on nothing more than the paper on which the treaties were written" (36). The community distinctions between several groups of Anishinaabe people were transformed not only by the allotment process that destroyed affiliations based on lines of cultural descent and marriage, but also by government legislation that distinguished people in terms of "competency" and "emancipation" based on blood-quantum distinctions that the *Zay Zah* decision and other cases revived.[17] Through the allotment process, social, cultural, and political differences among the Anishinaabe people understood through patterns of settlement, migration, intermarriage, and family were replaced by systems of classification determined according to "full-blood" and "mixed-blood" status. Recovering Indigenous women as agents of cultural transmission and tribal values requires approaching this history with a view to conceptualizing how colonialism and patriarchy participated in erasing Indigenous women's presence. The intergenerational effects of such a removal from history are made explicit in *The Antelope Wife* which shows how women's practices have been lost over time through the aggressive application of colonial policies that affect successive generations of Indigenous women and through the loss of tribal land.

Louise Erdrich's Indigenous-Feminist Literary Politics

The Antelope Wife builds on Erdrich's concern also explored in *The Round House* to demonstrate the way gender shapes land dispossession as these colonial relations contribute to the injustices suffered by Indigenous communities and as they participate in fostering sexual violence towards Indigenous women.[18] Erdrich's earlier fiction also expresses a profound concern for the loss of Indigenous women's knowledge practices and the removal of women from tribal lands by exploring their cultural isolation and community ostracization as social conditions that arise because these women lack access to tribal cultural inheritances and to socio-economic resources that are concretized in land. Erdrich's fiction shows how women's cultural disposability is directly connected to this loss of status as women are portrayed as victimized, exploited, or belittled by Indigenous men. In *Love Medicine*, one of Erdrich's best known and most popular texts, a book which enacts a similar story-telling style to the *The Antelope Wife* in highlighting the intersecting storylines of generations of women, Erdrich restores a sense of dignity and self-worth through intergenerational acceptance between women to Marie Lazarre. As one of the principal narrators of the story, Marie discloses her shame due to her family's lack of allotment land and tribal standing, which forces her to seek community acceptance, initially through the church, and subsequently through her marriage to Nector Kashpaw, a man whose tribal identity is beyond reproach because of his family lineage, yet whose excessive drinking and philandering have negative social consequences for his family. In one of the most moving scenes in the novel, Rushes Bear, Marie's mother-in-law, adopts Marie as her own daughter and disowns Nector as her son when his scandalous behaviour in disregarding his family responsibilities almost results in Marie's death in childbirth (104). Rushes Bear's poignant reminder of the burden that Indigenous women bear *as women* resonates powerfully when she states, "'You shame me . . . You never heard any wail out of her, any complaint. You never would know this birth was hard enough for her to die'" (104). Erdrich highlights Marie's narrow escape of death in childbirth to symbolize the social consequences of family abandonment and the loss to the tribe of women as mothers. Marie's status in the community is thus complicated by her isolation from her biological mother, Pauline, who forces her to fend for herself and her family as an adult, a consequence that her husband exploits through his indifference toward her. The emotional and physical exploitation of women emerges

as an important theme in Erdrich's other works of fiction,[19] and is especially important as a criticism of women's tribal disinheritance through
the loss of June Kashpaw (6), Marie's niece, whose "death as the object
of another's desire"[20] in the opening events of *Love Medicine* becomes
the mechanism through which Erdrich asserts compassionate affini-
ties between women, and tribal continuity through their storytelling
practices. Just prior to the moment when Rushes Bear transcends tribal
politics and community prejudice to claim Marie as her own daughter,
Marie expresses an identification with Rushes Bear's predicament in
finding herself alone and abandoned by her own children yet seeking
solace in the company of other women. Marie states, "She seemed to
have noticed the shape of my loneliness. Maybe she found it was the
same as hers" (99).

The necessity for women's identifications across generations as a
means to secure their survival and self-acceptance despite the systemic
dispossession of tribal peoples through the failure of land allotment
policies and widespread socio-economic impoverishment also arises
as a theme in Erdrich's novel *Tracks*. The story of the Chippewa community's land loss and their forced removal and assimilation as tribal
peoples[21] is recounted by Nanapush and Pauline to provide Lulu Nanapush with a narrative of personal history and identity in order that
she can understand and relate to her mother, Fleur, who was forced
from her land by the deception of the Indian Agent and the betrayal of
Rushes Bear. Sent by her from the socio-economic impoverishment of
the reservation to the loneliness and isolation of residential school (219,
226), Lulu outright refuses her mother as a family relation and the duty
of kinship that she owes through tribal inheritance to the community
and to herself (210). Lulu's disdain prompts Nanapush, the storytelling
elder, to explain the story of Fleur's family loss, her struggles to survive, and her tribal disinheritance. Through his explanation, and Lulu's
self-knowledge, Erdrich connects the microhistory of family relations
to the broad span of tragic historical events represented by allotment
practices to demonstrate the precarious and vulnerable positions that
Indigenous women occupy in response to external shifts in power relations. Not only does the novel begin with Fleur's loss of her family to
disease and death (3), through which she becomes an object of suspicion and is driven from the community to Argus where she is brutally
raped (26), it evolves through her return to Pillager land to pay the
annual allotment fee (36) in order to secure a place to give birth to her
daughter (44). Her exile and the loss of her sacred power are expressed

in her dispossession from the land for which she sacrifices so much of herself and her family. Fleur's story reveals how the story of land theft is also a narrative of women's more intimate losses, sacrifices, and vulnerabilities to sexual violence. The novel concludes with an explanatory account of gender disempowerment in order to tell a tale of cultural and social deprivation that explains how a woman in these circumstances could lose possession of her daughter (210). *The Antelope Wife* explores similar themes of loss, sexual violence, and family disinheritance by tracking the intersecting storylines of four generations of "Roy/Shawano women" (34) to illuminate their overlapping legacies of removal from the land through the violence of the settler-colonial encounter and the imposition of patriarchal cultural practices.

"Only the Names Survive": *The Antelope Wife*

Erdrich's novel contests the exclusions of Indigenous women from legal texts in their construction of tribal history and Indigenous intertribal relations by depicting women's absence as an historic act of displacement that occurs through the violence of colonial encounter. Set during the late nineteenth century, in a moment defined by a "spectacular cruel raid upon an isolated Ojibwa village mistaken for hostile during the scare over the starving Sioux" (3), the narrative begins with the story of Scranton Roy, a United States soldier scorned in love, who joins the cavalry in a fit of temper and discovers in battle a "sudden contempt" and "frigid hate" for the fleeing Ojibwa (4). In the chaos of "groaning horses, dogs screaming, [and] rifle and pistol reports," Roy stabs suddenly at an old woman who attacks him with nothing more than "a stone picked from the ground" (4). As he pulls his blade from her body, the woman utters the prophetic words "Daashkikaa. Daashkikaa," meaning "cracked apart" (213), calling into being an oath that sends him fleeing across the prairie in pursuit of a village dog who carries on its back the granddaughter of the dead medicine woman.

From this unconventional originary tale of violence and splitting, Erdrich constructs the narrative of colonial encounter as generating a decisive break in the social fabric of the Ojibwa community that ushers in distinct lines of cultural descent represented by the mixed-blood cultural inheritances of the Roy/Shawano women (34). These women embody the spirit, culture, and mythology of the people as they trace their connections to each other and to the land along the female line of descent through women who bear the "twins of twins, going back through the floating lines of time" (34). Their inheritances provide the essential knowledge in "names that gave the protection" and in understanding "the old ways ... and the traditions" that guard the people (35). The names establish an alternative line of descent in kinship relations and family memory in order to challenge the law's use of blood quantum lines of descent and property inheritance. They also represent the event marked by Scranton Roy's murderous act through a "pattern of destruction" that changes tribal relations and behaviour (36). The novel illustrates how the changes configured by this moment of colonial violence unleash a competing inheritance of social relations that contrast with those represented within the Ojibway community through the union of "Midassbaupayikway, Ten Stripe Woman, Midass," an Ojibway woman of the south descended from the "three-fires people" and "an Ivory Coast Slave" and a "Shawano man" from the "windigo, bear-walker, bad holy dream-man" people of the North (35). Cultural-tribal mixing in Erdrich's novel is thus both generative and exploitative, ushering in through the Anglo-American patrimony of the Roy line a legacy of violence towards women. Through this line, the novel conveys how Scranton Roy kills Midass's mother in a callous act of bravado that haunts him with guilt and anxiety until his last breath (239), and how this violence continues in his abduction of her granddaughter when he claims her as his own by renaming her in honour of his family relations (5). In a scene that thematizes the disorder and chaos engendered by Roy's abduction of Blue Prairie Woman's daughter from the Ojibway village, as a violent appropriation of gender as well as heritage, the narrative illuminates how in a desperate bid to halt the child's crying Roy slips the baby to his breast and suckles the infant (7). Critics who read this scene as a moment in which Roy "rescues an Indian baby" and "miraculously nurs[es] the infant at his own breast,"[22] overlook how Erdrich configures this act as an appalling sign of unnatural displacement that is surpassed only by a subsequent event in which, as Roy's wife, "Peace McKnight," lies dying in childbirth, about to "step from her ripped body into the utter calm of her new soul," she sees her husband "put his [newborn] son to his breast" (17).

By configuring these acts of patrimonial displacement as forms of disruption that bring about the exploitation and deaths of women, Erdrich illuminates how transformations in the power relations between men and women engender the conditions that lead to women's sexual vulnerability, establishing the common ground from which they inherit each other's intergenerational sorrow. Thus, when Rozina Whiteheart

Beads's grief for her daughter Deanna, who dies as a result of her father's failed suicide attempt (69), becomes unbearable and she no longer cares for her deathly ill, twin daughter Cally (89), she inherits a measure of "Ozhawashkwamashkodeykway/Blue Prairie Woman's" despairing grief for her lost "nameless" daughter who escaped from the dawn raid on the Ojibwa village on the back of a dog (12). Blue Prairie Woman, obsessed with sorrow for her lost child, leaves her community to search for her "nameless daughter," abandoning her children to the care of their grandmother, Midass, to be raised "as her own" (15), subsequently leaving them altogether when she dies of fever (19). Her loss figures a second break in the transmission of intergenerational knowledge that explains the power and authority of names. Erdrich thus draws parallels with the *Zay Zah* case to show how the loss of women's authority is directly connected to the absence of traditional knowledge and the absence of alternative sources of authority and connection in the defence of land. Consequently, when Cally is left to the care of her grandmothers Zosie and Mary, the twin descendents of the twins of Blue Prairie Woman (103), she experiences a sense of isolation and disconnection such that she is confused about her identity and cannot overcome her grief for her lost sister, Deanna (112).

One aspect of Cally's lack of connection between her selfhood and her cultural inheritance is expressed by her inability to distinguish between matters of cultural importance. When she loses her "turtle holder of soft white buckskin" containing "her birth cord," "dry sage," and "sweet grass" that she was supposed to "keep with [her] all [her] life" and have "bur[ied] with [her] on reservation land," she thinks "nothing of it" until "many years later" when she realizes that "over time the absence . . . will tell" (101). The "absence that tells" and that expresses Cally's feelings of family disconnection become a metaphor in the novel for the lack of emotional support and family dependence. Like Cally, who fails to appreciate the continuity of cultural ties represented by her "turtle holder," her grandmothers, who are also raised without a mother figure and grow up under the supervision of Midass,[23] rupture the family tradition initiated by Blue Prairie Woman. Instead of naming their twin daughters "Zosie and Mary" as they had been named, they call them "Rozin" and "Aurora" and break the "continuity" between family names that "gave the protection" (35). In yet another mirroring of the disavowal of family and tribal tradition, Rozin strays from the ritual of cultural continuity and names her daughters "Cally and Deanna" (35). The effect of these choices is devastating for each mother: Zosie loses Aurora when she dies of diptheria and has to be "pried" from the "five-year-old arms" of her sister (35); Rozina's daughter Deanna dies tragically when she follows her father as he plots his suicide, suffocating from carbon monoxide poisoning once he abandons the idea (70). That each woman's choice appears to be undertaken from an autonomous moment of self-determination indicates how Erdrich's novel privileges as a necessity acts of cultural continuity that enable a vision of Indigenous women's collective identity and social responsibility to each other. This obligation is premised in the intergenerational transmission of women's knowledge that teaches how culture, history, and family inheritance matter to the formation of collective social identity.

In one of the novel's most moving passages, Erdrich illustrates how Cally, Rozina's daughter, suffers from a one-sided view of her personal history, which includes guilt and concern for her mother's sorrow and utter contempt for her profligate father. Cally avoids feelings of compassion for her father's descent into alcoholism, blaming him for her sister's death, and preventing her recognition of the multiple strands of her cultural inheritances. When she arrives in Minneapolis in search of her grandmothers whom she hopes can explain the gaps in her understanding of her family's genealogy and aid her in uncovering the cultural inheritance that resides within her name that she hopes will ultimately allow her to overcome her grief for her sister, her grandmother Zosie confronts her with the knowledge that her father's alcoholism has become uncontrollable (121). Cally's first-person narration of her inner feelings and responses to her grandmother's inquiry about whether or not her mother "knows" illuminates her selfish desire to disidentify from the social embarrassment and shame of her family's past. While she thinks to herself, "Of course we know, in a way, but that is only a general way ... And I don't care, the truth is, [I] don't want to open up that piece of my heart that I locked shut after Deanna. All his fault, my heart says, all his fault and his alone," she replies to her grandmother, "'I never, and I mean never, want to see his face again'" (122). Contrary to Cally's emphatic denial of her father's existence, he appears as a figure in the bakery where Cally sits with her grandmother, an apparition "saggy-skinned and drooping like a week-old helium balloon" who "stands before the counter barely holding himself upright" (122). When he turns around suddenly and fixes Cally with a stare, he croaks out, "'Cawg ... Cawg ... Cawg,'" stops and says in a "terrible whisper," "'Deanna ... '" (122). The pain articulated in Richard Whiteheart Beads's misrecognition of his daughter and the overwhelming sense of despair evoked by this scene reverberate thematically with the feelings of identification Scranton Roy experiences when he stabs the old medicine woman who in her death reminds him of his mother. Neither man is recoverable in the narrative such that he can atone for his past behaviour: Richard dies from a gunshot wound self-inflicted in the hotel hallway of Rozin and Frank's honeymoon suite (180), and Scranton promises his son, Augustus, to Cally's great-grandmother as atonement for attacking the Ojibwa village but his grandson fails to make reparation and instead physically abuses and betrays Cally's grandmothers (238). Each man, nevertheless, plays an integral role in the recognition of family inheritances and tribal history that must be acknowledged and accepted if Cally is to overcome her grief and understand the pattern of loss and struggle through which each generation of women was forced to endure her life.

Erdrich illustrates the embeddedness of family history in Cally's need to recognize her relationship to a family inheritance of loss, sorrow, and violence related, in part, to the mysterious woman, "Sweetheart Calico," Blue Prairie Woman's first-born, who is drugged, assaulted, and raped by Klaus Shawano when he becomes so obsessed with her beauty that he kidnaps her and traps her in "Gakahbekong, Minneapolis" where she cannot find her way home (30). Cally's story, together with the "bitter milk" from a rescurer's breasts that bestow "disconcerting hatred" and "protection" (18) through the historic legacy of the Roy line, along with "the names of women" that belonged to "many powerful mothers" (13) emerging out of an Ojibwa past, enables her not only to understand how the many sides of cultural inheritance engender the "[f]amily stories [that] repeat themselves in patterns and waves generation to generation, across bloods and time," but also to accept "the pattern we go on replicating" that produces "a suicidal tendency, a fatal wish. On this side drinking. On the other a repression of guilt that finally explodes" (200). When Cally recognizes the broader pattern of historic displacement and loss through which women bear the responsibility within tribal culture for the unconscious acts of violence and selfishness that destroy the community's social fabric, she begins to grasp the senseless self-pity of her father's inheritance (64), the guilty complicity of her mother's abdication of responsibility in remaining with him (58), and her grief and sorrow for her absent sister (122). These acceptances compel her to forgive her parents for the incomprehensible violence that destroys their family. The connections that Erdrich articulates between the multiple strands of Cally's cultural inheritance and her ability to accept the family guilt and complicity that underlie her sister's death enable her to free Sweetheart Calico from the city that traps her (219) and to claim her inheritance as a descendant of Blue Prairie Woman with the power of the dreamer to restore the original names of women (217). Ultimately, through her description of Cally's recognition of the importance of tribal family history to a meaningful understanding of women's identities and their relations to the past, Erdrich's novel establishes that it is only through acceptance and integration rather than separation and denial that women are able to recover a sense of their inheritances and intergenerational community relations.

Erdrich's preoccupation in *The Antelope Wife* with the importance of family names to the restoration of cultural memory and historical community also arises in her non-fiction creative work. "The Names of Women" demonstrates a similar concern for imagining how to recover the significance of Ojibway women in history when their identities have been diffused through the dialectics and violences of colonial encounter. Erdrich writes: "*Ikwe* is the word for woman in the language of the Anishinabe, my mother's people, whose descendants, mixed with and married to French trappers and farmers, are the Michifs of the Turtle Mountain reservation in North Dakota. Every Anishinabe Ikwe, every mixed-blood descendant like me, who can trace her way back a generation or two, is the daughter of a mystery. The history of the woodland Anishinabe – decimated by disease, fighting Plains Indian tribes to the west and squeezed by European settlers to the east – is much like most other Native American stories, a confusion of loss, a tale of absences, of a culture that was blown apart and changed so radically in such a short time that only the names survive. And yet, those names" (132). In this provocative piece, Erdrich adopts a musing, intimate voice to characterize efforts to come to grips with a cultural inheritance of historical loss and disconnection, one that conceals the roles of Indigenous women even as it gestures to their fleeting presence in an archive represented by "the names of women." Rather than privilege her voice as the site for an unproblematized reconstruction of historical and cultural identity – one attributable to her experience alone to restore their identity – she proposes in this essay and in *The Antelope Wife* that the reconfiguration of Indigenous women's historically fractured lives must of necessity account for their social locations in history, the legacy of cultural inheritances and knowledge that they represent, and the restorative power embodied in language and naming through which to imaginatively reconstruct the cultural practices that lead to their empowerment and presence. Her vision of the cultural knowledge embodied in women's traditions and social relations articulates a dual inheritance of loss and recovery, yet it also demonstrates an overwhelming sense of the importance of restoring recognition of the site of language, intergenerational memory, and tribal and personal names to the social reconstruction of Indigenous women's lives and political identities.

The task that Erdrich proposes for Indigenous-feminist analysis in its project of historical recovery is thus twofold: on the one hand, we must rewrite the historical-legal archive by recovering the names of women who have been exiled from court records to demonstrate Indigenous women's resistances to colonial expansion and land expropriation; on the other hand, we are obligated to interpret the knowledge represented by Indigenous women's resistance to convey their struggles against dispossession in the present in order to accord ourselves a place in contemporary resistance movements. These political objectives represent precisely the decolonizing tasks undertaken by Winona LaDuke's political, legal, and literary activism.

Chapter Four

Land Claims, Identity Claims: *Manypenny v. United States* (1991) and *Last Standing Woman* (1997)[1]

The White Earth land claim dispute provides a gravitational centre to my book and the focus of this chapter because it demonstrates the complexity of Louise Erdrich's question – what does justice mean for Indigenous communities? – by highlighting the fact that no single answer is sufficient to address Indigenous peoples' land loss through settler-colonial occupation and dispossession. The land's status as a legal matter transcends the particular and the local to signify the symbolic, material, cultural, and emotional investments that concretize Indigenous peoples' regard for and commitment to its struggle. Its presence animates the collective source of being and aliveness, and its imaginary articulates the spiritual, political, ancestral, and aspirational logics that unite Indigenous peoples across time and place. As the occasion for Indigenous peoples' greatest strength, it is also the source of the greatest conflict and sorrow. In the post–civil rights period, its defence has ushered in a transnational and multifaceted oppositional framework that has motivated "a groundswell of movements of resistance" and the "emergence of struggles for collective self-determination" that have transformed "racial awareness, racial meaning, and racial subjectivity" (Frankenberg and Mani 293). Winona LaDuke's legal and literary activism have been at the forefront of this struggle. Through her creative and critical work, LaDuke's writing expresses a multidimensional approach to social justice for Indigenous peoples that foregrounds "the collective survival of all human beings" through their relations to each other and to the land (*All Our Relations* 5).[2] Her commitment to land sovereignty not only incorporates measures designed to overcome colonial laws' authority (*All Our Relations* 200) in order to recover "Indigenous systems of knowledge, jurisdiction, practice, and governance," it also facilitates "local self-reliance" (200) and gender empowerment through the restoration of Indigenous women's political and cultural status (127). In the complexity of her social justice stance, LaDuke's vision establishes the grounds for an Indigenous feminist literary activism through storytelling that makes possible Indigenous community regeneration.

In this chapter, I explore how *Last Standing Woman* crafts an oppositional consensual space from which to enact Indigenous decolonization by intervening through literature in the collective's social imaginary in order to alter the wider community's understanding of the conflict at White Earth. LaDuke not only participated with fellow tribal members in direct action to legally oppose the U.S. government's resolution to end the land conflict through a constitutional challenge launched in *Manypenny v. United States*, she also organized locally through *Anishinaabe Akiing* to demonstrate the widespread historical injustice and illegality of "reservation land takings" (*All Our Relations* 124). As community historian Holly Youngbear-Tibbetts explains, because the *Zay Zah* decision prompted the Minnesota Chippewa Tribe to undertake an investigation into land allotment practices on the White Earth Indian Reservation for the purposes of "identifying those land claims that followed the precedents established in the previous case of *Zay Zah v. Clearwater County*" (95), their tribe's search made public the pervasive practice of "illegally alienated" lands (117). Residents responded by organizing themselves into "broadly based citizen groups" that, on the one hand, "convened as the United Township Association (UTA)" for those individuals "whose property interests were directly challenged by the Department of Justice's determinations," and on the other hand, as "Anishinaabe Akeeng (The People's Land)," an organization that represented heirs to "alienated Indian allotments" (119). Before individual White Earth allottees could file suit, Congress passed special legislation entitled the White Earth Reservation Land Settlement Act of 1985 [WELSA] that purported to settle the question of disputed land titles on the White Earth Reservation, but in effect, "abrogated the rights of individual White Earth allottees to pursue their claims in court" (Youngbear-Tibbetts 130). To oppose WELSA's application, LaDuke and fellow members of Anishinaabe Akiing sought a court injunction challenging Congress's objective to halt the investigation into clouded titles at White Earth and to invalidate alternative dispute resolution processes that the community proposed to enter into (*All Our Relations* 124). The legal consequences of their failed challenge demonstrate the cultural and literary-political implications of this case. This chapter explores how the use of the term "mixed-blood" to describe Indigenous writers' literary activism works against the recognition of this writing's social justice objectives and oppositional stance. It proposes Indigenous feminism as an alternative framework through which to consider literature's social justice commitments, and shows how *Last Standing Woman* envisions an Indigenous feminist tribal politics that recognizes our common humanity through acts of solidarity undertaken by Indigenous women.

Manypenny v. United States

On 13 March 1991, Winona LaDuke and thirty-four enrolled members of the White Earth Band of Chippewa Indians appeared as appellants before the Minnesota Division of the United States District Court in an action to recover disputed land on the White Earth Indian Reservation in Northern Minnesota. Plaintiffs in the case, led by Marvin Manypenny and George Fineday, Sr, asserted approximately "40 claims involving title and possessory interests in 4087 acres of land" (*Manypenny v. United States* 948 F. 2d 1057 U.S. Ct. App. 1991, 1060). They sought "declaratory, injunctive, and monetary relief" against the federal government, including the Department of the Interior and several of its employees, the State of Minnesota and its agents, three Minnesota counties, and "numerous named and unnamed individual holders of, or claimants to, disputed property" (1058). They argued that by enacting the "White Earth Land Settlement Act (WELSA)" "Congress affirmatively and expressly waived the federal government's sovereign immunity" and "established a[n] independent cause of action for allottees and their heirs seeking return of the land and monetary damages" (1062). Plaintiffs stated furthermore that they "opposed the enactment of WELSA" and "continue to oppose the Act's provisions which divest them and other members of the White Earth Band of any interest in the disputed property" (1062).

As a contemporary land claim settlement Act passed by Congress to "settle claims to certain allotted lands on the White Earth Indian Reservation" (United States. Senate. "White Earth Indian Land Claims Settlement," v), WELSA consolidated imposed colonial definitions of Indigenous identity by distinguishing among community members on the basis of "full blood" and "mixed blood" inheritance and by grounding dispossessed allottees' claims to their allotment lands in the language of blood-quantum identity. "Full blood" status, for the purposes of legal verification within the Act, designated "a Chippewa Indian of the White Earth Reservation, Minnesota, who was designated as a full blood Indian on the roll approved by the United States District Court for the District of Minnesota on October 1, 1920 ... or who [was] the biological child of two full blood parents so designated on the roll or of one full blood parent so designated on the roll and one parent who was an Indian enrolled in any other federally recognized Indian tribe, band, or community" (vii). "Mixed blood" status was determined as "a Chippewa Indian of the White Earth Reservation, Minnesota, who was designated as a mixed blood Indian on the roll approved by the United States District Court of Minnesota on October 1, 1920 ... [and] also refer[ed] to any descendants of an individual who was listed on said roll providing that descendant was not a full blood under the definition in subsection (c) of this section" (viii).[3] Without reference to the imposed identity provisions of WELSA legislation, Judge John R. Gibson affirmed the decision of the District Court and dismissed the case against the federal government, the State of Minnesota, and the remaining counties and private landowners (*Manypenny v. United States* 948F. 2d 1057 U.S. Ct. App. 1991, 1060). Judge Gibson stated that since Congress proposed WELSA to settle "with finality" "unresolved legal uncertainties" arising out of clouded titles to allotted lands (1063), it could not also "establish a substantive basis for a cause of action" (1065) against the federal government as appellants claimed. For this reason, he stated, WELSA could not be read to imply a "waiver of sovereign immunity" of the federal government, and thus the District Court's decision to dismiss plaintiffs' claims on the grounds that they "failed to join" the United States "as an indispensable party to the case" (*Manypenny v. United States* 125 F.R.D. 497 U.S. Dist. Ct. D. Minn. 1989, 502) was held intact. With the failure of their appeal, appellants in the case exhausted all avenues of legal recourse for recovering tribal lands outside of the terms established in WELSA, and they forfeited all rights to receive compensation under the Act for lost allotments.

The background legal and legislative history of the White Earth Indian Reservation illustrates how the rulings by the Minnesota Supreme Court and Congress depend on identity categories that emerge out of federal policies of colonial management.[4] It also demonstrates that the problem of formulating community affiliations that do not conform to blood-quantum categories remains an important theoretical and practical issue in social justice criticism. This chapter argues that Indigenous-feminist literary criticism must remain vigilant over the conditions of cultural production from which emerge the identity categories we inhabit and employ in our cultural criticism. It argues for the importance of gender identity to a reading of community relations and tribal histories, and it proposes that contemporary creative writers and community activists, such as Winona LaDuke, offer a progressive vision for reimagining community values and inherited community relationships through Indigenous feminist practice.

Because the *Manypenny* case and WELSA legislation reveal the ways in which identity categories for Indigenous peoples have real, material implications, theorizing identity in Indigenous literature cannot remain an intellectual exercise divorced from social reality. For Indigenous peoples, identity categories mean all the difference between land and dispossession, restorative justice and continued oppression.[5] Thus, the study of Indigenous literature must be constituted through the terrain of political representation in order to transform the relationship between theory and practice and provide articulations for new and emerging political positions. As Laura Kipnis argues, "If the theoretical object prescribes a set of theoretical strategies, it simultaneously describes a field of political possibility" (152). At a historical juncture when land claims settlements coincide with the unrelenting persecution of Indigenous peoples, theorizing identity cannot be divorced from the legal and social implications of colonial identity formation and subjectification. It is out of an understanding of the crucial interlocking effects of the political, social, and theoretical for Indigenous peoples that this chapter attends to reasserting the necessity of gender analysis to Indigenous identity.

In what follows, I examine how Indigenous feminist critics have attempted to theorize a relationship between community identity, tribal history, and women's collective agency in connection with gender identity in order to create an oppositional space from which to restore gender identity as an analytical category to discussions of tribal politics and community values. In contrast to Congressional legislation that privileges as normative male tribal identity, Indigenous feminist writers and activists, as I have shown through this book, negotiate history and politics by examining the multiple imbrications of race and gender identity that shape the social subjectivities of Indigenous women. Their analyses of communal social arrangements include theorizing the valency of feminism and Indigenous identity for reconstructing history, and articulating forms of community identity that do not conform to blood-quantum status.

LaDuke's cultural politics demonstrate the imbrications of the literary with activist feminist aesthetics and social intervention. The connections that her activism articulates between tribal politics and gender relations suggest that, as a writer, she is beset by a dual and potentially conflicted set of critical and political demands: on the one hand, how to take issue with the call within literary studies for an unproblematized historical representation and reconstruction in Indigenous writing, and, on the other hand, how to participate in a process of cultural reinvention and renewal that illuminates how the revival and preservation of tribal identity must of necessity engage with the inheritances of a colonial past and the contributions of Indigenous women. In *Last Standing Woman*, issues of community identity and tribal relations are framed by the historical disruption of community ties and the social disintegration of community relations. The literary text not only stages debates about community identity, but also offers a problematization of these issues as they are represented through legal and legislative means.

For LaDuke, Indigenous feminist literary politics cannot be divorced from cultural and political alliances. Her work as a Green Party candidate, feminist organizer, and Indigenous and environmental activist demonstrates these commitments. One of the most widely recognized spokespeople on behalf of environmental, political, and economic issues, LaDuke served as Ralph Nader's vice-presidential candidate for the Green Party in the 1996 and 2000 elections, was chosen by *Time Magazine* in 1994 as one of America's fifty most promising leaders age forty and under, was selected by *Ms. Magazine* in 1997 as one of its women of the year, and, in 1988, received a $20,000 award by Reebok in recognition of her human rights activism, which she used to buy back nearly 1000 acres of reservation land at White Earth (Cronin n.p. and LaDuke, *All Our Relations* 126). LaDuke has also been instrumental in forming community-based organizations, such as the White Earth Land Recovery Project, to explore other mechanisms for recovering tribal lands after participating as a claimant in the *Manypenny* case that exhausted all legal recourse available to the community, and in establishing the Indigenous Women's Network, a non-governmental organization that advocates a collective identity for all women as representatives of "Mothers of our Nations" ("Indigenous Women's Network" 1).

The potentially misunderstood "new ageism" of LaDuke's account of women's collective agency as representative of "Mother Earth in human form" is further complicated by her public activism which displays a conscientiousness for the collective "marginalization of all women" from environmental collapse, and for the erosion of women's self-determination through "colonialism" and "rapid industrialization" in fledgling nations ("Indigenous Women's Network" 1). Although LaDuke defends her views on "the living wage, health care, [and] welfare reform" as "women's issues," she has failed to secure the support of mainstream feminist groups, particularly during the 2000 election in the United States when she was accused by prominent women activists not only of discussing "motherhood" issues at the expense of a concern for "feminis[t]" ones, but also of dividing support for the left by running on behalf of the Green Party and "taking votes away from the Democratic Party" (Rampell, "Towards an Inaugural Pow-Wow" n.p.).[6] While it is probably more accurate to describe LaDuke's commitments to mainstream feminist concerns as a form of "green feminism" in keeping with her support for the Green Party's core values on women's issues,[7] her engagements with tribal history and gender representation in *Last Standing Woman* demonstrate a form of *feminist* "indigenism" that connects the erosion of intertribal historical ties with transformations to the status of women as a result of the disruption of power relations within Indigenous communities. My claims for LaDuke's novel are informed by Marie Anna Jaimes Guerrero's definition of "indigenism," which she describes as a "struggle against American colonization from the premise of collective human rights" ("Civil Rights" 102), but I am restoring the term "feminist" to her analysis of the relationship between "native women and feminism" (101) even though Guerrero claims that the "priorities and sociopolitical agendas" expressed by the "white, middle-class women's movement" are "individualist rather than communal in orientation" leading to a polarization of interests that she expresses as "feminism versus indigenism" (102). Instead of adopting "Eurocentric paradigm[s]," Guerrero insists on a "universal indigenist worldview" that facilitates the recognition of "struggle[s] between Indian nations and the American state over questions of sovereignty and incorporation into the U.S. polity [as] most visible when one examines the contradictions that emerge over the tribal status of native women" (103). While I agree with her claims that "patriarchal structures" operate "both inside and outside the tribe" (103), I am concerned with Guerrero's definition of both colonialism and tribalism as undifferentiated forms of "patriarchy" (103). If colonialism is patriarchal and tribalism is patriarchal, then what difference does "race" identity make to the subjectivity of Indigenous women? LaDuke's novel articulates this question by offering an intersectional analysis of the relationship between race and gender identity through its exploration of the effects of colonialism as a disruption that occurs in the structural relations within the tribe, thus shifting relations of power, and through its examination of the subordination of Indigenous women as a function of the loss of power now associated with Indigenous men, thus transforming relations of gender. Her literary activism can thus be understood as strategically reconfiguring aspects of the cultural imaginary that are not accessible through legal, legislative, and political means, the material implications of which I have laid out at the beginning of this chapter.[8]

Indigenous cultural criticism must also ask what implications an imposed colonial past has for Indigenous identity that is increasingly determined according to demands for its expression of "authenticity." Debates about the status of mixed-blood literature that deploy an organizing binary of "insider/outsider" status to privilege forms of literary expression that construct Indigenous literatures as sites for the "identification" of tribally specific cultural practices, or as "authentic" expressions of tribal culture, exist alongside claims that foreground the literature's reflection of tribal communities historically to privilege its mimetic function. At one end of this spectrum of demands for authenticity, Elizabeth Cook-Lynn's criticisms of the "mixed-blood literary movement" for its repudiation of "tribally specific literary traditions" that are formulated within "the hopeful, life-affirming aesthetic of traditional stories, songs, and rituals" (76, 67) take issue with the "major self-described mixed-blood voices of the decade" who, Cook-Lynn claims, offer "few useful expressions of resistance to the colonial history at the core of Indian/White relations" (67). The assemblage of writers from distinct tribal and national inheritances who represent the claim that "mixed-blood" writing has become a movement include "Gerald Vizenor, Louis Owens, Wendy Rose, Maurice Kenny, Michael Dorris, Diane Glancy, Betty Bell, Thomas King, Joe Bruchac, and Paula Gunn Allen" (67). Aside from arranging this list according to mixed-blood status, it is unclear how these writers are constitutive as a group especially when they share no common ground according to gender, tribal origin, or national identity. In thus foregrounding these writers as mixed-blood rather than through another organizing category, Cook-Lynn appears to be complicitous with her own critique in so far as her discussion of "mixed-blood identity" foregrounds identity categories instituted through federally imposed blood-quantum distinctions, thus lending critical weight to the terms, rather than through other categories of social enablement that might include tribal identity or political affiliation.

In contrast to Cook-Lynn's position, Louis Owens argues for a reading of mixed-blood literature that posits its resistant politics as representative of its "exterior" location beyond the literature itself, presumably in the "real" of social relations as a "place of contact between cultural identities, a bidirectional, dynamic zone of resistance" from which to confront the dominant discourse (*Mixedblood Messages* 47). The site of political engagement that Owens claims for a "hybridized, polyglot, transcultural frontier" that is "quite clearly internalized" by mixed-blood authors, yet provides the common ground from which "Native Americans . . . continue to resist [an] ideology of containment and to insist upon the freedom to imagine themselves within a fluid, always shifting frontier space" (27), relies on the "fixity" of the concept of mixed-blood identity as a transhistorical signifier that asserts its timelessness without reference to the literature's internal variation or to its implication in different socio-historical context. In a critical style similar to Cook-Lynn's, Owens analyses a range of mixed-blood texts for their consistency with his advocacy of a social/constructivist approach to Indigenous writing.

The literary-critical positions represented by Cook-Lynn and Owens articulate two ends of a spectrum in a debate that is concerned to legitimate the literary politics and oppositional practices of Indigenous writing by illustrating how it participates in or fails to reflect tribal practices. I have drawn attention to these critical positions in order to illuminate the ways in which identity politics organizes these discussions. Both critics claim an interventionary space for mixed-blood literature in cultural discourse, yet in so doing, they homogenize distinctions between tribally distinct Indigenous writers.

What remains unspoken in these considerations of the category of mixed-blood writing is the term's implication in a colonial history of land allotment practice through which the federal government imposed forms of colonial identity on Indigenous communities. This recognition and its historical specificity to the dispersal of tribal lands during the allotment period are crucial to understanding how the literary-critical practices we deploy as cultural critics circumvent and thus perpetuate analytical terms that benefit colonial policies. The kind of criticism that I have been demonstrating and one that I would call for eschews the self-evident in critical engagements with Indigenous literary texts to formulate a critical discourse that reads across the genres of literary, legal, and social positioning. As the social justice implications of the *Manypenny* cases disclose, not to do so is to absent ourselves from a field of engagement that is critical to the social and cultural histories of Indigenous communities. An Indigenous-feminist literary practice that identifies the social effects of cultural work and its political imbrications in colonial history would move beyond the self-evident form of discursive practice that relies *solely* on "telling our story" criticism. In this sense, it is equally as important to consider Indigenous writing for its self-consciousness with regard to staging the limitations of singular identities privileged at the expense of other aspects of relational self-hood. My reading of LaDuke's writing for its intersectional staging of race and gender consciousness represents an attempt to think through the social implications and political alternatives proposed by a critical stance that illuminates the imbrications of race and gender identifications and disidentifications under different historical conditions. I have done so by privileging a cultural analysis of law approach that articulates the relationship between congressional legislation as it has been imposed within Indigenous communities, and a "standpoint feminist perspective" that privileges subordinate group claims in order to politicize identity categories within the material histories of Indigenous anti-colonial struggle.

By "standpoint feminist perspective," I invoke Nancy Hartsock's elaboration of the term as not "simply an interested position" which she qualifies as a "bias," but rather a critical stance that is invested in "the sense of being engaged" (107). For Hartsock, a standpoint structures knowledge formations in an invested way that "posits a duality of levels of reality, of which the deeper level or essence both includes and explains the 'surface' or appearance, and indicates the logic by means of which the appearance inverts or distorts the deeper reality" (108). In addition, the concept of a standpoint, according to Hartsock, "depends on the assumption that epistemology grows in a complex and contradictory way from material life" (108). Hartsock's definition of "standpoint thinking" is important not only to my analysis of the relationship between gender and history in Indigenous women's critical practices, but also to my foregrounding of colonial politics through legal and legislative representations in which the presence of Indigenous identity in colonial legal texts serves as a distorting narrative of social reality that displaces recognition of ongoing practices of land dispossession through colonial legal means. For the Indigenous women writers whose work I explore in this book, the loss of

Indigenous lands represents a deeply historical and material power consequence that is theorized according to several organizing sets of transnational criteria that connect Indigenous peoples through their political struggles against dispossession – tribal membership disbarment, the out-adoption of Indigenous children, violence against Indigenous women, and the restoration of equitable gender relations.

The call for a recognition of the reciprocal relationship that exists between Indigenous women's traditions, and a standpoint Indigenous-feminist perspective that can illuminate how feminism's commitment to analysing the reproduction of gender relations facilitates the reconstruction of Indigenous women's historically fractured lives, has been raised by critics Paula Gunn Allen, Laura Tohe, and Kathryn Shanley, whose important insights I build on here. Allen's analysis represents one of the earliest attempts by a cultural critic to restore gender analysis to a consideration of the organizing politics of community practices. Allen argues that "[a]nalysing tribal cultural systems from a mainstream feminist point of view allows an otherwise overlooked insight into the complex interplay of factors that have led to the systematic loosening of tribal ties, the disruption of tribal cohesion and complexity, and the growing disequilibrium of cultures that were anciently based on a belief in balance, relationship, and the centrality of women, particularly elder women. A feminist approach reveals not only the exploitation and oppression within the tribes by whites and by white government but also areas of oppression within the tribes and the sources and nature of that oppression. To a large extent, such an analysis can provide strategies for the tribes to reclaim their ancient gynarchical, egalitarian, and sacred traditions" (223). Allen proposes a "gynocratic" reading of Indigenous traditions that emphasizes the concepts of balance and interconnectedness and that foregrounds the values of personal autonomy, communal harmony, and egalitarianism found within oral narrative forms. Her reading, however, of the feminist content within the traditional Keres ritual "How Kochinnenako Balanced the World" seems to enact a form of "tribal feminism" that privileges a self-actualizing feminist consciousness as enabling social transformation, at the expense of illustrating how tribal communal cultural values connect with feminist agency. If it is the case that tribal consciousness differs from yet illuminates aspects of feminist standpoint analysis, then on what grounds is this difference staged, and how is a "tribal-feminist" perspective different from an "information-retrieval" approach to feminist consciousness that provided the basis for second-wave feminist work?[9] These questions remain unanswered in Allen's model, yet they are crucial to articulating the differences in social and cultural location that Allen argues for.

In a similar manner to Allen's focus on a tribal "matrilineal" consciousness as self-actualizing and privileged within Indigenous communities and through which Indigenous women organize and articulate for themselves a place within Indigenous culture, Laura Tohe asserts the prominence of "Diné women" and "Diné matrilineal culture" to the survival and continuity of women's cultural practices, despite the "[disruptions of] five hundred years of Western patriarchal intrusion" (103). In a provocative essay entitled "There is No Word for Feminism in My Language," Tohe articulates the relationship between the continuity of Diné cultural traditions, such as the "Kinaaldá, Walking into Beauty" or "coming-of-age ceremony" (106), a ceremony that "celebrates [an initiate's] transformation from girl to woman" (106), and matrilineal deities, such as "Changing Woman" or "White Shell Woman," the "principal mythological deity" through which the "matriarchal system of the Diné was established," to the reconstruction of positive self-images for Diné women that have enabled them to resist their portrayal as "'those poor' Indian women who were assimilated, colonized, Christianized, or victimized," and to the establishment of their self-identities as "women who cling to the roots of their female lineage" (104). Tohe demonstrates how Diné women have sustained each other during disruptive socioeconomic changes that have altered their social positions in terms of gender relationships. She argues that these women have continued to rely on "kinship" patterns and "clan relationships" to secure positive relational connections. She refuses, however, to represent or identify these practices as "feminist" in scope or ideology.

Indeed, Tohe seems determined to eschew a relationship between the cultural practices of Diné women as they sustained them through "five hundred years of colonialism," and feminism as a movement that she characterizes as ethnocentric and performative, that prompted white feminists of the 1970s to "burn their bras" and ignore the "issues that were relevant to [Diné women's] tribal communities" (109). While it is possible to dismiss as reductive the representation of the women's movement of the 1970s in order to recognize the problems of ethnocentrism and strategic performativity that Tohe is pointing to, it is much more difficult to disregard the issue of essentialism through which she argues for the exceptionality of Diné women's cultural systems, more difficult, because the exceptionality of Diné women legitimates a relational identity that connects Diné women through *identity as sameness* with women "from other tribes" (110). It is important to recognize Tohe's argument as privileging a form of cultural resistance that recognizes tribal identity as enabling for Indigenous women even though tribal identity and matrilineal culture are not discussed in terms of their historical and political specificity, yet it is hard to forget the "exceptionality" of *Chippewa women* from the White Earth Indian Reservation who were so different from other women that when they married non-Indigenous men they were excluded from federal recognition.[10] An explanation of the self-actualizing consciousness of Diné matrilineal culture, together with an understanding of why colonial policies targeted this cultural consciousness in other locations, provides a broader recognition of the systematic and uneven colonial processes that affect Indigenous women in discrete yet relational cultural locations. Tohe concludes that "[t]here was no need for feminism because of our matrilineal culture. And it continues. For Diné women, there is no word for feminism" (110). This claim rings as a somewhat rhetorical argument for the exceptionality of Diné women's matrilineal culture as it disavows a larger commitment to building a future for Indigenous women's feminist community, one that can work against asymmetrical power relations in several cultural and/or tribal locations.

In contrast to Allen's focus on feminist consciousness and Tohe's emphasis on tribal women's exceptionalism, Kathryn Shanley calls for a shifting, local analysis that can attend to "the gulf" that exists between "feminism as we theorize and practice it in the academy ... and the way women live their lives in postcolonial times and places" ("Blood Ties" 209). Shanley argues for a cross-cultural feminist perspective that considers the common denominators and communal ties in the experiences and continuing traditions of contemporary Indigenous women. She writes, "[w]hether living off-reservation in rural America, on-reservation in America's internal colonies that could be sovereign, or in America's cities, Indian women and their histories cannot be adequately represented or understood if we do not also understand their centuries-old oppressions" (210). The standpoint for Shanley's practice exists in the provisionally known but intimately familiar space of emplacement within her family. She writes: "[my] 'Indianness' is more than blood heritage – it is a particular culture, Nakota, and a history of the place where I grew up, and more. I am also a mixed-blood, though I prefer [the] term 'crossblood' ... Woman, however, is the first skin around me, and I do not entirely know what it is or even how to talk about it. I do know it is not my story alone; my story belongs also to my mother, grandmother, sisters, friends, relatives, and so many others, including non-Indians, and all their perspectives must be respected in whatever I say. So my approach to the subject of American Indian women and history requires a shifting discourse, one that circles its subject and even circles my own subjectivity" (205). The genealogy that Shanley constructs of a gendered identity dispersed across multiple inheritances of history and family provides a model of Indigenous identity that is circular and provisional, yet conceives of the space of feminist critical work as a site for reconstruction and reimagining connections among women through the cross-cultural work of the critic. It is a space that contrasts, on the one hand, with imposed forms of tribal identity that privilege blood-quantum quotas, and thus collude with federally enforced identification policies, and on the other, with a self-constituting feminist subject that privileges individual agency. The question that remains, however, is how to conceive of women's gendered identity over time. Or to phrase the question somewhat differently in accordance with Shanley's recognition of the role of the cultural critic, what critical frameworks within contemporary feminist criticism can read the multiple intersections of Indigenous identity in the context of an inherited colonial history?

To provide a provisional answer, I turn to the work of feminist historian Joan Scott, whose analysis of gender as an organizing category in women's scholarship proposes a two-part theorization of gender identity that depends upon conceiving of gender relations both as "constitutive element[s] of social relations based on perceived differences between the sexes" and as "a primary way of signifying relationships of power" (42). Scott argues for a materialist analysis of gender identity as "substantively constructed and [related] to a range of activities, social organizations, and historically specific cultural representations," in order to extend considerations of gender as an analytic category beyond what she characterizes as the "descriptive stage" of gender identifications to a conceptual level of analysis that explains how gender relations occur systematically (44). For Scott, feminist critics need to pursue not "universal general causality" but "meaningful explanation" through which to understand how gender relations interact with social organizations so as to articulate not only "a concept of human agency as the attempt ... to construct an identity, a life, a set of relationships, a society within certain limits and with language," but also "[a] conceptual language that at once sets boundaries and contains the possibility for negation, resistance, reinterpretation, the play of metaphoric invention and imagination" (42). Scott's conceptualization of gender both as a site of subject constitution and as a language through which relations of power are articulated thus provides an understanding of "the individual subject" in relation to "social organization[s]" and an explanation for "the nature of [these] interrelationships" towards a recognition of "how gender works, how change occurs" (42).

In drawing on Scott's theorization of gender relations as a conceptual apparatus for reading LaDuke's *Last Standing Woman*, my purpose is not to engage in a form of feminist privileging that deploys one set of critical thinkers against another. That is, I am not arguing for a reading of Joan Scott's work as more interventionary/resistant/enabling than the theorizations of gender and race identity offered by Indigenous feminist critics and writers. This is not a form of "identity politics" as it is practised in Susan Gubar's analysis of feminist criticism.[11] Rather, my aim here is to illustrate how these critical thinkers struggle with a similar set of organizing questions. In Scott's view, "gender as an analytic category" enables feminist historicism in so far as it "explain[s] the origins of patriarchy" based on "analogies to the opposition of male and female," acknowledges the centrality of a "woman question" to recovery work in women's history by accommodating "feminism within a Marxian tradition," and recognizes "the formation of subjective sexual identity" in "different schools of psychoanalysis so as to explain the production and reproduction of the subject's gendered identity" (41, 33). Nevertheless, Scott argues, "gender as a way of talking about systems of social or sexual relations d[oes] not appear" (41). She claims, rather, that feminist historians, in pursuing "single origins" in terms of gender analysis, have given little attention to the imbrications of the "individual subject [with] social organization" and to "articulat[ing] the nature of their interrelationships" (41). Yet, her explanation for this neglect – that feminist critics have had "[difficulty] incorporating the term 'gender' into existing bodies of theory and convincing adherents of one or another theoretical school that gender belongs in their vocabulary" (41) – continues to resonate as an important materialist insight for feminist criticism, especially in light of ongoing reformulations of history that are being written with what Gayatri Chakravorty Spivak calls the "tools for developing alternative histories," that is, with analytic frameworks that read history through the multiple determinations of "gender, race, ethnicity, [and] class" ("Who Claims Alterity?" 271). To recognize the conceptual similarities between the issues raised by Indigenous feminist critics in conjunction with the formulation of these questions in feminist historical work is to undertake a form of cross-cultural engagement that prioritizes the common ground and conceptual terrain through which to envision a form of Indigenous feminist community. Such an endeavour, as well as their political importance and potentially socially transformative justice goals, are represented in fiction by Indigenous women writers.

"Protect the Land": *Last Standing Woman*

In *Last Standing Woman*, Winona LaDuke negotiates a space for the recognition of gender identity to community relations and tribal history by configuring the story of the disruption of the Anishinaabe social order through invasive policies of colonial management as a series of interruptions that lead to the erosion of Anishinaabe cultural values and to the sexual exploitation of women. Set during the nineteenth century in the waning moments of Indigenous resistance to the United States government's treaty-making process and to settler incursions on Indigenous land, the novel begins with the story of "Ishkwegaabawiikwe," an Anishinaabe woman "drawn to the border" between Anishinaabe and Dakota territory and "drawn to battle" by the discord that surfaces in her marriage when she realizes her mistake in marrying a man "at war" with "himself," "the spirits," the Creator," and "his wife," who "beat[s] her and cut[s] her ... until she c[an]not see and c[an]not feel" (27). Isolated from her family who "would have avenged such an act" by her husband's hunting and trading practices, and to escape from the physical abuse of her spouse, Ishkwegaabawiikwe travels with her brother to the border zone that divides Anishinaabe land from Dakota territory and there witnesses the devastating effects of "Little Crow's War" with the United States (33). Confronted by the "charred remains" of the Dakota village, Ishkwegaabawiikwe searches for the Dakota woman whom she had observed and admired during a previous visit, and weary of the "battles between the Dakota and the *Anishinaabeg*, the battles between the Indians and the white men, [and] the war in her own lodge," she rescues the Dakota woman, "Situpiwin, Tailfeathers Woman," and claims her as her "sister" (34).

By asserting a connection with the Dakota woman as her kin through a courageous act of self-determination, Ishkwegaabawiikwe disavows her community's injunction against offering help to the Dakota people and restores a sense of self-respect to the woman who is bereft of her family and tribe, for in spite of Dakota expectations to the contrary,

Ishkwegaabawiikwe acts to bring aid to the Dakota people out of respect for their prior affiliations as the Anishinaabe people's "most honored enemies," even though the Anishinaabeg leaders rejected the Dakota's call for support in their war against the United States government for fear of violating Anishinaabe treaty arrangements (32). The decision by the Anishinaabeg war chief "Shingobay" in refusing assistance to the Dakota people and in insisting on the Anishinaabeg people's autonomy results not in their future protection but in a form of administrative extermination that leads to the "terminat[ion] [of] the *Anishinaabeg* reservations of Gull Lake, Sandy Lake, Pokegama, Oak Point, and others" within a year (32). The novel privileges Indigenous women's acts of resistance as engendering an alternative vision of community identity that focuses on intertribal communal relations rather than autonomous ones, and foregrounds the necessity for a dual approach to reconfiguring the history of the Anishinaabe community, one that not only illustrates the multiple identifications through which community affiliations occur, but also represents as constitutive the relationship between the cultural and sexual exploitation of tribal women and the political and territorial dispossession of the Anishinaabe people.

In a novel that relentlessly explores the issue of community fragmentation for several generations of Anishinaabe people who struggle to resist the physical erosion of the community's land base by "the white man's law" and his "treaty" (24) and the spiritual destruction of their ceremonies through the people's religious conversion by the "Episcopal and Catholic priests" (46), LaDuke deploys the kinship union between Ishkwegaabawiikwe and Situpiwin as a symbolic act of resistance to the erosion of community values. Their kinship signifies Indigenous women's cultural connection and interdependence and conveys an ethical consciousness that transcends tribal dissolution and community antagonisms to assume both material and spiritual dimensions within the novel. Thus, when Ishkwegaabawiikwe and Situpiwin learn of the proposal by the "pine cartel"[12] and the Indian Agent Simon Michelet to deforest several allotments at Many Point and eliminate the seasonal round of trapping and wild rice harvesting at Round Lake (70), they are able to unite with traditional community members to protect the land and destroy the logging equipment in an act of defiance that re-establishes a resistant consciousness within the tribe and that consolidates the spiritual renewal of the community that began with Ishkwegaabawiikwe's recreation of the drumming ceremonies (40). Although the community does not go unpunished for its behaviour – several families starve to death when government rations are withheld by the Indian Agent (57) and members of the drumming circle are arrested and incarcerated for practising the ceremonies (59) – Ishkwegaabawiikwe's opposition to the Indian Agent and the timber barons together with the spiritual regeneration initiated within the community by the resurgence of "Ojibway ceremonies" provide a touchstone for subsequent generations at White Earth. The younger people learn of Ishkwegaabawiikwe's courage and her kinship with Situpiwin through intergenerational storytelling and recover the ceremonies as an alternative symbolic framework for countering the material and spiritual devastation that occurs on the reserve through economic disparity and rampant poverty.

Indeed, one of the most compelling features of LaDuke's novel is her representation of the social problems of alcoholism and drug addiction as a transhistorical phenomenon perpetuated by the fragmentation of community ties and the social isolation of community members. Through the story of Janine Littlewolf, set in the contemporary moment, LaDuke links the concept of intergenerational disinheritance and social isolation represented by Situpiwin's deprivation of her family and the loss of Anishinaabe members through death, disease, and residential schools (72–80) to the contemporary predicament of Anishinaabe women who endure systemic poverty and emotional despair as a result of their "accumulation of intergenerational grief" (117). LaDuke illustrates how the expression of Janine Littlewolf's desperation in "drown[ing]" in alcohol her "pain of loss" for her children who have been taken by social workers continues the legacy of disinheritance and isolation that women endure historically through the loss of their children to boarding schools. In keeping with her personal history of absent parents and an institutional upbringing where her only "memories of intimacy" were represented by "the nuns of nine years of boarding school" (117), Littlewolf suffers from a similar legacy of abjection for "having signed over her parental rights" such that "she never could locate [her children], and they could never know of her, their blood family, or even of each other" (117). The resonances between Littlewolf's physical act of repudiation in signing away her children to the welfare agency reverberates symbolically with the political act of dispossession resulting from the treaty and allotment arrangements through which the Anishinaabeg people were perceived to have sealed away their allotment land with "the stroke of a pen on a sheet of paper" to "the white man's government" (24). Yet, LaDuke's novel struggles to reconfigure the abjection of this reading of Anishinaabe history by articulating a form of social solidarity between community members that is organized through "the crises and contingencies of historical survival" (Bhabha 199).[13] The figure of George Ahnib, Janine Littlewolf's only remaining son who "huffs" gasoline to escape their impoverishment and to enter the world of the drum (115) exemplifies LaDuke's commitment to expressing a form of community that is not bound by federally imposed identity provisions or paternalistic categories of biological inheritance but emerges out of the community's accumulated identifications with each other and their collective struggles in history. In LaDuke's view, George belongs to the reservation through bonds of personal and group history and political priority, not only because "[it] was his home," but also because "he [was] related by blood to many families ... related by the tragedy and joy of the village's collective history" (119).

The central conflict in the novel illustrates LaDuke's concern to articulate a form of collective community identity that enables the social reconstruction of members' historically fractured lives without reassembling them at the expense of individual interest groups and without reconfiguring social justice issues as identity status relations. The decisive moment occurs during a stand-off between a community-based group known as "Protect Our Land" – an organization reminiscent of "Anishinaabe Akeeng" – and FBI officials supported by the tribal council and several non-Indigenous community members brought together by their resentment of the demands made by Protect Our Land and from a growing sense of frustration and vulnerability due to the clouded title status of their property on reservation land (133).[14] When Alanis Nordstrom, an "Indian reporter" for the *Rocky Mountain News* who grew up off-reserve and whose identifications with her inheritances from the Anishinaabe community are "conveniently Indian" (183), returns to White Earth to cover the story of the occupation of the White Earth Reservation tribal offices by members of Protect Our Land, she learns of the oppositional efforts by members of the group who resist the tribal council's decision to construct a mill for logging purposes on sacred reservation land. Following the repeated dismissal of their objections by the tribal council, they resolve to voice their protest through confrontational means, for from the perspective of Protect Our Land, the threat from clear cutting represents both a spiritual and material assault that not only jeopardizes their social resources through the possible elimination of their "hunting and trapping lands" and "medicin[al] plants" (148), but also risks their cultural past and future inheritances through the desecration of "grave sites" that house the artefacts of "beadwork," "medicine pouches," and "bones" of the Anishinaabeg dead whose residence on White Earth land preceded the configuration of it through allotment boundaries (143).[15] The participation in the resistance of Elaine Mandamin, the great-great-great granddaughter of Mindemoyen, a woman who lost her land in 1915 when the government's representative from the Smithsonian Institution claimed that her "cranial measurements" and "scarable skin"[16] determined that she was "of mixed blood descent" (65), together with the garrison strategies undertaken by Moose Hanford, the great-grandson of Ishkwegaabawiikwe, whose grave site had been desecrated by archaeology students from the university (138), illustrate how LaDuke represents the conflict over clear cutting as a social justice issue. This issue, for LaDuke, foregrounds the oppositional consciousness associated with Indigenous women's collective cultural disinheritance, but builds solidarity within the feminist community through inclusive gender politics.

Indeed, one of the most excruciating scenes in the novel occurs in response to the abdication of responsibility to an Indigenous feminist community by Alanis Nordstrom. Frightened by the threat of guns arrayed on both sides of her as she enters the tribal offices to report on the activities of Protect Our Land, yet confident that her "adopted survival strategy" of passing as Indian during the cultural events of pow-wows and rallies participated in "from the stands" will distinguish her from the group (183), Alanis is stunned by the realization that someone has mistaken her for a "militant" member of the community organization and fired on her as she attempted to leave the tribal offices to retrieve her belongings from her car (185). The moment of recognition and self-emplacement that Alanis experiences demonstrates LaDuke's uncompromising stance towards Indigenous identity as a social position that cannot be appropriated as a site of privilege dissociated from its imbrication in hierarchical social relations, for as Alanis struggles to hold back her recognition of her complicity with the material advantages that accrue through passing[17] as a "weekend Indian," the narrative voice of the storyteller intervenes to assert the epistemic violences associated with Indigenous identity and resistance:

> The bullets had not hit her, had not torn into her physical body and shattered bones and spilled blood, but the bullets had hit her just the same, hit her somewhere else deep inside. She was in shock as she stood still, silently fighting to regain her composure. *I am not you,* she had almost said, yet

obviously to whomever had leveled the rifle to his shoulder, closed one eye to sight it, placed his finger on the cool steel of the trigger and pulled, obviously to that person she was *one of them*. And that person – whether he had tried to kill her and missed or merely had tried to scare her with a close shot – had taken away a part of her. And now her image of herself as the objective, professional newspaper reporter became confused with her image as the gunman saw her, as an Indian, as an enemy, as someone to shoot. The bullets had destroyed the boundaries in her mind, and the ricochet reverberated through her very soul. (187)

LaDuke resolves the conflict associated with Alanis's experience of disidentification and misrecognition by illustrating how her experience of physical violation prompts her to abandon her position of objectivity. She begins to identify with the vision of community and economic sustainability adopted by Protect Our Land (179), to broadcast the conflict publicly so as to expose the social and ethical commitments of the group (213), and to return to the reservation as a prodigal member to re-establish connections in the aftermath of the resolution to the conflict that includes the cancellation of the "logging permit and mill construction lease" (219), as well as funeral arrangements for Hawk Her Many Horses, a member of Protect Our Land who was killed during the standoff (216). LaDuke settles Alanis's confusion by demonstrating a transformation to her community consciousness as she recognizes the material costs of perceiving subordinate group identity and Indigenous resistance as *optional* issues for political commitment.

Many of the political sentiments expressed in the novel are also reflected in LaDuke's public statements about the relationship between activist engagements and ethical responsibility. In an interview with the *Seattle Times*, when asked how she felt about "white people who want to participate in native-land, environmental or social-justice causes," LaDuke replied, "'Do it because it's the right thing ... Don't do it because of guilt. Do it because it encourages your own humanity'" (Cronin n.p.). That LaDuke articulates a vision of Indigenous feminist community that is inclusive in terms of gender identity yet organized through a politics of affiliation signals her responsibility to work exhaustively towards her goals of rebuilding community identifications and transforming relations of power in order to establish a desirable and enabling collective future.

One of the most compelling features of LaDuke's novel is her configuration of a site for the establishment of a community formulated on the basis of its "common humanity" and ethical responsibility in her claim for the White Earth Indian Reservation as an "Anishinaabe homeland" (23). Narrated through the transhistorical feminist consciousness of "Ishkwegaabawiikwe, the Storyteller" (17), the narrative restores to the Anishinaabeg people a vision of their common origins and historical agency that begins with the arrival of the people at "Gaawaawaabigan-ikaag," "White Earth," a place "named after the white clay you find [there]," as the consummate end to a spiritual journey that began with their "thousand year" migration from the "big waters in the *Waaban aki*, the land of the east" and concluded with their arrival "*Ningaabii'anong*, [in] the west" (23). LaDuke's vision of the formation of White Earth as a place constructed through divine intervention that transports the Anishinaabe people from a liminal state of existence where they "undulated between material and spiritual shadows" to a new beginning in the observance of the "Creator's law" and in recognition of a "season[al] round" (24) not only connects the Anishinaabe to the land through a spiritual purpose that disavows its formation as a remnant of the treaty process in which the Anishinaabe people become the victims of colonial management, but also articulates their relationship to the land as a material fact in recognition of their historical agency.[18] Thus, in LaDuke's view, the *Anishinaabeg* people's right to the land cannot be superseded by secular issues that privilege the relations of law and government over the relations of the metaphysical. For LaDuke, the Anishinaabeg people's material and spiritual connections to the land are fused such that they cannot be distinguished through quantifiable blood connections or illegally imposed colonial patterns of ownership.

The concluding events of the novel emphasize this view as they illustrate the return to the White Earth community of the bones of ancestors and their cultural belongings that resided for decades in the Smithsonian Institution in Washington (270). Organized through the efforts of Elaine Mandamin and Danielle Wabun, two members of Protect Our Land who discover an "inventory of the people and belongings missing from the reservation through the years" (269), and with the aid of Alanis Nordstrom, who researches the "anthropologists and Indian agents' records for White Earth" to match "people [with] documents and sacred items," the community prepares for the return of "funerary objects, human remains, and objects of cultural patrimony" to be reburied on the land (271). The scene in which Moose Hanford's van breaks down while he is travelling from Washington to White Earth with the remains of "ancestors" from the Anishinaabeg community located in the back (274), his feelings of vulnerability when several people stop to assist him including a police officer whom he worries might arrest him (276), and his buoyant response when he realizes that the people surrounding him have offered their help because they support the rights of Indigenous peoples to repatriate their cultural artefacts (278), demonstrate the future moment of cooperation and understanding that LaDuke envisions between Indigenous and non-Indigenous peoples. The novel thus offers the issue of repatriation,[19] and its attendant recognition of the rights of Indigenous peoples to reclaim their lands and their cultural effects, as a contemporary problem whose resolution all people can work towards. Such a recognition on LaDuke's part reconfigures the boundaries of identity politics from an oppositional stance that privileges asymetrically organized Indigenous relations towards a communal position that envisions a common humanity. What resides at the forefront of this vision of community relations is an Indigenous feminist network organized through the values of mutual respect and cultural obligation.

For an Indigenous-Feminist Literary Criticism

A question that runs through Louise Erdrich's *The Antelope Wife* concerns the meaning associated with the necklace of blue beads that Blue Prairie Woman bequeaths to her daughter as protection against the U.S. cavalry in its dawn raid on the Ojibway village from which her child is spared. As the beads exchange hands between women, they figure the broader themes of women's intergenerational longing, loss, and sorrow that the novel explores to convey Erdrich's message about how time and memory conceal women's identities. Erdrich associates longing for the necklace with a desire to "hold time" (215) and to recover from the historical past an object that will make known to us how Indigenous women endure, in order to give meaning and significance to our own struggles. This desire, expressed in the "northwest trader blue" of the beads (215), is double-edged: to grasp the beads one must also accept the names; to claim the names, one must also assume the events that make up the pattern that Blue Prairie Woman's life depicts – its grief, struggles, madness, passions, love, and sorrows; to assume the pattern one must also live the life. Erdrich's narrative cautions against this desire, which reiterates the message offered by other Indigenous women writers: forego the desire to appropriate the life; accept the story instead. Leslie Marmon's Silko's *Ceremony* echoes Erdrich's sentiments. As the presider over the ceremony explains, "I will tell you something about stories … They aren't just entertainment … They are all we have" (n.p.). Thomas King is even more philosophical about the relationship between knowledge, storytelling, and social power. "The truth about stories," he writes, "is that that's all we are."

This book has focused on Indigenous women's writing in the post-civil rights period in order to hear the stories that Indigenous women tell as they craft through narrative a consensual space from which to recount their struggles for social authority and political rights. Its objective has been to analyse their commitments to storytelling practices, as these practices reflect an Indigenous-feminist critical vision concerning women's efforts to achieve community acceptance, to protect the importance of family relations, to understand the meaning of their intergenerational inheritances, and to activate a wider social consciousness about the protection of tribal lands. Its premise of analysis and comparison has adapted Marie Anna Jaimes Guerrero's conceptualization of "indigenism" as a struggle against settler-colonialism and patriarchy by giving priority to the intersectional framework that Guerrero calls for. As she observes, "patriarchal structures can, in concert, literally determine whether native women's claims to membership within tribes are honored or ignored" ("Civil Rights" 103). Guerrero's focus on tribal membership and its associated rights is crucial to recognizing how Indigenous women are dispossessed by being confined and ignored by Indigenous communities and the wider society. In broadening Guerrero's analytic beyond an attention to membership issues, I have sought to explain how the state-sanctioned out-adoption of Indigenous children and Indian residential schooling also dispossess women from social status and Indigenous rights. April Raintree's haunting voice as she searches for meaning to explain the loss of her family demonstrates Mosionier's awareness that rights alone are inadequate to compensate for women's historical exploitation and marginalization, even as her novel raises the question to ask where these rights exist in order to signal our failure to be vigilant about these matters. The stories of generations of Roy/Shawano women that Erdrich's novel portrays to illuminate Indigenous women's vulnerability to gender violence distinguish the intersection between sexual violence and the violence of settler-colonial dispossession. Erdrich's novel recognizes these dual legacies in the "Czech beads called northwest trader blue" that capture the "depth of the spirit sky" (214), beads that are carried by the Antelope Wife beneath her tongue, amid the broken teeth that signify her abduction and rape, beads that she exchanges for her freedom by breaking the silence that their implication in a colonial past imposes. The silencing of Indigenous communities through colonial-legal means is also foundational to LaDuke's novel which rewrites the history of the White Earth Reservation's dispossession to challenge the history established by legal texts which write out of view White Earth's historical allegiances with other tribal peoples. Affirming this legacy through

Indigenous women's activism permits recognition of a transhistorical feminist consciousness that this literature establishes. Its mythological and secular structure also informs the quest for land protection that Silko's *Ceremony* depicts through Tayo's search as he embraces his inheritances from women by acknowledging the sacrifices they have made on his behalf.

Writing by Indigenous women is thus exemplary in constructing the literary parameters of Indigenous feminism, permitting an important subcategory within Indigenous literature that recognizes a wide range of authors, including Joy Harjo, Paula Gunn Allen, Maria Campbell, Janet Campbell Hale, and Eden Robinson, in addition to those studied here, writers for whom the distinctiveness of gender relations and their imbrication in the colonial, cultural, and economic positions that Indigenous women are forced to occupy in social relations are central. How to account for the ways in which Indigenous women are dispossessed of social and political authority has been an important objective of this book. In addition to advocating for the power and potentiality of Indigenous women's literary activism, it has also sought to make apparent the social inequalities established by colonial law and patriarchal society that disempower women.

To do so, it has taken up a twofold method of analysis building from Gayatri Spivak's crucial formulation of subaltern gender dynamics a legal-literary dialect of comparison that shows how legal texts both "proxy" and "portray" Indigenous women: on the one hand, through an attention to conceptualizing how legal mechanisms participate in "rendering visible the mechanisms [of colonial control] [in order] to render[] vocal the individual [of colonial management]" (Spivak, "Can the Subaltern Speak" 255); on the other hand, by illustrating how Indigenous women writers articulate voice and agency to permit Indigenous women "to know and speak for themselves" (247). The enormous degree to which colonial law impacts the lives of Indigenous women and their communities and the social and political consequences that follow from its imposition have provided the social and political ground for reading Indigenous women's texts, in their contestations against discriminatory tribal membership codes, their critique of the dispossession of women from their children, their troubling of law's circulation of dehumanizing identity categories through blood-quantum codes, and their protests against law's continuation of injustice through revived colonial forms of land dispossession. My book builds on earlier work in the field of transnational Indigenous studies that has laid an important foundation for understanding the implication of law and legislation to the marginalization and silencing of Indigenous peoples in social and political discourses.[1] Indigenous women's writing counters these acts of silencing and erasure. It creates new forms of political community and social identity by crafting Indigenous-feminist literary models that re-articulate Indigenous women's inheritances across intergenerational and tribal lines, establishing recognition of the ways in which Indigenous women contribute to gender, tribal, and social transformation.

One of its most important efforts has been to show how storytelling in law – legal stories that depend on the organization of "particular issue, relevant fact, controlling law, and entailed conclusion" also disclose a "human story – the concrete narrative of who did what to whom, where, when, how, and why" (Henderson 905). My project is implicated in law and legal reasoning through its concern for recovering the agency of Indigenous women. It has attempted to show the implications of this reliance by highlighting the failures that law practises against Indigenous women, especially in the story of Ms Martinez's legal activism, by also foregrounding her conviction that law may do better to facilitate and protect Indigenous women's rights. In this regard, much critical work remains to be done, especially in recovering the traditions of Indigenous legal systems that may be put into dialogue with contemporary law practices. Such a project is beyond the scope of this book, but it does indicate the progressive ground of research and social intervention represented by law and humanities scholarship. The storytelling practices represented by the Indigenous women writers studied here speak directly to colonial-legal texts, illuminating how Indigenous women's lack of access to tribal and community cultural resources perpetuates their socio-economic disempowerment and often violent sexual exploitation. These writers articulate an alternative political grounding for law as it scrutinizes its own future goals and objectives. Consequently, Indigenous women's writing in the post–civil rights period undertakes an important social justice task, one that I have defined as Indigenous feminist in its summoning of an Indigenous feminist literary activism through engagements with law and cultural discourses. Hearing these women's voices but also learning from them about what social justice projects Indigenous feminists should aim to achieve, I have argued in this book that literary texts also participate in a social justice project by opening up a creative-critical space for the re-imaginings necessary to bring social and legal justice to Indigenous women.

Notes

Introduction

1 For an excellent analysis of the structural organization and cultural contexts of "Storyteller," see Lorenz 59–75.

2 For accounts of the term "gender justice," see Smith, "Native American Feminism" 121, and Cunningham, "Indigenous Women's Visions of an Inclusive Feminism" 55–9. Studies exploring how Indigenous writing engages legal matters include works by Beth Piatote, Maureen Konkle, Robert Warrior, and David J. Carlson.

3 Robert Cover's classic text, "Violence and the Word," contends that there are strict limits to legal interpretation's capacity to achieve "common and coherent meaning" because of its role in justifying state violence (1628). Cover argues that legal interpretation is best understood through its participation in generating *"conditions of effective domination"* (Cover's emphasis) that engender "cris[es] of credibility" (1615–16), that is, of analysing, through interpretive dissent, state law's monopoly on violence and its coercive role in securing our consent to its practices. He observes that the two fields of law and literature function as separate disciplines because their political outcomes achieve dramatically different social effects. Alan Hunt's clarification of the relationship between law and literature as one concerned primarily with the task of interpretation argues for their interconnections. Hunt states, "what links literary criticism and legal studies is that both are significantly concerned with the interpretation of texts" (513).

4 Episkenew's *Taking Back Our Spirits* provides an important analysis in the Canadian context of how Indigenous literatures "give … voice and validity to [Indigenous peoples'] collective experience" (16).

5 One of the most important articulations of this idea that literature matters to the pursuit of political and social justice is expressed by Hodge in "Challenges of the Struggle for Sovereignty" (494).

6 Delgado's strategy of using stories to construct an alternative "community-building function[]" in law was developed further by Indigenous legal scholar Robert Williams, who urged critical race scholars to practise "outsider jurisprudence" (1019) in order to disclose the ways in which dominant forms of legal meaning were experienced as "alien and alienating" to a community of scholars "who identify with outsider groups" (1019, n.1). Rebecca Tsosie expanded this claim by linking "outsider group" status to the existing sovereignty that Indigenous communities retain within the ambit of "America's legal ideology" as "separate sovereigns" and "outsiders" to the "myth of American national origin" ("Separate Sovereigns" 498, 500).

7 Two important accounts of intersectionality that highlight its political stakes for women include Kimberle Crenshaw's foundational research, which argues that Black women's experiences of injustice in the workplace are misunderstood by legal accounts that focus on "single-axis" sources of discrimination that emphasize either race or gender discrimination when, in fact, these women are "multiply-burden[ed]" as Black women (140), and Rita Kaur Dhamoon, who argues that discourses of difference and power must be analysed in their specific locales in order to understand that the privileging of one set of identity markers involves the underprivileging of another category of difference that is assumed by, but not constitutive of, the category as a source of identity discrimination. The arguments and the disagreements within the field of intersectional-type studies concerning its areas of priority are explored further by Dhamoon in "Considerations" 230, and *Identity/Difference* 61–6.

8 See Suzack et al., *Indigenous Women and Feminism*.

9 Indigenous-feminist research that makes explicit the relationship between Indigenous-feminist analysis and intersectionality includes Altamirano-Jimenez, "Indigenous Women"; Huhndorf and Suzack, "Indigenous Feminism"; Lawrence and Anderson, "Introduction"; Redbird, "Honouring"; Smith, "Native American Feminism," and Smith and Kauanui, "Native Feminisms."

10 Guerrero proposes the concept of "Native Womanism" to "reenvision[] a pre-patriarchal, pre-colonialist, and pre-capitalist U.S. society" that affirms "Native women's self-determination in reclaiming their indigenous roles [to] empower them with respect and authority in indigenous governance" ("Patriarchal Colonialism" 67).

11 I am indebted to Shari Huhndorf for this point.

12 For an in-depth analysis of First Nations sovereignty, legal status, and its constitutional guarantees, see Macklem, "First Nations Self-Government" 384–5; for analysis of the United States' recognition of "Indian tribes" as "first sovereigns," see Duthu, *American Indians* xxv.

13 Andrea Smith expresses this idea somewhat differently when she states, "we must understand that attacks on Native women's status are themselves attacks on Native sovereignty" (123).

14 In contrast, Joseph Bauerkemper highlights Indigenous transnationalisms as "consonant configuration[s]" to signal their movement away from "oppositional" logics (6). He argues, with Heidi Kiiwetinepinesiik Stark, that "peoplehood" rather than "nationhood" grounds the integrity of tribal peoples' territorial borders (2).

1 Gendering the Politics of Tribal Sovereignty

1 The membership ordinance that affected Ms Martinez came into effect in 1939 when the Santa Clara Pueblo organized under the provisions of the Indian Reorganization Act. It adopted membership requirements that stated, "hereafter the following rules shall govern the admission to membership to the Santa Clara Pueblo:

   (1) All children born of marriages between members of the Santa Clara Pueblo shall be members of the Santa Clara Pueblo.
   (2) All children born of marriages between male members of the Santa Clara Pueblo and non-members shall be members of the Santa Clara Pueblo.
   (3) Children born of marriages between female members of the Santa Clara Pueblo and non-members shall not be members of the Santa Clara Pueblo.
   (4) Persons shall not be naturalized as members of the Santa Clara Pueblo under any circumstances."

Martinez v. Santa Clara Pueblo, 402 F. Supp. 5, 7 (D.N.M. Jun. 25, 1975; Resnik, "Dependent Sovereigns," 704). Judith Resnik explains that the tribe's 1935 constitution altered prior membership practices in two ways that changed the community's governing structure: first, the membership criteria had to be submitted for approval to the Secretary of the Interior; and second, initially membership had been extended to "four groups of people" according to the following criteria: "1) those 'of Indian blood' whose names appeared on the 1935 census roll; 2) all 'persons born of parents both of whom are members of the Santa Clara pueblo'; 3) all 'children of mixed marriages between members of the Santa Clara pueblo and nonmembers, provided such children have been recognized and adopted by the council'; and 4) all 'persons naturalized as members of the pueblo'" ("Dependent Sovereigns" 704–5, citing the Constitution and Bylaws of the Pueblo of Santa Clara, New Mexico, reprinted in Supreme Court Brief of the Petitioners, *Santa Clara Pueblo v. Martinez*, No 76–682, Appendix at 1 [Oct Term, 1976]). Resnik observes that when the statement of membership rules was amended subject to the approval of the Assistant Secretary of the Interior on 21 November 1939, the Pueblo altered and thereby effectively "extinguished two other membership routes set forth in the 1935 constitution," eliminating "with those provisions" the possibility that members of the Pueblo could exercise discretion in according membership to individuals (705).

2 *Martinez v. Santa Clara Pueblo*, 402 F. Supp. 5 (1975) 14. Although her children lived on land belonging to her, Ms Martinez was barred from conveying the land to any person who was a non-member of the Pueblo. See Brief for Petitioners, 1977 WL 189105, 6.

3 It argued that "the equal protection guarantee of the Indian Civil Rights Act should not be construed in a manner which would authorize th[e] court to determine which traditional values will promote cultural survival and therefore should be preserved and which of them are inimical to cultural survival and should therefore be abrogated" (F.Supp. 18).

4 The Court of Appeals rejected the tribe's claim that the ordinance established the transmission of culture through patriarchy, a claim viewed by the court as the Pueblo's "'strongest argument' (the importance of education by a Santa Claran male in Pueblo traditions) because the court held that 'there could have been a solution without discrimination'" (Memorandum for the United States as Amicus Curiae, 1977 WL 189104, 4; citations omitted; see also 540 F.2d 1039, 9). In their brief to the Supreme Court, the Pueblo expanded this argument by characterizing the entire "social makeup of the tribe" as "patrilineal, patrilocal and patricultural," based on testimony by community members and expert witnesses (Brief for Petitioners, 1977 WL 189105, 12).

5 J. White dissenting; J. Blackman did not participate (U.S. 107).

6 Resnik's important essay "Dependent Sovereigns" introduced this characterization; see, for example, her statement, "For those of us who believe in women's rights and are also concerned about federal government imperialism, the case becomes hard" (727).

7 As Klint Cowan notes, the tribe "did not contest the law's discriminatory nature but rather asserted that it represented the tribe's patriarchal cultural heritage" (21).

8 Scholars who foreground their sense of being perplexed by its outcome include Robert Lawrence, who characterizes it as "the single most interesting case in all of Anglo-American jurisprudence" (307), Judith Resnick, Klint Cowan, Rina Swentzell, and Lucy Curry.

9 As Butler explains, "It would be a mistake to understand such productions as 'merely cultural' if they are essential to the functioning of the sexual order of political economy – that is, if they constitute a threat to its very workability" ("Merely Cultural" 42).

10 See note 7 above.

Several tribal communities affirmed this view. In their support for the intervenant National Tribal Chairman's Association, they argued against the interference of the Tenth Circuit Court by criticizing the court for its presumption to "sit in judgment over Pueblo tradition and custom" (1977 WL 189110 6), on the one hand, and by asserting the need to protect the community's "cultural survival" (1977 WL 189110 6) as it was expressed through dominant male culture, on the other. Their argument, that the "gender-based … distinction between classes," objected to by the Tenth Circuit, is "not *per se* a gender distinction, but is a distinct classification of alien fathers as opposed to native fathers," a classification necessary to ensure that the "Santa Clara Pueblo's patrilineal and patrilocal tradition survives" (1977 WL 189110 12–14), presumes the silence of women in their capacity for transmitting cultural values through marriage. Such silencing has been theorized by Floya Anthias as necessary to securing an "autonomous realm of patriarchal social relations" (373). Paradoxically, the illegitimate children of Santa Claran women are "granted full rights and cared for by the Pueblo" (Brief for Petitioners, 1977 WL 189105, 15). This inconsistency suggests that marriage symbolically represents the containment of women through domestic relations, a confinement that carries tremendous ideological weight given the number of tribes that intervened in the case.

11 Important work by Philip P. Frickey, Frank Pommersheim, and N. Bruce Duthu (*American Indians* 23) in the federal Indian law context shows how courts erode tribal sovereignty by undermining tribal political identity. Frickey characterizes the court's decision-making as undertaking "judicial missionary work" in "domesticat[ing] tribal power by harmonizing federal Indian law with basic Anglo-American legal values and assumptions" (73). The court's modern stance, he notes, is tellingly silent with regard to past policies that severely eroded tribes' "self-governing authority" (11). One of its most pernicious stances, according to all three scholars, is the predominance of the modern colonial law era with protecting non-Indian residents and parties from "tribal authority" (4). This colonial-legal reality

is the direct result of the federal government's assimilative laws that were forced onto Indigenous peoples, the most "dramatic and drastic" of which concerns "the allotment policy which brought a significant number of non-Indian people into Indian country as permanent residents" (Pommersheim 460). The political irony of *Martinez* is that the ordinance's gender discriminatory practices actually generate more non-member residents of Santa Clara Pueblo by disallowing the enrollment of children of women's mixed marriages. Non-member residents, as Frickey, Pommersheim, and Duthu note, are precisely the citizenry for whom the Supreme Court has adopted its modern federal Indian law rationale of eroding tribal sovereignty by rationalizing the protection of "non-Indian" interests.

12 The classic literary text in this regard is Momaday's *House Made of Dawn*, a novel that demonstrates the revival of community traditions through the incorporation of the Bahkyush people, a community of "old men and women that survived a journey along the edge of oblivion" (14–15). Their story augments and empowers new storytelling traditions that aid the community in decolonizing ways. In the Canadian law context, Val Napoleon demonstrates this capacity for renewal through the incorporation of Western law practices into Gitskan storytelling traditions and ceremonial practices represented by the *Delgamuukw* decision and the legal actors who played a role in its outcomes; see "*Delgamuukw*: A Legal Straightjacket for Oral Histories?" *Canadian Journal of Law and Society* 20.2 (May 2005): 123–55. For Silko's legal training and awareness of its traditions, see Chavkin 4.

13 Silko's reference is to her short story "Tony's Story." Two of the best accounts of the law and literature dialectic engaged by Silko's short fiction are Evers, "The Killing of a New Mexico State Trooper," and Hoilman, "The Ethnic Imagination."

14 Dr Florence Hawley Ellis, an Emeritus Professor of Anthropology from the University of New Mexico, provided expert testimony to support the Pueblo's claim that Santa Clara was traditionally patrilineal in kinship and thus its ordinance supported the goals of cultural preservation.
Dr Ellis stated that a foreseeable result for the Pueblo of "allow[ing] their women to marry non-Santa Clarans, and … their children [to] bec[o]me members," would be that "the culture would eventually break down and be lost" because of the "importance of men in connection with carrying on of the culture [and] the training of the children in socio-religious situations" (National Tribal Chairman's Association Amicus Curiae Brief, 1977 WL 189110 18). Ms Martinez took issue with this characterization of men's roles by noting that the connection between male-line membership and cultural transmission asserted by the Pueblo to further religious instruction

was inconsistent since a witness for the Pueblo testified that he did not participate in the Pueblo religion, nor teach his children of a mixed marriage the Tewa language, practices which were considered crucial by the Pueblo for religious participation (Respondents' Brief 1977 WL 189106, 19).

15 Prior to the ordinance coming into effect, the Pueblo, for religious purposes, was divided into "Winter" and "Summer" peoples with children from different moieties belonging to their father's affiliation under "usual circumstances," but not in all cases (Respondents' Brief 1977 WL 189106, 21). The alternative community identifications and membership criteria established by these traditions were not assessed by the Supreme Court as culturally agreed upon paradigms of community identity, although they were noted as important by the lower court, and played a key role in the Court of Appeal's assessment of the dispute (see *Martinez v. Santa Clara Pueblo* 402 F. Supp. 5, 8). They suggest a greater fluidity and evolving interactions between family, culture, and spiritual traditions that were altered by the tribe's forced adoption of the ordinance, a point noted by Resnik in "Dependent Sovereigns" at 705–6.

16 Not all advocates of tribal sovereignty agree with the *Martinez* holding. Ezekiel J.N. Fletcher contends that "The discriminatory overtones of the *Martinez* decision ... scar its power as testament to tribal sovereignty" (41). In Lucy Curry's view, the case asserts the Pueblo's acceptance of "a sovereign's racist and sexist criteria for excluding undesirables," rather than an affirmation of the Pueblo's right to defend membership rules as a form of tribal sovereignty (205). Klint Cowan argues that the *Martinez* decision has wider implications in calling into question the United States government's international obligations because the "discriminatory Pueblo membership law violates several international human rights provisions that bind the United States" (21). He notes that these international human rights obligations include "non-discrimination, equal protection, and effective remedy under the ICCPR and the American Declaration" (22).

17 Resnik offers the most succinct claim about the opposition between sovereignty and gender subordination when she states, "In *Santa Clara Pueblo*, the Court held that sovereignty interests trumped inquiry into the legality, under federal law, of rules that (at least from a feminist perspective) subordinate women" (702).

18 Zizek's "Multiculturalism," from which I borrow this idea, explains that the universal ideological coding of culture "is always hegemonized by some particular content which colours its very universality and accounts for its efficiency" (28). He notes that what circulates as the "typical" works through an act of translation in which the "transcendental schematism" accords meaning

to content that "directly relates and applies to our 'actual experience'" (29), thus concealing its origins in local and specific cultural terms.

19 Ms Martinez's respondent's brief distinguished the necessity for tribal communities to exercise forms of "internal sovereignty" to determine their tribal membership by arguing that she did not seek to authorize the courts "to say what the Pueblo's membership must be – only to prohibit an invidious discrimination" (1977 WL 189106, 25), a discrimination that, as she argued, served no purpose in protecting Pueblo culture because the Martinez children were not "cultural outsiders," as the Pueblo contended, but rather members of the community who had "known no home but the Pueblo" (1977 WL 189106, 20). Rina Swentzell, a member of Santa Clara Pueblo, observes that the implications of the ordinance "did not make sense," that it was not "just or fair," and that it represents "blatant gender discrimination" (97), but states that it is defensible on its merits.

20 Smith notes this assumption as the political quietism engendered by the idea that "If we successfully decolonize … then we will necessarily eliminate the problems of sexism as well" (121).

21 For the "unbearable" as a crucial entry point to political activism, see Bersani 201.

22 The Court noted that "[a] detailed summary of the efforts [by] Julia and Audrey Martinez [to remedy their situation within the Pueblo] would fill several pages" (F. Supp. 6).

23 The case was re-argued before the Supreme Court of the American Indian Nations in 2003. The Court upheld the U.S. Supreme Court's ruling that the Indian Civil Rights Act of 1968 "did not waive tribal sovereign immunity for suit in federal courts" (92). It argued that its reason for upholding the decision was based on the "foremost factor" concerning the "self-determination of the Santa Clara Pueblo" (95). Richard B. Collins, in writing the petitioner's brief, raised the key point that "the relief sought by petitioners will promote and accommodate recognition of tribal jurisdiction over non-members" (75), by extending tribal jurisdiction and non-member rights into the civil realm (76), a point unaddressed by the Court's analysis. Alex Tallchief Skibine, in the respondents' brief, noted that allowing the federal courts "to rule on such challenges" would subject "every internal aspect of tribal self-governance" to federal scrutiny and thus alter a tribe's sovereign status by forcing them to become "federal instrumentalities" (87). Skibine argues this point in addition to raising the dilemma that one might "disagree with this particular ordinance" (87), yet support it in the legal realm, a point also not taken up by the Courts' analysis. For the published record of the Court's decision, see Leeds.

24 Ms Martinez's respondents' brief notes that her children were regarded as "persons within the cultural group" (as cited by the Court of Appeal 540 F.2d 1048). By contrast, Ms Martinez noted that "male-line children of half or less ancestry" are admitted to membership in the Pueblo despite "knowing nothing of its language, culture, religion, or traditions" and notwithstanding the fact of their having been "raised away from the Pueblo" (Respondents' Brief 1977 WL 189106, 20). This distinction lead to her assertion that the "dispute is not over the legitimacy of the Pueblo's claimed purpose to maintain the Santa Clara religion and culture" but rather to the "means chosen to promote those ends" (20).

25 Several configurations of membership identity are authorized by the ordinance. The children born out of wedlock to Santa Claran mothers are permitted to become members based on the rationale that "they have no other place to go, and [they are] recognize[d] to be half Santa Clara on the mother's side" (Brief of the National Tribal Chairman's Association as Amicus Curiae 1977 WL 189110 17).

26 Restoring dignity represents a key feature of reparation and redress movements that link the achievement of social justice to social, political, and individual restoration efforts that legal mechanisms are increasingly required to uphold (see Teitel, *Transitional Justice* 120). I discuss this aspect of transitional justice and its implications for the development of an Indigenous feminist critical practice in chapter 2.

27 See Denise Reaume's important use of this term to distinguish a person's attachment to particular knowledge and concrete practices that inhere through socialization. These attachments are distinct from purely liberal or individualistic notions of a "context of choice" rationale that privileges the abstract ability to "choose" rather than defend an understanding of why a particular cultural context is meaningful to a person ("Justice between Cultures" 127). Reaume's distinction explains why "opting-out" of a culture or protecting the right to "opt-out" are not viable choices for Indigenous women whose commitments to their culture of upbringing exceed the values that "choice" advocates espouse.

28 Reaume critiques this slippage between subjective responses and objective principles as "mistak[ing] a symptom of the violation of the relevant interest for the interest itself" ("Indignities" 75). Ms Martinez's focus on the implications of the sex discrimination for herself and her children distinguished between the ordinance's objective effects that impersonally submitted herself, her children, and other women similarly situated to greater vulnerability, from subjective effects that individualized these consequences at the personal level which may have been expressed through "hurt feelings"

(see Reaume, "Discrimination" 39). This distinction is crucial for understanding how harms to dignity are objective harms that "inhere in the denial of respect" to personhood, rather than to subjective responses in the form of "feelings of worthlessness" which may be related to the subject's demeanour in light of such a denial. The distinction recognizes, as Reaume notes, that the "evil to be prevented or remedied is conveying the implication of worthlessness" in the first place ("Discrimination" 39).

29 Several scholars cited herein note this important insight. See, for example, Berger, "Indian Policy"; Green, "Native American Women"; Guerrero, "Civil Rights"; Huhndorf and Suzack, "Indigenous Feminism"; and Medicine, "North American" 127–9. Bethany Berger's legal analysis of the ways that federal and state legislatures marginalized Indigenous women by denying them "treaty rights," "rights of descent," "stable marriages," and "power within the family" that they held prior to colonization provides a comprehensive and insightful historical account of these dynamics to show how "The history … supports the argument that state and federal actions were responsible for the diminished view of Indian women in the eyes of their tribes" (2, 52).

30 Law practices are the focus of Kimberle Crenshaw's formative account of intersectionality in her analysis of how legal discourses "multiply-burden" Black women in anti-discrimination cases. Especially important to her critique is the recognition that "formal equality" fails to address collective forms of discrimination by treating "likes alike" (Reaume, "Discrimination" 4), according to an implicit norm that does not specify the gender or race terms of comparison (Crenshaw 144). Critical race scholar Angela Harris applies Crenshaw's analysis to her anti-essentialist feminist stance that uses the concept of "multiple consciousness" (584) to challenge "all kinds of oppression based on seemingly inherent and unalterable characteristics" (612) and to go beyond feminist theory's presumptions about identity essentialism. Identity essentialism, Harris notes, obtains one of its most harmful effects in positing identity as "inherent" rather than "relational" (608) to establish how women's roles reflect aspects of their gender personalities. Harris argues that this position "leaves women open to the same old patterns of discrimination, only now justified as choice" (605, citing Joan Williams 801–21).

31 See also Silko's short story, "The Man to Send Rain Clouds."

32 The novel is not explicit about how Laura dies although Silko implies that she suffers a violent death at the hands of a current male lover. Silko draws this association through Tayo's point of view when he is left with the family and recalls that "she had come after dark and wrapped him

in a man's coat … and that there were men in the car with them" (66). Displaced to a child's point of view, the narrative suggests vulnerability and violence that Laura's actions, in leaving Tayo with her family, appear to save him from.

33 By characterizing Old Grandma's authority as situated in the past (33), Silko suggests that women and mothers also bear responsibility for the socialization of other women and their daughters in ways that enable practices of gender socialization to evolve in order to address new demands rather than to conform to existing practices. Silko opens up a space for women's community by implying that although Old Grandma's influence has been superseded, other women are expected to take up the responsibility of forming gender relations that empower and support women.

34 For an important reading of this passage depicting Laura as a figure who interacts with the sacred world inhabited by the "Katsina," see Purdy 125.

35 Silko's portrayal of community suspicion and condemnation towards women who do not fit in intersects with other writers' examination of this issue, such as James Welch, who depicts how the Blackfeet community turns against the narrator's grandmother in its desperation to find a source for the "death and despair" they suffer from during the "desperate times" brought about by the invading U.S. forces (155, 154). Welch shows the tragic effects of this hostility in the community's efforts to "look for signs" to explain "the curse" of the invading U.S. soldiers and their discovery of meaning in the "beauty" of this woman which "made a mockery of their situation" (155).

36 Jane Robinett argues that Silko's reference to "Root Woman" invokes "Mexican curandera practices" to align Tayo's healing practices with Navajo traditions in order to assert a broad interconnected tradition among writers from the southwest (4–5).

37 In the canon of American Indian writing, Louis Owens' *Bone Game* articulates this dual heritage through the trans-historical agency of Venancio Asisara.

2 The Legal Silencing of Indigenous Women

1 See Kirby 77, borrowing this term from Kathleen Jamieson 30. Kirby explains that, legally, "marrying out" means: "an Indian woman who marries a person who is not an Indian is 'not entitled to be registered' or … loses status" (77, citing Indian Act, R.S.C. 1970, c. 106). King's novel incorporates several historical references to Indian Act legislation as it affects Indigenous women; for a study of how colonial policies contribute to Indigenous

women's vulnerability to patriarchal and social violence, see Stratton, "There is no Bentham Street in Calgary."

"Marrying out" remains an important political and social issue for Indigenous women in Canada and continues to receive critical attention by Indigenous feminist activists and scholars. Joyce Green provides an important account of the consequences of legal banishment authorized by the Indian Act in her essay "Sexual Inequality"; for an analysis of the legislation's interlocking legal, cultural, and gender-discriminatory effects, see McIvor, "The Indian Act as Patriarchal Control of Women"; for an examination of "marrying out" in a comparative transnational framework, see Huhndorf and Suzack, "Indigenous Feminism."

2 I discuss Robinson's portrayal of gender violence and women's confinement due to competing social harms at greater length in "The Transposition of Law and Literature."

3 Frederic Jameson argues that the "political unconscious" of a text may be detected by restoring to its surface a "repressed and buried reality" that "leads to the unmasking of cultural artifacts as socially symbolic acts" (20). By contextualizing the text in this way, its circulation as "merely cultural" (Butler, "Merely Cultural" 33), rather than political and social, may be contested and may make apparent the underlying conditions and social discourses out of which the text arises, while also contesting the privatization and psychologizing of experience and politics which, Jameson asserts, separate the individual from recognition of his or her implication in the social field. Not to contest this separation, Jameson warns, is to participate in a form of depoliticization that "maims our existence as individual subjects and paralyzes our thinking about time and change just as surely as it alienates us from our speech itself" (20). How to contextualize speech acts to highlight their political intent, as Jameson urges, represents an important concern within transitional justice for actors concerned to reconcile the truth-claims of women with their experiences of domestic and social violence. Dina Al-Kassim theorizes this issue as a structural barrier within Western legal institutions that "deny 'voice' while granting the rights of speech" (179). One of the goals of this chapter is to show how literary texts counter this omission and erasure by establishing an alternative ground for assessing women's individual and collective experience of violence as it is depicted through literary texts.

4 The Court of Appeal case made headlines in Manitoba and across Canada; see "Girl Is Ward of Court after Legal Tug of War."

5 This section of the Act "dispenses with parental consent in the case of a *de facto* adoption" (*Racine v. Woods* 185).

6 The Court of Appeal also found that the adoption notice filed by Mr and Mrs Racine was inconsistent in the dates indicated for having received a "child for private adoption" (*Woods v. Racine and Racine* para. 40), a fact that was important to the Court's assessment of the issue because the notice required the consent of the parent or guardian to the adoption application.

7 Justice Matas described the cultural circumstances of the parties as "transracial" rather than "interracial"; see *Woods v. Racine and Racine* para. 5 (for "interracial," as an element of assessment, see paras. 11, 71, and 94), and *Racine v. Woods* para. 180.

8 As Kline explains, "When judges determine 'best interests' in First Nations child welfare cases, facts and arguments are constructed and organized so as to give credence and legitimacy to the removal of First Nations children from their families and communities. By constructing the child *conceptually* as separate from her culture, the *actual* removal of the child from it is made to seem unproblematic" (396).

9 The story of Ms Woods's reunion with her daughter appeared in the *Globe and Mail* with the caption "The Indian Child Welfare Mess." It described Ms Woods's case as a "*cause celebre* for Manitoba native people" that expanded to involve "the chiefs of the eight bands of the Dakota Ojibway Tribal Council in southwestern Manitoba" who "vowed to pay Mrs. Woods's legal expenses all the way to the Supreme Court" (Krotz). The Supreme Court also used the expression "*cause célèbre*" in quoting the Trial Judge as stating, "The media incident, in Judge Krindle's view, manifested an incredible indifference to the effect such an incident might have on her child. It made … a very private little girl, into a '*cause célèbre*' in her school and community" (*Racine v. Woods* 179). A follow-up article published on 10 April 1984, six months after the Supreme Court's ruling, suggests that both courts misunderstood the intensity of Ms Woods's determination to recover her daughter. It indicates that Ms Woods was informed by Justice Scollin of the Manitoba Court of Queen's Bench that she "should not have any contact with her daughter" and that her "persistent court applications regarding [her daughter] are an abuse of the rights of the adoptive parents" ("Court Tells Mother to Stop").

10 Two additional facts are omitted from the Supreme Court's account that point to its objectifying analysis of the case, facts that are given weight before the Court of Appeal: the Trial Judge's characterization of Ms Woods's attempts to recover her daughter in 1980 which are described as "half-baked" (*Woods v. Racine and Racine* para. 142) and Ms Woods's First Nation status as a member of the Long Plain First Nation (para. 136).

11 "Real Indians," according to Kline, do not exist because they are relegated by the Courts to the historical past (Kline, "The Colour of Law" 455).

12 The Committee considered Ms Lovelace's complaint because the outcome of the Lavell/Bedard case, established as the highest law of the land, left Ms Lovelace with no domestic remedies through which to appeal from the state's decision against her; thus she and other Indigenous women similarly situated had no local state means by which to contest Canada's discriminatory treatment of them.

13 For an important analysis of the sexual violence of this language, see Cummings 317.

14 The classic text in law and literature studies exploring law's multivocality is Felman's *The Juridical Unconscious*. Brook Thomas also draws attention to law as a multilayered discourse, observing that "The law is perhaps above all a *praxis*, a way of doing things, a language of shared references and intentions, and an enterprise very much directed towards an outcome: some form of adjudication, with winners, losers, settlements, sentences" ("Literature" 352).

15 On the international stage, transitional justice is best described as "a process" for "dealing with the aftermath of violent conflicts and systemic abuses in order to provide conditions for a peaceful future" (Buckley-Zistel and Zolkos 1). It achieves this purpose by adopting "a number of instruments and mechanisms, including national and international tribunals, truth commissions, memory work, reparations and institutional reforms, which aim at uncovering the truth about past crimes, putting past wrongs right, holding perpetrators accountable, vindicating the dignity of victims-survivors and contributing to reconciliation" (1, citations omitted).

16 See Momaday's *House Made of Dawn* which is crafted to portray Abel's point of view as he sits in court listening as "Word by word by word these men were disposing of him in language" (90).

17 Scarry explains that the displacement and appropriation of the "felt-characteristics of pain" occurs not only because "the person in great pain experiences [one's] own body as the agent of [one's] agony" (47), but also because "the referential powers of the human voice" (8) mediate the interaction between "the body [as] the locus of pain and the voice [as] the locus of power" (51), directing our attention away from the body and permitting pain's "felt-attributes [to be] lifted into the ... world ... and attached to a referent other than the human body" (13).

18 Mosionier's recognition of this absence is signalled by the concern for law and justice explored by her text and by the acknowledgment that it extends to The Honorable Chief Justice Murray Sinclair, with whom she consulted

when he served as an Associate Judge in Manitoba. Until recently, the Honorable Chief Justice served as the Chair of the Truth and Reconciliation Commission of Canada. Mosionier's non-fiction work, *Come Walk With Me*, explores her family's experience of out-adoption and the reunion that occurred with her mother in which her mother shared the alienating and indignant experience of sitting in the courtroom, listening to "everyone … speaking out against them" as her children were taken from her ("Mosionier Details Experience").

19 Julie Rak and James Dawes provide important insights into the complexities of non-fiction testimonial writing as it negotiates its claims to expressing the "real" and opening up a space to examine how artistic forms express justice and victims' rights. Rak argues that scholars of non-fiction witness narratives explore the paradox of selfhood and agency by choosing "not … to conform to all the conditions of intelligibility that master narratives (and their readers) require" but by constructing their stories so that the "event itself stands in for interiority," thus enabling the event and witnessing to provide the contours of the communal act (232). Dawes observes that asking how "art constitute[s] the human" in relation to expressing a commitment to justice (400–1) permits culture to maintain its integrity by not collapsing the complexity of cultural acts into the universal reach of human rights' discourse expressed through abstract norms. These scholars permit an important shift from a focus on the identity of texts to a study of their status as cultural objects that allows for a transnational discourse of justice to take place in public discourse by focusing on voice, experience, and artistic form rather than solely on identity.

20 Letters as "disruptive" devices played a role in the *Racine* case. A letter written by Mrs Racine to Mrs Woods was withheld by the Brandon Children's Aid Society due to its view that the letter's "tone and content … d[id] not present as particularly stable" (*Woods v. Racine and Racine*, 19 Man. R. (2d), para. 31 and 33). By incorporating letters from Cheryl to form a dialogue with April's verbal narrative, Mosionier enacts solidarity with Indigenous women who "write letters to themselves" in order to undertake writing as an empowering creative task. The classic text in the field of Indigenous women's writing in this regard is Campbell's *Halfbreed*.

21 For contrasting readings of Cheryl's character, see Sharon Smulders's analysis of the novel's engagement with the relationship between a "culturally deprived survivor of foster care" (75) and Metis experience in urban Canada, and Aubrey Hanson's essay which explores the novel's portrayal of violence in the context of its treatment of "Aboriginality and whiteness" (17).

22 See Nightingale for a tremendously important analysis of the differential treatment Indigenous women are subjected to by the courts and police and for her conclusion that Indigenous women are "less likely to report a sexual assault committed by a White man if they fear their complaint would not be believed" (81).

3 Colonial Governmentality and Gender Violence

1 N. Bruce Duthu offers a sustained analysis of this decision's implications for tribal nations in *American Indians and the Law*; see especially 19–24 and 43–5. He argues further that law enforcement for Indigenous women is haphazard and inconclusive at best; see "Broken Justice in Indian Country." Ann Tweedy's "Unjustifiable Expectations" examines the *Oliphant* case by undertaking a historically rigorous account of allotment era writings concerning the Cheyenne River Sioux Tribe in order to challenge the Supreme Court's use of non-Indian purchasers "justifiable expectations" to support rulings that rescind tribal jurisdiction and enable reservation diminishment (131).

2 For two important readings of the novel for its engagements with federal Indian law, see Julie Tharp, who examines the novel for its treatment of sexual violence, and Christopher Bracken, who notes that Erdrich's text raises a key moral problem by asking "how to act where no law applies" (8).

3 A quiet title action represents a legal process that constitutes evidence of a right to property.

4 The United States government officially suspended nation-to-nation treaty-making relations with Indian tribes in 1871, and replaced the treaty process with a new approach that depended upon "agreements" considered by Congress to be similar in kind to treaties (Cohen 127). These "agreements" constituted legislation that gradually moved away from a tribe-by-tribe relationship towards a more general comprehensive program of administration that "increased the statutory power vested in Indian service officials, and stead[ily] narrow[ed] the rights of individual Indians and tribes" (128). One of the first policies to emerge under this new system was the General Allotment Act of 1887 (also known as the "Dawes Act," for Senator Henry Dawes who sponsored the bill), a policy that conjoined assimilationist federal legislation with demands for economic expansion and development in the West. As Felix Cohen explains, "proponents of assimilation policies maintained that if Indians adopted the habits of civilized life they would need less land, and the surplus would be available for white settlers. The taking of these lands was justified as necessary for the progress of

civilization as a whole" (128). The Allotment Act, as is generally recognized, had devastating consequences for American Indian peoples in eroding traditional systems of collective land tenure and tribal autonomy, and instituting an arbitrary system of blood classification known as "blood-quantum" codes through which tribal land was distributed (Churchill and Morris 14). Of the several purposes behind the assimilationist intent of the allotment policy, one objective aimed "to have the same laws applied to Indians that applied to whites," while another intended to eradicate "the difference[s] [between] Indian and white concepts of property" (Cohen 131). In order to institute the Dawes Act for reservations nationwide, Congress passed special legislation designed to enforce the allotment policies in specific tribal communities. This legislation would then supersede previous arrangements between the tribes and the federal government. The Nelson Act of 1889 represented the requisite legislation for the Chippewa Tribe of Minnesota. Under the terms of the Act, "the Anishinaabeg were to cede all reservations in the state except White Earth and Red Lake and relocate to the White Earth Reservation to farm individual allotments ... A three-member commission [set up to initiate land allotment] would negotiate with each band and have responsibility for compiling censuses, taking votes, securing removals, and making allotments" (Meyer 52).

5 The "trust patent," established under the terms of the 1889 Nelson Act, disallowed the sale or incumbrance of Zay Zah's allotment for twenty-five years by vesting title to the land in the United States government until such time as Zay Zah proved or was accorded competency by the Indian Claims Commissioner. The intent behind the stipulation of competency was "to allow Indians to learn to regard land as real estate and [to] manage their own affairs before they would be allowed to sell the land or be required to pay property taxes" (Meyer 51). In this manner, U.S. citizenship, which attached to "patents issued in fee simple," represented a determination that the "Indian" was competent to "adopt the habits of civilized life" (Churchill and Morris 14). The "trust patent" stipulated that at the end of the twenty-five year period the allottee would be issued a "fee patent" by the United States which would convey title to the land to "said Indian" "discharged of said trust and free from all charge and incumbrance whatsoever" (*State v. Zay Zah* 584). The *Zay Zah* case is significant in comparison with previous suits in that both parties agreed – and the court recognized – that at no time had Zay Zah applied for a patent in "fee simple" for his land. For an examination of several court cases that prove the *Zay Zah* decision as an exception in this regard, see Holly Youngbear-Tibbetts's historically rigorous analysis in "Without Due Process."

6 The Clapp Amendment, dated 21 June 1906 and introduced by Senator Moses Clapp from Minnesota, secured inclusion of a rider to the 1906 Indian Appropriations Act, and followed from the Burke Act, passed nationwide in May 1906, which designated as "competent" those allottees who wished to undertake management of their own affairs (Meyer 152). It concerned only the lands of mixed-blood residents on the White Earth Reservation and applied only to the State of Minnesota. The Rider determined competency among tribal members in terms of full-blood and mixed-blood identity by permitting the sale, encumbrance, and taxation of allotted land within the White Earth Reservation held by "adult mixed bloods" (153). Meyer notes that "the text of the Clapp Rider and its further elaboration in 1907 were carefully drawn to achieve the broadest possible application"; the Rider's terms "would apply 'heretofore' and 'hereafter' to adult mixed-bloods and to those full-bloods declared 'competent' by the Secretary of the Interior" (153). The legislation also extended further authority to the Secretary of the Interior to "terminate the trust period and issue fee patents whenever he was convinced of an allottee's 'competence'" (152). Although this "competency clause" (Meyer 152) required that allottees apply for a patent in fee simple, the Clapp Amendment heightened rather than resolved tenuous distinctions among the Chippewa in terms of "full-blood" and "mixed-blood" identity. Moreover, it intensified a policy of indiscriminate determination of Indian identity based on blood-quantum codes practised nationwide. Felix Cohen notes that during the period from 1916 to 1920, "the Interior Department undertook a wholesale program to issue fee patents to Indians without their consent" (427). He adds further "the Department established 'competency commissions' which travelled about and issued large numbers of fee patents unilaterally, sometimes over the open opposition of the Indians" (427n205). The effect of this practice was that by 1928 "four-fifths of the Indians declared 'competent' no longer owned their land" (427n205). The indiscriminate practice of retracting the federal trusteeship relationship through the application of blood-quantum codes, together with the moralizing appraisal of American Indians through competency determinations, instituted a far-reaching pattern of land dispossession among American Indian communities, one consequence of which is observable in the problematic practice of asserting claims to American Indian identity through the terms "full-blood" and "mixed-blood" status as enabling accounts of Indian identity that displace historically varied and locally organized tribal concepts.

7 Appellants argued that there would be no "trust status" to continue beyond the stipulated 25-year period (583).

8 Justice Yetka (concurring specially) raised the problem of the shifting and contradictory nature of federal policies towards American Indian communities in his statements following the decision in the case. He noted that the decision "contributes to the still unresolved problems which are the product of shifting Federal policies towards Indian tribes" (589), and he argued that in addition to "rais[ing] serious due process considerations" the decision also heightened the "state's dilemma" with regard to its legal jurisdiction, since, on the one hand, the trusteeship agreement between the United States and American Indian tribes vested power of attorney in Congress, yet, on the other, Public Law 280 (enacted in 1954 with regard to unterminated Indigenous nations, without tribal agreement; see Churchill and Morris 15) asserted the State's authority over criminal and civil matters on several reservations, including those in Minnesota.

9 For an analysis of the legal history of clouded land titles at White Earth, see Edward Michael Peterson Jr, "That So-Called Warranty Deed," and Holly Youngbear-Tibbetts, "Without Due Process."

10 Emphasis in original. Scott's analysis builds on Michel Foucault's theorization of governmentality as a process of disposition requiring both oversight and social regulation that permits a relationship between government and the body to be governed. As Foucault explains, "Government is defined as a right manner of disposing things so as to lead not to the form of the common good ... but to an end which is 'convenient' for each of the things that are to be governed" (95).

11 The idea that title to the land attached to "competence" which was assessed by the federal government and determined through blood-quantum distinctions indicates the process of moral regulation to which American Indian peoples were subjected. Through the application of the procedures for land allotment in the General Allotment Act, blood-quantum codes also became the means to acquiring citizenship (see Cohen 142).

12 In their discussions of the policies of land allotment and the significance of mixed-blood status to its administration, both Meyer and Cohen note the widespread pattern of dispossession that followed from attaching blood status to land distribution. Melissa Meyer explains that although the 1889 Nelson Act "made no distinctions between 'mixed-bloods' and 'full-bloods'" in terms of Indian identity (191), government legislation imposed by the U.S. Chippewa Commission set up to enforce the allotment legislation among the White Earth residents relied on a ruling by the Assistant Attorney General dated 24 May 1895 that "a 'Chippewa Indian' must be of 'Chippewa Indian blood'; must have a recognized connection with one of the bands in Minnesota; must have been a Minnesota

resident when the act was passed; and must move to one of the reservations with the intention of residing there permanently" (60). Meyer notes that the ruling "discriminated against the children of Anishinaabe women who married U.S. citizens after 9 August 1888 denying them rights under the Nelson Act," and "extended Nelson Act benefits to those who had received 'half-breed scrip' under the 1854 and 1855 treaties" (60). Erdrich's novel *Tracks* invokes this history of involuntary migration and removal as people were forced to follow the land by relocating to their allotments in other territories, leading to women's social isolation when they were abandoned by their families. Erdrich explores this issue through the character Rushes Bear, a figure whose desire to own the land and whose destitute status, as a consequence of her family isolation, leads to the breakdown of her relations with Fleur, whose task is guardianship of the land. In the portrayal of women's affiliations and conflicts, Erdrich shows how changes to the status of the land lead to disruptions in relations among women, a theme explored by Silko in *Ceremony*. Like Silko, Erdrich also examines the differential ways in which Indigenous women articulate land sovereignty and its defence. For a fuller treatment of the *Zay Zah* case, sexual violence and dispossession, and *Tracks*, see Huhndorf, "Contested Images, Contested Lands."

13 See their comment, "No one disputes that decades ago local Indians were unfairly deprived of hundreds of thousands of acres that were guaranteed to them in perpetuity by solemn treaty; yet no one can agree about what should be done to correct that injustice today" (n.p.).

14 They state, "we cannot agree with the authors' conclusions" (n.p.).

15 Thomas notes that law and literature as disciplines had a prior history of connections in the formation of governance and ethical citizenry (514).

16 See *Tracks* in this regard, especially the dispute between Rushes Bear and Fleur that leads to Fleur's self-imposed exile from the community.

17 A compelling example of the interpretive lengths that courts went to in order to maintain the logic of blood quantum as reasonable grounds for characterizing tribal identity arises in *United States v. First National Bank*, 234 U.S. 257 (1914), wherein the court describes "Indian allottees" as members of classes made up of "full blood," "mixed blood," "half blood," "pure blood," "thoroughbred," and "foreign blood" (258) admixtures in order to establish the meaning of identity through which the court could apply the Clapp Amendment and subject tribal land to taxation.

18 Erdrich's best-known novel in this regard is *Tracks* (1988) which explores the late nineteenth-century removal of the Chippewa people to reservation

lands in Minnesota. The novel's generative centre for land protection is the character Fleur who is brutally raped when she ventures to a neighbouring non-Indigenous town for employment in order to pay taxes on Pillager land. Erdrich's thematization of Indigenous women's vulnerability to sexual assault and racialized, predatory violence resonates with Silko's portrayal of this issue in *Ceremony* through her depiction of Helen Jean's story when she leaves the reservation to find employment, and in her portrayal of Tayo's mother, Laura, who flees from the village to escape community condemnation of her behaviour. The connection between economic exploitation and gender violence in *Tracks* and *Ceremony* also arises in Erdrich's portrayal of the kidnapping and sexual assault of Sweetheart Calico in *The Antelope Wife*, an issue I discuss in more detail below.

19 *Shadow Tag* is especially complex in this regard, best described in its plot as a first-person retrospective account by a daughter of how her father stalks and kills her mother.

20 Jeanne Perreault generously shared this insight with me in arguing for a reading of June's death as the generative condition within which the novel as a whole functions.

21 Chadwick Allen provides an excellent analysis of Erdrich's novel *Tracks* as a form of "(post)colonial hybridity" in its appropriation and deployment of "treaty discourse … as metaphor and metonymy" (63) and in its consideration of the relationship between the rhetorical tropes of orature and the inscription of treaty documents as metonyms for "broken promises" in American Indian historical literature.

22 See Postlethwaite's review of *The Antelope Wife* in "A Web of Beadwork," and Kakutani, "'Antelope Wife.'"

23 The narrative does not explain what happened to Zosie and Mary's mother.

4 Land Claims, Identity Claims

1 Republished with permission of University of Oklahoma Press, from *Reasoning Together: The Native Critics Collective*, ed. Craig S. Womack, Daniel Heath Justice, and Christopher B. Teuton. Norman: University of Oklahoma Press, 2008. 169–92.

2 Glen Coulthard argues that Indigenous resurgence and decolonization require multi-faceted and diverse approaches to counter and overcome the dispossession of Indigenous peoples from their lands. See *Red Skin, White Masks,*" 165–9.

3 In an attempt to smooth over the uneven historical contradictions inherent in the term, and to forestall recognition of community social practices determining membership, Congress included an additional qualifier that

defined "mixed-blood" status as follows: "The term 'mixed blood' shall not include an Indian enrolled in any federally recognized Indian tribe, band, or community other than the White Earth Band" (viii). For an excellent account of how the U.S. government uses "theories of race" to "articulate political goals," see Garroutte, "The Racial Formation of American Indians."

4 For a history of the land transactions, public policies, and government enactments that illustrate the mismanagement of White Earth Reservation lands by federal and state governments, see pages 1060–2 of *Manypenny v. United States* 1991. Melissa L. Meyer provides a historical-materialist account of the ways in which differences in cultural, social, and religious practices were consolidated at White Earth in terms of "mixed-blood" and "full-blood" distinctions through government legislation and internal political dissension, see *The White Earth Tragedy*. An invaluable analysis of the "equity suits" by White Earth heirs together with an examination of the legal and legislative dispossession of allottees and a synopsis of WELSA occurs in Youngbear-Tibbetts's "Without Due Process." For a general legal history of the White Earth Indian Reservation and the complicated categories of legal claims that emerged following the *Zay Zah* decision, see Peterson, "That So-Called Warranty Deed." The *Zay Zah* case represents the foundational quiet action title by George Aubid Jr that challenged the tax-delinquent status of a White Earth allottee, and made clear in its decision that "the language of the Clapp Amendment cannot be taken on its face" (Peterson 178).

5 See Alfred and Corntassel 597–614.

6 Support was withheld from the Green Party by Gloria Steinem, a board member of the Feminist Majority Foundation, and Dolores Huerta, cofounder of *United Farm Workers*, both of whom, according to Ed Rampell, "vigorously backed Gore and called upon women not to vote for Nader" ("Feminist Dream or Nightmare" n.p.). "Many leading feminist organizations and individuals," Rampell notes, were concerned that "a Bush victory would result in the appointment of anti-abortion Supreme Court justices, and the enactment of legislation curtailing or ending women's reproductive rights" (n.p.). He claims that "many female voters apparently agreed [with mainstream feminist demands] since in the majority of states more men than women voted for Nader, according to gender voting results released by the Feminist Majority" (n.p.).

7 These include "the replacement of the cultural ethics of domination and control with more cooperative ways of interacting that respect differences of opinion and gender" and "[h]uman values such as equity between the sexes, interpersonal responsibility, and honesty ... with moral conscience" (Rampell, "Towards an Inaugural Pow-Wow" n.p.).

8 In this regard, LaDuke's writing does not distinguish her from a tradition of Indigenous authors who have taken up the politics of redress both through writing and political critique, but rather firmly locates her within a network of Indigenous intellectual activism. Robert Warrior's *Tribal Secrets* assesses the work of Vine Deloria Jr and John Joseph Matthews as early examples of this strategy of engagement. Warrior argues convincingly for the politicization of literary aesthetics in his contention that Indigenous literary practices need to be considered from a materialist perspective that engages both the historical circumstances from which they emerge and the political commitments of their producers (xx). The recovery and expansion of these traditions and their implications in colonial law are also central to Carlson, *Sovereign Selves*, Deloria, *Indians in Unexpected Places*, Konkle's *Writing Indian Nations*, and Piatote's *Domestic Subjects*.

9 My use of the term "information-retrieval approach" is indebted to Gayatri Spivak's ground-breaking formulation of this problem in "Three Women's Texts and A Critique of Imperialism." Spivak argues that the organizing features of feminist recovery work in their focus on recuperating the "self-authorizing" female heroine of feminist criticism from the archive of British women's history depends upon the disavowal of the feminist agent's complicity with the discourses of Western imperialism (798–9).

10 During the allotment of land among White Earth residents, the United States Chippewa Commission, set up to enforce the allotment legislation enacted by the 1889 Nelson Act, relied on a ruling by the Assistant Attorney General dated 24 May 1895 that "a 'Chippewa Indian' must be of 'Chippewa Indian blood': must have a recognized connection with one of the bands in Minnesota; must have been a Minnesota resident when the act was passed; and must move to one of the reservations with the intention of residing there permanently" (Meyer 60). The ruling, according to Melissa Meyer, "discriminated against the children of Anishinaabe women who married U.S. citizens after 9 August 1888 denying them rights under the Nelson Act" (60).

11 See "What Ails Feminist Criticism?" Gubar claims that "a number of prominent advocates of racialized identity politics and of poststructuralist theories have framed their arguments in such a way as to divide feminists, casting suspicion upon a common undertaking that remains in dispute at the turn of the twentieth century" (880). She notes the work of "feminists of racial identity politics," such as "bell hooks, Hazel Carby, and Chandra Mohanty," as particularly egregious examples of the tendency to "promote consternation among white women" (890).

12 This term belongs to Holly Youngbear-Tibbetts. See "Without Due Process" 97.

13 The conceptualization of community through "the crises and contingencies of historical survival" and the compelling project of "enacting historical agency through the slenderness of narrative" both belong to Homi Bhabha's formulation of resistance through narrative in his provocative reading of Toni Morrison's novel *Beloved* in "By Bread Alone" 198–9.

14 The novel makes explicit reference to the *Zay Zah* case argued in 1977 on behalf of "George Agawaateshkan," a figure reminiscent of "George Aubid" from the *Zay Zah* decision, who refuses to "sign papers issued to him by a county agent which would relinquish his rights to a parcel of land" at White Earth (133). Like Aubid, Agawaateshkan pursues the matter in court and legitimates his claim to the land when the Supreme Court of Minnesota rules in his favour and acknowledges that the "county and state had illegally taken the *Anishinaabeg* land almost sixty years before" (133). Rather than authenticate Agawaateshkan's land claim *solely* through mixed-blood status and lines of descent in keeping with the Supreme Court decision in the *Zay Zah* case, LaDuke illustrates how Agawaateshkan's title emerges out of his affiliations with a tranhistorical resistant consciousness that ties him as a descendant to "Bugonaygeeshig, the war chief of the southwestern *Anishinaabeg*" (133), who was the only Anishinaabeg leader during the last of the "Indian wars" with the courage to commit the Anishinaabeg people to Dakota aid (31).

15 LaDuke's recognition of the dehumanizing treatment that White Earth members were subjected to emerged in the research undertaken by Anishinaabe Akeeng. Youngbear-Tibbetts explains that because the allotment process disrupted community relations over an extended period of time, it made it difficult for individual allottees to act on their claims or even recognize that they might have one. Of the several administrative problems that arose for Anishinaabe Akeeng in contacting their potential constituency, several occurred as a result of the administrative procedures inherited by them from the Bureau of Indian Affairs. These problems included the fact that "only 40 percent of potential membership was resident on the reservation, and few of these even knew if their ancestors had trust allotments, much less where such lands might have been located" Youngbear-Tibbetts 122). Additionally, "the original record of allotments [was] fraught with duplicity and error, as [was] the designation of allottees in the land claims enumeration," while "[s]ometimes Christian names were used, sometimes Indian names. In too many cases, nicknames and vernacular names, such as the Anishinaabemowin (Chippewa language) equivalent of 'old lady,' 'young man,' or 'little girl,' were used" (122).

16 LaDuke's description of the methods of "scientific racism" painfully cap-
tures the humiliating experience of embodiment that White Earth members were forced to endure through their objectification by government
officials and scientists. When Mindemoya appears before Dr Ales Hrdlicka
to decide whether or not she is of "mixed-blood" or "full-blood" descent
so as to determine if her land is "saleable," she is forced to endure several
uncomfortable minutes while the doctor measures her cranial size and
records her physical features. The most distressing moment occurs when
she is ordered to disrobe while the doctor "pull[s] his thumb and fore-
finger across her chest in a deep scratch" in order to discover whether or
not her skin is tough enough to resist penetration by sharp objects, which
was believed, at the time, to be an indication of "full-blood" status. The
debasing psychological and emotional violations are second only to the
act of physical dispossession from her land that accompanies Hrdlicka's
pronouncement that Mindemoya is of "mixed-blood descent" (65).

17 Cheryl Harris examines the relationship between "white privilege" and
"racial passing" in relation to her grandmother's experience in negotiating
passing as race privilege in "Whiteness as Property"; see pages 1710–12.

18 The connections between LaDuke's representation of the formation of the
White Earth Indian Reservation as an "Anishinaabe homeland" and the
search for a Jewish homeland through the epic journey of the Israelites
are most likely not accidental. LaDuke is half Jewish on her mother's side,
although she identifies solely as Anishinaabe and has lived on the White
Earth Reservation since 1981 when she moved to the community to become
principal of the local school. She was born in East Los Angeles in 1959
to Anishinaabe activist and later actor Vincent LaDuke, who was origi-
nally from White Earth and who divorced from LaDuke's mother, Betty
Berstein from the South Bronx, five years after their daughter was born.
After the divorce, LaDuke and her mother relocated to Oregon where she
was raised. Her post-secondary education interests demonstrate an early
investment in both political science and economics, both of which have
been central to the social reconstruction work that she has undertaken
on the White Earth Reservation. She attended Barnard College in New
York City before attaining an economics degree from Harvard University,
and holds a Master's degree in rural development from Antioch College.
She has also been a fellow at the Massachusetts Institute of Technology
(Baumgardner 49).

19 Of the several articles and special journal issues devoted to the issue of
repatriation of Native American remains, the most succinct in terms of its
treatment of government policy, legal objectives, and community concerns

is by Rebecca Tsosie, who examines the issue in relation to the discovery of "Kennewick Man," the development of the *Native American Graves Protection and Repatriation Act*, and the consideration of repatriation as a political policy in its historical, cultural, and legal contexts in "Privileging Claims to the Past."

Conclusion

1 See especially Barker, *Native Acts*; Blackhawk, *Violence over the Land*; Rifkin, *Manifesting America*; and King, *The Inconvenient Indian*.

Works Cited

Books and Articles

Aboriginal Justice Implementation Commission. *Report of the Aboriginal Justice Inquiry of Manitoba.* Volume 2. November 1999. http://www.ajic.mb.ca/ volume.html. Accessed 4 July 2013.

Alfred, Taiaiake, and Jeff Corntassel. "Being Indigenous: Resurgences against Contemporary Colonialism." *Government and Opposition* 40.4 (Autumn 2005): 597–614.

Al-Kassim, Dina. "Archiving Resistance: Women's Testimony at the Threshold of the State." *Cultural Dynamics* 20.2 (2008): 167–92.

Allen, Chadwick. "Postcolonial Theory and the Discourse of Treaties." *American Quarterly* 52.1 (2000): 59–89.

Allen, Paula Gunn. *The Sacred Hoop: Recovering the Feminine in American Indian Traditions.* Boston: Beacon Press, 1986.

Altamirano-Jiménez, Isabel. "Indigenous Women, Nationalism, and Feminism." *States of Race: Critical Race Feminism for the 21st Century.* Ed. Sherene Razack, Malinda Smith, and Sunera Thobani. Toronto: Between the Lines, 2010. 111–26.

Amnesty International Canada. "No More Stolen Sisters." September 2009. http://www.amnesty.ca/sites/default/files/ amr200122009enstolensistersupdate.pdf. Accessed 20 December 2009.

Amnesty International USA. *Maze of Injustice: The Failure to Protect Indigenous Women from Sexual Violence in the U.S.A.* New York: Amnesty International USA, 2007.

Angel, Naomi. "Before Truth: The Labors of Testimony and the Canadian Truth and Reconciliation Commission." *Culture, Theory and Critique* 53.2 (2012): 199–214.

Anthias, Floya. "The Material and the Symbolic in Theorizing Social Stratification: Issues of Gender, Ethnicity, and Class." *British Journal of Sociology* 52.3 (September 2001): 367–90.

Authers, Benjamin. "Truth in the Telling: Procedure, Testimony, and the Work of Improvisation in Legal Narrative." *Critical Studies in Improvisation/Etude critiques en improvisation* 6.1 (2010): 1–6.

Barker, Joanne. *Native Acts: Law, Recognition, and Cultural Authenticity.* Durham, NC, and London: Duke UP, 2011.

Bauerkemper, Joseph. "Indigenous Trans/Nationalism and the Ethics of Theory in Native Literary Studies." *Oxford Handbook of Indigenous American Literature.* Ed. James H. Cox and Daniel Heath Justice. Online Publication: February 2014. DOI: 10.1093/oxfordhb/9780199914036.013.014.

Bauerkemper, Joseph, and Heidi Kiiwetinepinesiik Stark. "The Trans/National Terrain of Anishinaabe Law and Diplomacy." *Journal of Transnational American Studies* 4.1 (2012): 1–21.

Baumgardner, Jennifer. "Kitchen Table Candidate." *Ms.* 11.3 (April/May 2001): 47–53.

Bedolla, Lisa Garcia. "Intersections of Inequality: Understanding Marginalization and Privilege in the Post–Civil Rights Era." *Politics & Gender* 3.2 (2007): 232–48.

Bell, Christine, and Catherine O'Rourke. "Does Feminism Need a Theory of Transitional Justice? An Introductory Essay." *International Journal of Transitional Justice* 1 (2007): 23–44.

Berger, Bethany R. "Indian Policy and the Imagined Indian Woman." *Kansas Journal of Law & Public Policy* 14 (2004–5): 103–20.

Bersani, Leo. "Is the Rectum a Grave?" *October* 43 (Winter 1987): 197–222.

Bhabha, Homi. "By Bread Alone: Signs of Violence in the Mid-Nineteenth Century." *The Location of Culture.* London and New York: Routledge, 1994. 198–211.

Blackhawk, Ned. *Violence over the Land: Indians and Empires in the Early American West.* Cambridge, MA, and London: Harvard UP, 2006.

Booth, W. James. "The Unforgotten: Memories of Justice." *American Political Science Review* 95.4 (December 2001): 777–91.

Bracken, Christopher. "Reconciliation Romance: A Study in Juridical Theology." *Qui Parle: Critical Humanities and Social Sciences* 24.1 (Fall/Winter 2015): 1–29.

Brooks, Peter. "Literature as Law's Other." *Yale Journal of Law & the Humanities* 22 (2010): 349–67.

Buckley-Zistel, Susanne, and Magdalena Zolkos. "Introduction: Gender in Transitional Justice." *Gender in Transitional Justice*. Ed. Susanne Buckley-Zistel and Ruth Stanley. Basingstoke; Hampshire; New York: Palgrave-Macmillan, 2011. 1–33.

Butler, Judith. "Is Kinship Always Already Heterosexual?" *Differences: A Journal of Feminist Cultural Studies* 13.1 (2002): 14–44.

– "Merely Cultural." *New Left Review* I/227 (Jan.–Feb. 1998): 33–44.

Campbell, Maria. *Half-breed*. Toronto: McClelland and Stewart, 1973.

Carillo, Jo. "Tribal Governance/Gender." *Readings in American Indian Law: Recalling the Rhythm of Survival*. Ed. Jo Carillo. Philadelphia: Temple UP, 1998. 205–10.

Carlson, David J. *Sovereign Selves: American Indian Autobiography and the Law*. Urbana and Chicago: U of Illinois P, 2006.

Chavkin, Allan. Introduction. *Leslie Marmon Silko's Ceremony: A Case Book*. Ed. Allan Chavkin. New York: Oxford UP, 2002. 3–15.

Cheyfitz, Eric. "The Colonial Double Bind: Sovereignty and Civil Rights in Indian Country." *Journal of Constitutional Law* 5.2 (Jan. 2003): 223–40.

Chopra, Tanja, and Deborah Isser. "Access to Justice and Legal Pluralism in Fragile States: The Case of Women's Rights." *Hague Journal on the Rule of Law* 4 (2012): 337–58.

Christofferson, Carla. "Tribal Courts' Failure to Protect Native American Women: A Reevaluation of the Indian Civil Rights Act." *Yale Law Review* 101 (1991–2): 169–85.

Churchill, Ward, and Glenn T. Morris. "Table: Key Indian Laws and Cases." *The State of Native America: Genocide, Colonization, and Resistance*. Ed. M. Annette Jaimes. Boston: South End, 1992. 13–21.

Code, Lorraine. "The Perversion of Autonomy and the Subjection of Women: Discourses of Social Advocacy at Century's End." *Relational Autonomy: Feminist Perspectives on Autonomy, Agency, and the Social Self*. Ed. Catriona Mackenzie and Natalie Stoljar. New York and Oxford: Oxford UP, 2000. 181–209.

Cohen, F. *Handbook of Federal Indian Law*. Charlottesville: Michie: Bobbs-Merrill, (1942) 1982.

Collins, Richard B. "*Petitioner's Brief, Martinez v. Santa Clara Pueblo*, before the Supreme Court of the American Indian Nations, 2003 Term." *Kansas Journal of Law & Public Policy* 14.1 (2004–5): 67–78.

Cook-Lynn, Elizabeth. "American Indian Intellectualism and the New Indian Story." *American Indian Quarterly* 20.1 (Winter 1996): 57–76.

Coulthard, Glen Sean. *Red Skin, White Masks: Rejecting the Colonial Politics of Recognition*. Minneapolis and London: U of Minnesota P, 2014.

"Court Tells Mother to Stop Trying to See the Daughter She Gave Up." *The Globe and Mail* 10 April 1984: p. 8. Accessed 14/07/2012.

Cover, Robert. "Foreword: Nomos and Narrative." *Harvard Law Review* 97 (1983–4): 4–68.

– "Violence and the Word." *Yale Law Journal* 95 (1985–6): 1601–29.

Cowan, Klint. "International Responsibility for Human Rights Violations by American Indian Tribes." *Yale Human Rights & Development Law Journal* 9 (2006): 1–43.

Crane, Gregg. "The Path of Law and Literature." *American Literary History* 9.4 (Winter 1997): 758–75.

Crenshaw, Kimberle. "Demarginalizing the Intersection of Race and Sex: A Black Feminist Critique of Antidiscrimination Doctrine, Feminist Theory and Antiracist Politics." *University of Chicago Legal Forum* (1989): 139–67.

Cronin, Mary Elizabeth. "Activist/Author Looks to the Future." *Seattle Times* 23 April 1998. http://community.seattletimes.nwsource.com/archive/?date=19980423&slug=2746765.

Cubilié, Anne, and Carl Good. "Introduction: The Future of Testimony." *Discourse* 25.1 & 2 (Winter and Spring 2004): 4–18.

Cumming, Peter. "'The Only Dirty Book': The Rape of April Raintree." In *Search of April Raintree: Critical Edition*, by Beatrice Culleton Mosionier. Ed. Cheryl Suzack. Winnipeg: Portage & Main, 1999. 307–22.

Cunningham, Myrna. "Indigenous Women's Visions of an Inclusive Feminism." *Development* 49.1 (2006): 55–9.

Curry, Lucy A. "A Closer Look at *Santa Clara Pueblo v. Martinez*: Membership by Sex, by Race, and by Tribal Tradition." *Wisconsin Women's Law Journal* 16 (2001): 161–214.

Das, Veena. "Cultural Rights and the Definition of Community." *The Rights of Subordinated Peoples*. Ed. Oliver Mendelsohn and Upendra Baxi. Oxford UP, 1997. 117–59.

Dawes, James. "Human Rights in Literary Studies." *Human Rights Quarterly* 31 (2009): 394–409.

Delgado, Richard. "Storytelling for Oppositionists and Others: A Plea for Narrative." *Michigan Law Review* 87 (August 1989): 2411–41.

Deloria, Philip J. *Indians in Unexpected Places*. Lawrence: UP of Kansas, 2004.

Desbiens, Caroline. "'Women with no femininity': Gender, Race, and Nation-Building in the James Bay Project." *Political Geography* 23 (2004): 347–66.

Dhamoon, Rita Kaur. "Considerations on Mainstreaming Intersectionality." *Political Research Quarterly* 64.1 (2011): 230–43.

– *Identity/Difference Politics: How Difference is Produced, and Why It Matters.* Vancouver: U of British Columbia P, 2010.

Dirlik, Arif. "The Global in the Local." *Global/Local: Cultural Production and the Transnational Imaginary.* Ed. Rob Wilson and Wimal Dissanayake. Durham, NC: Duke UP, 1996. 21–45.

Duthu, N. Bruce. *American Indians and the Law.* New York: Penguin, 2008.

– "Broken Justice in Indian Country." *New York Times* 11 August 2008, A17.

Episkenew, Jo-Ann. *Taking Back Our Spirits: Indigenous Literature, Public Policy, and Healing.* Winnipeg: U of Manitoba P, 2009.

Erdrich, Louise. *The Antelope Wife.* New York: Harper, 1998.

– *Love Medicine.* 1984. New and Expanded Version. New York: Harper, 1993.

– "The Names of Women." *Granta* 41 (Autumn 1992): 131–8.

– "Rape on the Reservation." *The New York Times* 26 February 2013. Accessed September 2015. http://www.nytimes.com/2013/02/27/opinion/native-americans-and-the-violence-against-women-act.html?_r=0

– *The Round House.* New York: HarperCollins, 2012.

– *Shadow Tag.* New York: HarperCollins, 2010.

– *Tracks.* New York: Harper, 1988.

Erdrich, Louise, and Michael Dorris. "Who Owns the Land?" *New York Times Magazine.* 4 Sept. 1988: 32+.

Evers, Lawrence J. "The Killing of a New Mexico State Trooper: Ways of Telling a Historical Event." *Wicazo Sa Review* 1.1 (1985): 17–25.

Felman, Shoshana. "Forms of Judicial Blindness, or the Evidence of What Cannot Be Seen: Traumatic Narratives and Legal Repetitions in the O.J. Simpson Case and in Tolstoy's *The Kreutzer Sonata.*" *Critical Inquiry* 23 (Summer 1997): 738–88.

– *The Juridical Unconscious: Trials and Traumas in the Twentieth Century.* Cambridge, MA, and London: Harvard UP, 2002.

Fletcher, Ezekial J.N. "Trapped in the Spring of 1978: The Continuing Impact of the Supreme Court's Decisions in *Oliphant, Wheeler,* and *Martinez.*" *Federal Lawyer* (March/April 2008): 36–43.

Foucault, Michel. "Governmentality." *The Foucault Effect: Studies in Governmentality with Two Lectures by and an Interview with Michel Foucault.* Ed. Graham Burchell, Colin Gordon, and Peter Miller. Chicago: U of Chicago P, 1991. 87–104.

Franke, Katherine M. "Gendered Subjects of Transitional Justice." *Columbia Journal of Gender and Law* 15.3 (2006): 813–28.

Frankenberg, Ruth, and Lata Mani. "Crosscurrents, Crosstalk: Race, 'Postcoloniality' and the Politics of Location." *Cultural Studies* 7.2 (May 1993): 292–310.

Frickey, Philip P. "A Common Law for Our Age of Colonialism: The Judicial Divestiture of Indian Tribal Authority over Nonmembers." *Yale Law Journal* 109 (1999–2000): 1–85.

Fuller, Lon L. *The Morality of Law*. New Haven: Yale UP, 1969.

Fyfe, R. James. "Dignity as Theory: Competing Conceptions of Human Dignity at the Supreme Court of Canada." *Saskatchewan Law Review* 70 (2007): 1–26.

Garroutte, Eva Marie. "The Racial Formation of American Indians." *American Indian Quarterly* 25.2 (Spring 2001): 224–39.

"Girl Is Ward of Court after Legal Tug of War." *The Globe and Mail*, 1 January 1983: 13.

Green, Joyce. "Sexual Inequality and Indian Government: An Analysis of Bill C–31 Amendments to the *Indian Act*." *Native Studies Review* 1.2 (1985): 81–95.

– "Taking Account of Aboriginal Feminism." *Making Space for Indigenous Feminism*. Ed. Joyce Green. Blackpoint, NS, and London: Fernwood & Zed Books, 2007. 20–32.

Green, Rayna. "Native American Women." *Signs: Journal of Women in Culture and Society* 6.2 (1980): 248–67.

Gubar, Susan. "What Ails Feminist Criticism?" *Critical Inquiry* 24 (Summer 1998): 878–902.

Guerrero, Marie Anna Jaimes. "Civil Rights versus Sovereignty: Native American Women in Life and Land Struggles." *Feminist Genealogies, Colonial Legacies, Democratic Futures*. Ed. M. Jacqui Alexander and Chandra Mohanty. New York and London: Routledge, 1997. 101–21.

– "'Patriarchal Colonialism' and Indigenism: Implications for Native Feminist Spirituality and Native Womanism." *Hypatia* 18.2 (Spring 2003): 58–69.

Hanson, Aubrey Jean. "'Through White Man's Eyes': Beatrice Culleton Mosionier's *In Search of April Raintree* and Reading for Decolonization." *Studies in American Indian Literatures* 24.1 (Spring 2012): 15–30.

Harris, Angela. "Race and Essentialism in Feminist Legal Theory." *Stanford Law Review* 42 (February 1990): 581–616.

Harris, Cheryl. "Whiteness as Property." *Harvard Law Review* 106.8 (June 1993): 1707–91.

Hartsock, Nancy C.M. "The Feminist Standpoint: Developing the Ground for a Specifically Feminist Historical Materialism." *The Feminist Standpoint Revisited & Other Essays*. Boulder: Westview Press, 1998. 105–32.

Henderson, Greig. "The Cost of Persuasion: Figure, Story, and Elegance in the Rhetoric of Judicial Discourse." *University of Toronto Quarterly* 75.4 (Fall 2006): 905–24.

Hodge, Merle. "Challenges of the Struggle for Sovereignty: Changing the World versus Writing Stories." *The Routledge Reader in Caribbean Literature.* Ed. Alison Donnell and Sarah Lawson Welsh. London and New York: Routledge, 1996. 494–7.

Hoilman, Dennis. "The Ethnic Imagination: A Case History." *Canadian Journal of Native Studies* 2 (1985): 167–75.

Huhndorf, Shari. "Contesting Images, Contested Lands: The Politics of Space in Louise Erdrich's *Tracks* and Leslie Marmon Silko's *Sacred Water.*" *Oxford Handbook of Indigenous American Literature.* Ed. James H. Cox and Daniel Heath Justice. Oxford Handbooks Online: February 2014. DOI: 10.1093/oxfordhb/9780199914036.013.012

– *Mapping the Americas: The Transnational Politics of Contemporary Native Culture.* Ithaca and London: Cornell UP, 2009.

Huhndorf, Shari M., and Cheryl Suzack. "Indigenous Feminism: Theorizing the Issues." *Indigenous Women and Feminism: Politics, Activism, Culture.* Ed. Cheryl Suzack, Shari Huhndorf, Jeanne Perreault, and Jean Barman. Vancouver: U of British Columbia P, 2010. 1–17.

Hunt, Alan. "The Big Fear: Law Confronts Postmodernism." *McGill Law Journal/Revue De Droit De McGill* 35.3 (1989–90): 507–40.

International Center for Transitional Justice, "Gender Justice." http://ictj.org/publications, Date 2010, http://ictj.org/publications?keys=gender+justice&language%5B%5D=en. Accessed 8 August 2012.

Irlbacher-Fox, Stephanie. *Finding Dahshaa: Self-Government, Social Suffering, and Aboriginal Policy in Canada.* Vancouver: U of British Columbia P, 2009.

Iyer, Nitya, "Categorical Denials: Equality Rights and the Shaping of Social Identity." *Queen's Law Journal* 19 (1993–4): 179–207.

Jaggar, Alison M. "Transnational Cycles of Gendered Vulnerability: A Prologue to a Theory of Global Gender Injustice." *Philosophical Topics* 37.2 (2009): 33–52.

Jameson, Frederic. *The Political Unconscious: Narrative as a Socially Symbolic Act.* Ithaca, NY: Cornell UP, 1981.

Jamieson, Kathleen. *Indian Women and the Law in Canada: Citizens Minus.* Ottawa: Advisory Council on the Status of Women, Indian Rights for Indian Women, 1978.

Jung, Courtney. "Canada and the Legacy of the Indian Residential Schools: Transitional Justice for Indigenous People in a Nontransitional Society." *Identities in Transition: Challenges for Transitional Justice in Divided Societies.* Ed. Paige Arthur. Cambridge: Cambridge UP, 2013. 217–50. Cambridge Books Online. http://ebooks.cambridge.org. DOI:http://dx.doi.org/10.1017/CBO9780511976858. Accessed 31 May 2013.

– "Transitional Justice for Indigenous People in a Non-transitional Society." International Center for Transitional Justice. https://www.ictj.org/ publications. Date 2009, https://www.ictj.org/sites/default/files/ICTJ-Identities-NonTransitionalSocieties-ResearchBrief-2009-English.pdf. Accessed 15 July 2013.

Kahn, Paul W. *The Cultural Study of Law: Reconstructing Legal Scholarship.* Chicago and London: U of Chicago P, 1999.

Kakutani, Michiko. "'Antelope Wife': Myths of Redemption amid a Legacy of Loss." *The New York Times* 24 March 1998.

King, Thomas. *The Inconvenient Indian: A Curious Account of Native Peoples in North America.* Minneapolis: U of Minnesota P, 2013.

– *Medicine River.* Toronto: Penguin, 1991.

– *The Truth about Stories: A Native Narrative.* Minneapolis: U of Minnesota P, 2008.

Kipnis, Laura. "Feminism: The Political Conscience of Postmodernism?" *Social Text* 21 (1989): 149–66.

Kirby, Peter. "Marrying Out and Loss of Status: The Charter and New Indian Act." *Journal of Law and Social Policy* 1 (1985): 77–95.

Kline, Marlee. "Child Welfare Law, 'Best Interests of the Child' Ideology, and First Nations." *Osgoode Hall Law Journal* 30.2 (1992): 375–425.

– "The Colour of Law: Ideological Representations of First Nations in Legal Discourse." *Social & Legal Studies* 3.4 (1994): 451–76.

Konkle, Maureen. *Writing Indian Nations: Native Intellectuals and the Politics of Historiography, 1827–1863.* Chapel Hill and London: U of North Carolina P, 2004.

Krotz, Larry. "Manitoba: The Indian Child Welfare Mess." *The Globe and Mail* 27 February 1982: 8. Accessed 14 July 2012.

Kuokkanen, Rauna. "Self-Determination and Indigenous Women's Rights at the Intersection of International Human Rights." *Human Rights Quarterly* 34 (2012): 225–50.

LaDuke, Winona. *All Our Relations: Native Struggles for Land and Life.* Cambridge, MA: South End P, 1999.

– "The Indigenous Women's Network: Our Future, Our Responsibility." United Nations Fourth World Conference on Women. Beijing, China. 31 August 1995. https://ratical.org/co-globalize/WinonaLaDuke/ Beijing95.html.

– *Last Standing Woman.* Vancouver: Rainforest Books, 1997.

Laurence, Robert. "A Quincentennial Essay on *Martinez v. Santa Clara Pueblo.*" *Idaho Law Review* 28 (1991–2): 307–47.

Lawrence, Bonita, and Kim Anderson. "Introduction to 'Indigenous Women: The State of Our Nations.'" *Atlantis* 29.2 (2005): 1–10. https://journals.msvu.ca/index.php/atlantis/article/view/1041/998.

Leeds, Stacy L. "*Martinez v. Santa Clara Pueblo,* before the Supreme Court of the American Indian Nations, 2003 Term." *Kansas Journal of Law & Public Policy* 14 (2004–5): 91–6.

Lorenz, Paul H. "The Other Story of Leslie Marmon Silko's 'Storyteller.'" *South Central Review* 8.4 (Winter 1991): 59–75.

Macklem, Patrick. "First Nations Self-Government and the Borders of the Canadian Legal Imagination." *McGill Law Journal* 36 (1990–1): 382–456.

McIvor, Sharon D. "The Indian Act as Patriarchal Control of Women." *Aboriginal Women's Law Journal* 1.1 (1994): 70–88.

Medicine, Beatrice. "North American Indigenous Women and Cultural Domination." *American Indian Culture and Research Journal* 17.3 (1993): 121–30.

Meyer, Melissa L. *The White Earth Tragedy: Ethnicity and Dispossession at a Minnesota Anishinaabe Reservation, 1889–1920.* Lincoln and London: U of Nebraska P, 1994.

Momaday, N. Scott. *House Made of Dawn.* New York: HarperCollins, 1966.

Monture-Angus, Patricia. *Thunder in My Soul: A Mohawk Woman Speaks.* Halifax, NS: Fernwood Publishing, 1995.

Mosionier, Beatrice. *Come Walk with Me: A Memoir.* Winnipeg: High Water P, 2009.

Mosionier, Beatrice Culleton. *In Search of April Raintree: Critical Edition.* Ed. Cheryl Suzack. Winnipeg: Portage & Main, [1983] 1999.

"Mosionier Details Experience in Plainspoken Memoir." *Winnipeg Free Press.* 31 Oct. 2009: H. 9.

Nagy, Rosemary. "Transitional Justice as Global Project: Critical Reflections." *Third World Quarterly* 29.2 (2008): 275–89.

Napoleon, Val. "*Delgamuukw*: A Legal Straightjacket for Oral Histories?" *Canadian Journal of Law and Society* 20.2 (May 2005): 123–55.

Nesiah, Vasuki, et al. "Truth Commissions and Gender: Principles, Policies, and Procedures." International Centre for Transitional Justice, Gender Justice Series. (July 2006): 1–56. https://www.ictj.org/sites/default/files/ICTJ-Global-Commissions-Gender-2006-English_0.pdf. Accessed 4 July 2013.

Ní Aoláin, Fionnuala, and Eilish Rooney. "Underenforcement and Intersectionality: Gendered Aspects of Transition for Women." *International Journal of Transitional Justice* 1 (2007): 338–54.

Nightingale, Margo L. "Judicial Attitudes and Differential Treatment: Native Women in Sexual Assault Cases." *Ottawa Law Review* 23.1 (1991): 71–98.

Orford, Anne. "Commissioning the Truth." *Columbia Journal of Gender and Law* 15.3 (2006): 851–83.

Otto, Dianne. "'Gender Comment:' Why Does the UN Committee on Economic, Social and Cultural Rights Need a General Comment on Women?" *Canadian Journal of Women & the Law* 14.1 (2002): 1–52.

Owens, Louis. *Bone Game*. Norman: U of Oklahoma P, 1994.

– *Mixedblood Messages: Literature, Film, Family, Place*. Norman: U of Oklahoma P, 1998.

– "'The Very Essence of Our Lives:' Leslie Silko's Webs of Identity." *Leslie Marmon Silko's Ceremony: A Casebook*. Ed. Allan Chavkin. New York: OUP, 2002. 91–116.

Peterson, Michael Edward, Jr. "That So-Called Warranty Deed: Clouded Land Titles on the White Earth Indian Reservation in Minnesota." *North Dakota Law Review* 59 (1983): 159–81.

Piatote, Beth. *Domestic Subjects: Gender, Citizenship, and Law in Native American Literature*. New Haven: Yale UP, 2013.

Pommersheim, Frank. "Democracy, Citizenship, and Indian Law Literacy: Some Initial Thoughts." *Thomas M. Cooley Law Review* 14.3 (1997): 457–71.

Postlethwaite, Diana. "A Web of Beadwork." Rev. of *The Antelope Wife* by Louise Erdrich. *New York Times Book Review* 12 Apr. 1998, late ed., sec. 7: 6.

Povinelli, Elizabeth. "The State of Shame: Australian Multiculturalism and the Crisis of Indigenous Citizenship." *Critical Inquiry* 24.2 (Winter 1998): 575–610.

Purdy, John. "The Transformation: Tayo's Genealogy in *Ceremony*." *Studies in American Indian Literatures* 10.3 (Summer 1986): 121–33.

Rak, Julie. "Doukhobor Autobiography as Witness Narrative." *Biography* 24.1 (Winter 2001): 226–41.

Rampell, Ed. "Feminist Dream or Nightmare: The Green Party." *Women's International Net Magazine* 38 11 June 2001.

– "Towards an Inaugural Pow-Wow." *Women's International Net Magazine* 4 June 2001. http://www.winmagazine.org.

Ratner, Michael D., and Mahlon Perkins. "Who Owns the Land?" *New York Times Magazine* 2 October 1988. http://www.nytimes.com/1988/10/02/magazine/l-who-owns-the-land-322388.html.

Razack, Sherene. "Speaking for Ourselves: Feminist Jurisprudence and Minority Women." *Canadian Journal of Women and the Law* 4.2 (1990): 440–58.

Réaume, Denise. "Comparing Theories of Sex Discrimination: The Role of Comparison."*Oxford Journal of Legal Studies* 25.3 (2005): 547–64.
- "Discrimination and Dignity." *Louisiana Law Review* 63 (2003): 1–51.
- "Indignities: Making a Place for Dignity in Modern Legal Thought." *Queen's Law Journal* 28 (2002): 61–94.
- "Justice between Cultures: Autonomy and the Protection of Cultural Affiliation." *University of British Columbia Law Review* 29.1 (1995): 117–42.
Redbird, Elsie B. "Honouring Native Women: The Backbone of Native Sovereignty." Ed. Kayleen M. Hazlehurst. *Popular Justice and Community Regeneration: Pathways of Indigenous Reform*. London: Praeger, 1995. 121–41.
Resnik, Judith. "Dependent Sovereigns: Indian Tribes, States, and the Federal Courts." *University of Chicago Law Review* 56 (1989): 671–759.
Rifkin, Mark. *Manifesting America: The Imperial Construction of U.S. National Space*. New York: OUP, 2009.
Riley, Angela R. "(Tribal) Sovereignty and Illiberalism." *California Law Review* 95 (2007): 799–848.
Robinett, Jane. "Looking for Roots: Curandera and Shamanic Practices in Southwest Fiction." Academic.edu. 1–22. Accessed June 2015. http://www.academia.edu/9225291/Looking_for_Roots_Curandera_and_Shamanic_Practices_in_Southwest_Fiction.
Robinson, Eden. *Monkey Beach*, Toronto: Random House, 2000.
Sarat, Austin, and Jonathan Simon. "Cultural Analysis, Cultural Studies, and the Situation of Legal Scholarship." *Cultural Analysis, Cultural Studies, and the Law: Moving beyond Legal Realism*. Ed. Austin Sarat and Johnathan Simon. Durham, NC, and London: Duke UP, 2003. 1–34.
Scarry, Elaine. *The Body in Pain: The Making and Unmaking of the World*. New York and Oxford: OUP, 1985.
Scott, David. *Refashioning Futures: Criticism after Postcoloniality*. Princeton: Princeton UP, 1999.
Scott, Joan. "Gender: A Useful Category of Historical Analysis." *Gender and the Politics of History*. New York: Columbia UP, 1988. 29–50.
Scurfield, Maureen. "Mosionier Details Experiences in Plainspoken Memoir." Rev. of *Come Walk with Me* by Beatrice Culleton Mosionier. Winnipeg Free Press 31 October 2009, H 9.
Shanley, Kathryn. "Blood Ties and Blasphemy: American Indian Women and the Problem of History." *Is Academic Feminism Dead?* Ed. The Social Justice Group at the Center for Advanced Feminist Studies, University of Minnesota. New York and London: New York UP, 2000. 204–32.

– "Thoughts on Indian Feminism." *A Gathering of Spirit: A Collection by North American Indian Women*. Ed. Beth Brant. Toronto, ON: The Women's Press, 1984. 213–15.

Shih, Shu-Mei. "Global Literature and the Technologies of Recognition." *PMLA* 119.1 (2004):16–30.

Silko, Leslie Marmon. *Ceremony*. New York: Penguin, 1977.

– "Cottonwood *Part Two: Buffalo Story*." *Storyteller*. New York: Arcade Publishing, 1981. 67–76.

– "Language and Literature from a Pueblo Indian Perspective." *English Literature: Opening Up the Canon*. Ed. Leslie A. Fiedler and Houston A. Baker. Baltimore, MD: Johns Hopkins UP, 1981. 54–72.

– "The Man to Send Rain Clouds." *The Man to Send Rain Clouds: Contemporary Stories by American Indians*. Ed. and intro. Kenneth Rosen. New York: Vintage, 1974. 3–8.

– "Storyteller." *Storyteller*. New York: Arcade Publishing, 1981. 17–32.

– "Storytelling." *Storyteller*. New York: Arcade Publishing, 1981. 94–8.

– "Tony's Story." *The Man to Send Rain Clouds: Contemporary Stories by American Indians*. Ed. and intro. Kenneth Rosen. New York: Vintage, 1974. 69–78.

– "Yellow Woman." *Storyteller*. New York: Arcade Publishing, 1981. 54–62.

– "Yellow Woman and a Beauty of the Spirit." *Yellow Woman and a Beauty of the Spirit: Essays on Native American Life Today*. New York: Touchstone, 1997. 60–71.

Skenandore, Francine R. "Revisiting *Santa Clara Pueblo v. Martinez*: Feminist Perspectives on Tribal Sovereignty." *Wisconsin Women's Law Journal* 17 (2002): 347–70.

Skibine, Alex Tallchief. "*Respondents' Brief, Martinez v. Santa Clara Pueblo*, before the Supreme Court of the American Indian Nations. 2003 Term." *Kansas Journal of Law & Public Policy* 14.1 (2004–5): 79–90.

Smith, Andrea. "Native American Feminism, Sovereignty, and Social Change." *Feminist Studies* 31.1 (Spring 2005): 116–32.

Smith, Andrea, and J. Kehaulani Kauanui. "Native Feminisms Engage American Studies." *American Quarterly* 60.2 (2008): 241–9.

Smulders, Sharon. "'What is the proper word for people like you?': The Question of Metis Identity in *In Search of April Raintree*." *ESC: English Studies in Canada* 32.4 (December 2006): 75–100.

Spivak, Gayatri Chakravorty. "Imperialism and Sexual Difference." *Oxford Literary Review* 8.1–2 (1986): 225–40.

– "The Rani of Sirmur: An Essay in Reading the Archives." *History and Theory* 24.3 (1985): 247–72.

– "Three Women's Texts and a Critique of Imperialism." *Critical Inquiry* 12.1 (Autumn 1985): 243–61. Rpt. in *Feminisms: An Anthology of Literary Criticism.* Ed. Robyn R. Warhol and Diane Price Herndl. New Brunswick, NJ: Rutgers UP, 1991. 798–814.

– "Who Claims Alterity?" *Remaking History.* Ed. Barbara Kruger and Phil Mariani. Dia Art Foundation Discussions in Contemporary Culture No. 4. Seattle: Bay Press, 1989. 269–92.

Stetson, C.L. "Equal Protection under the Indian Civil Rights Act: *Martinez v. Santa Clara Pueblo.*" *Harvard Law Review* 90 (1976–7): 627–36.

Stratton, Florence. "There is no Bentham Street in Calgary: Panoptic Discourses and Thomas King's *Medicine River.*" *Canadian Literature* 185 (Summer 2005): 11–27.

Suzack, Cheryl. "Land Claims, Identity Claims: Mapping Indigenous Feminism in Literary Criticism and in Winona LaDuke's *Last Standing Woman.*" *Reasoning Together: The Native Critics Collective.* Ed. Craig S. Womack, Daniel Heath Justice, and Christopher B. Teuton. Norman: U of Oklahoma P, 2008. 169–92.

– "The Transposition of Law and Literature in *Delgamuukw* and *Monkey Beach.*" *South Atlantic Quarterly* 110.2 (Spring 2011): 447–63.

Suzack, Cheryl, et al. *Indigenous Women and Feminism: Politics, Activism, Culture.* Vancouver: U of British Columbia P, 2010.

Swan, Edith. "Feminine Perspectives at Laguna Pueblo: Silko's *Ceremony.*" *Tulsa Studies in Women's Literature* 11.2 (Autumn 1992): 309–28.

Swentzell, Rina. "Testimony of a Santa Clara Woman." *Kansas Journal of Law & Public Policy* 14.1 (2004–5): 97–102.

Teitel, Ruti G. "Global Transitional Justice." *Project on Human Rights, Global Justice and Democracy.* Working Paper No. 8, Center for Global Studies. Ed. Jo-Marie Burt (Spring 2010): 1–19. https://www.gmu.edu/centers/globalstudies/publications/hjd/hjd-wp-8.pdf.

– *Transitional Justice.* Oxford and New York: OUP, 2000.

– "Transitional Justice Genealogy." *Harvard Human Rights Journal* 16 (2003): 69–94.

Tharp, Julie. "Erdrich's Crusade: Sexual Violence in *The Round House.*" *Studies in American Indian Literatures* 26.3 (Fall 2014): 25–40.

Thomas, Brook. "Literature as Law's Other." *Yale Journal of Law & the Humanities* 22.2 (2010): 349–67.

– "Reflections on the Law and Literature Revival." *Critical Inquiry* 17.3 (Spring 1991): 510–39.

Tohe, Laura. "There Is No Word for Feminism in My Language." *Wicazo Sa Review* 15.2 (2000): 103–10.

Truth and Reconciliation Commission of Canada. The Honourable Justice Murray Sinclair, Chair. "Meet the Commissioners." Truth and Reconciliation Commission of Canada, 1500-360 Main Street, Winnipeg, Manitoba R3C 3Z3. https://www.trc.ca/websites/trcinstitution/index.php?p=5. Accessed 29 July 2013.

– "Indian Residential School Survivor Committee (IRSSC)." Our Mandate. https://www.trc.ca/websites/trcinstitution/index.php?p=5. Accessed 12 August 2013.

Tsosie, Rebecca. "Privileging Claims to the Past: Ancient Human Remains and Contemporary Cultural Values." *Arizona State Law Journal* 31.2 (Summer 1999): 583–677.

– "Separate Sovereigns, Civil Rights, and the Sacred Text: The Legacy of Justice Thurgood Marshall's Indian Law Jurisprudence." *Arizona State Law Journal* 26 (1994): 495–533.

Tweedy, Ann E. "Unjustifiable Expectations: Laying to Rest the Ghosts of Allotment-Era Settlers." *Seattle University Law Review* 36.1 (2012): 129–88.

Valencia-Weber, Gloria. "*Santa Clara Pueblo v. Martinez*: Twenty-five Years of Disparate Cultural Visions." *Kansas Journal of Law & Public Policy* 14 (2004–5): 49–66.

Valencia-Weber, Gloria, and Christine P. Zuni. "Domestic Violence and Tribal Protection of Indigenous Women in the United States." *St. John's Law Review* 69 (1995): 69–135.

Warrior, Robert Allen. *Tribal Secrets: Recovering American Indian Intellectual Traditions*. Minneapolis: U of Minnesota P, 1995.

Welch, James. *Winter in the Blood*. New York: Penguin, 1974.

Wilkinson, Charles F. *American Indians, Time, and the Law*. New Haven and London: Yale UP, 1987.

Williams, Joan C. "Deconstructing Gender." *Michigan Law Review*. 87.4 (Feb. 1989): 797–845.

Williams, Robert A. "Gendered Checks and Balances: Understanding the Legacy of White Patriarchy in an American Indian Cultural Context." *Georgia Law Review* 24 (1989–90): 1019–44.

Wright, Melissa W. *Disposable Women and Other Myths of Global Capitalism*. New York and London: Routledge Taylor & Francis Group, 2006.

Young, Iris Marion. *Justice and the Politics of Difference*. Princeton, NJ: Princeton UP, 1990.

Youngbear-Tibbetts, Holly. "Without Due Process: The Alienation of Individual Trust Allotments of the White Earth Anishinaabeg." *American Indian Culture and Research Journal* 15.2 (1991): 93–138.

Zizek, Slavoj. "Multiculturalism, Or, the Cultural Logic of Multinational Capitalism." *New Left Review* I/225 (Sept.-Oct. 1997): 28–51.

Legal Cases and Statutes

Attorney General of Canada v. Lavell-Isaac v. Bédard [1974]. 2 S.C.R. 1349. Supreme Ct. of Can. 27. August 1973.

Sandra Lovelace v. Canada. Communication No. R.6/24, U.N. Doc. Supp. No. 40 (A/36/40) at 166. 1981.

Manypenny v. United States. 125 F.R.D. 497 U.S. Dist. Ct. D. Minn. 1989.

Manypenny v. United States. 948 F. 2d 1057 U.S. Ct. App. 1991.

Martinez v. Santa Clara Pueblo. 402 F.Supp. 5 (D.N.M. Jun 25, 1975) (NO. CIV. 9717).

Martinez v. Santa Clara Pueblo. 540 F.2d 1039 (10th Cir(N.M.) Aug 16, 1976) (NO. 75–1615).

Oliphant v. Suquamish Indian Tribe. 435 U.S. 191 (1978).

Racine v. Woods, [1983] 2 S.C.R. 173.

Santa Clara Pueblo v. Martinez. 436 U.S. 49, 98 S.Ct. 1670, 56 L.Ed.2d 106 (U.S.N.M. May 15, 1978) (NO. 76–682).

State of Minnesota v. Zay Zah. 259 N.W. 2d 580. Minn. Supr. Ct. 1977.

United States. Senate. Select Committee on Indian Affairs. "White Earth Indian Land Claims Settlement." *Hearing before the Select Committee on Indian Affairs.* 99 Cong., 1st sess. S. 1396. Washington: GPO, 1985.

United States v. First National Bank. 234 U.S. 245 Syllabus 1914.

Woods v. Racine and Racine [1982]. 19 Man. R. (2d) 186.

Appellate Court Documents (US)

U.S. Appellate Briefs

Santa Clara Pueblo and Lucario Padilla, individually and as Governor of Santa Clara Pueblo, Petitioners, v. Julia Martinez, on behalf of herself and all others similarly situated, and Audrey Martinez, on behalf of herself and all others similarly situated. Respondents., 1976 WL 181159 (Appellate Brief) (U.S. Dec. 22, 1976) Motion to File Brief Amici Curiae and Brief of Amici Curiae of the Pueblo de Cochiti, the Pueblo of Isleta, the Pueblo of Jemez, the Pueblo of Laguna, the Pueblo of Sandia, the Pueblo of San Felipe, t (NO. 76–682).

Santa Clara Pueblo, et al., Petitioners, v. Julia Martinez, et al., 1977 WL 189104
    (Appellate Brief) (U.S. Apr. 26, 1977) Memorandum for the United States as
    Amicus Curiae (NO. 76–682).
Santa Clara Pueblo, et al, Petitioners, v. Julia Martinez, et al, Respondents.,
    1977 WL 189105 (Appellate Brief) (U.S. Jul. 15, 1977) Brief for Petitioners
    (NO. 76–682).
Santa Clara Pueblo, et al., Petitioners, v. Julia Martinez, et al., Respondents.,
    1977 WL 189106 (Appellate Brief) (U.S. Aug. 27, 1977) Respondents' Brief
    (NO. 76–682).
Santa Clara Pueblo, et al., Petitioners, v. Julia Martinez, et al., Respondents.,
    1977 WL 189110 (Appellate Brief) (U.S. Jul. 15, 1977) Brief of the National
    Tribal Chairmen's Association as Amicus Curiae in Support of Petitioners
    (NO. 76–682).

Index

abjection, 75, 116

Aboriginal justice. *See* Indigenous justice

abuse: domestic, 50, 68, 76, 79, 114; emotional, 54; of Indigenous peoples, 79–80; physical, 96, 114; physical and verbal, 67; physical, verbal, and sexual, 45

acculturation, 10, 25

Acoma Pueblo, 25

activism: civil rights, 5; community, 9, 103; environmental, 104, 119; ethical responsibility and, 119; Indigenous, 76, 104; Indigenous women's, 4, 8–9, 11–14, 18, 31, 48, 87, 124; legal, 13, 14, 18, 21, 30–1, 48, 98–9, 125; literary, 5, 79, 87, 98–101, 106, 124–5; political, 14, 98; social justice, 79; social and political, 8, 11; storytelling, 80. *See also* Indigenous women's writing

adoption, 52, 54–5, 57, 65, 69, 90–1. *See also* Indigenous children: out-adoption of

alcohol, 60, 68

alcoholism, 52, 73, 80, 90, 95, 96, 116. *See also* substance abuse

Al-Kassim, Dina, 138n3

Allen, Chadwick, 147n21

Allen, Paula Gunn, 106, 109–11, 124

allies, 79

allotment: Allotment Period, 107, 142n1; General Allotment Act ("Dawes Act"), 142–3n4, 145n11; lands, 83–5, 90, 101–2, 116, 143n5, 144n6, 150n15; legal and legislative dispossession of allottees, 148n4; policies (United States), 83, 89, 91, 131–2n11, 143n5, 144n6, 145n11, 145–6n12, 146n17; practices, 91, 100, 107; White Earth Reservation and, 83, 100–1, 148n4, 149n10, 150n15

All-Pueblo Agency, 30

alternative dispute resolution processes, 86, 100

American Indian historical literature, 147n21

American Indian peoples: Clapp Amendment, land dispossession and, 144n6; competency determinations of, 89, 143n5, 144n6, 145n11; Congressional intent towards, 84, 86; citizenship,

slave, 93
Smith, Andrea, 129n13, 134n20
Smithsonian Institution,
   representation in *Last Standing
   Woman* (Winona LaDuke), 118, 120
Smulders, Sharon, 141n21
social discourse, 21, 34, 51, 75, 138n3
social isolation, 10, 14, 50, 53, 67–8,
   70–3, 116, 145–6n12
social justice, 135n26; activist
   engagement with, 119; clear cutting
   and, 118; criticism, 102; Indigenous,
   11; Indigenous community and,
   6, 8–9, 12–13, 47; Indigenous
   feminism and, 8, 12; Indigenous
   literature and, 101, 125; for
   Indigenous peoples, 99; Indigenous
   women and, 47, 49, 78; Indigenous
   women's writing and, 8–11, 15,
   125 (*see also* Indigenous women's
   writing); institutional commitment
   to, 56; law and literature and,
   6–7; legal, 9; liberal-democratic
   countries and, 63; literature and,
   5–8, 11, 15, 128n5; *Manypenny v.
   United States* and, 108; movements,
   5; reconfiguration as race relations,
   117; theorists, 7
social texts, 4, 12, 78
sons, 38, 50, 80, 90, 96
spiritual: agency and political
   agency, 45; aid, 46; blight, 23;
   community, 35, 115–16; and
   domestic isolation, 40; land
   and, 38, 99, 117, 120; legacy,
   41–2; order, 35–6, 38; power, 3,
   91; reclamation, 3–4; resistance, 9;
   traditions, 133n15; world, 25, 37,
   43–5, 137n34. *See also* Indigenous
   women: spiritual power of

Spivak, Gayatri, 88, 113, 124, 149n9
stalking, 79, 147n19
state, 15, 22, 31, 65; colonial
   legal policies of, 63; colonial
   practices of, 14, 72; control,
   69; demeaning treatment
   authorized by, 67; democratic
   aims of, 71; discrimination, 59;
   governmentality, 88; intrusions
   on Indigenous land, 10; liberal-
   democratic, 53, 63–4; mechanisms,
   57; nation, 15; out-adoption and,
   12, 52; transitional justice and,
   63–4, 71, 74; violence, 127n3; voice
   and, 71
State of Minnesota v. Zay Zah, 12,
   82–6, 89, 94, 100, 143n5, 144n7,
   145n8, 145–6n12, 148n4, 150n14
statute of limitations, 86
Steinem, Gloria, 148n6
Stevens, Eugene and Laurie, 83–4
stories: colonialism and, 97;
   community decolonization and,
   41–2; countering gender injustice,
   47–8; of female disposability, 29;
   Indigenous communities and,
   9, 26; Indigenous women and,
   6, 12, 24, 36, 41–6, 92, 96, 123;
   Indigenous women writers and,
   11, 122–3; law and, 11–12, 21,
   128n6; limits of legal reasoning
   and, 87; "memory-justice" and, 72;
   as microhistory, 91; origin, 29, 82;
   silencing in official, 6; traditional,
   106. *See also* legal narrative;
   narrative
storytelling, 9, 11–12, 24–6, 46,
   50, 53, 62, 77; Indigenous
   community regeneration and, 100;
   intergenerational, 116; knowledge,

social power, and, 122; law and, 125, 132n12
subaltern, 14, 124
subjectivity, 5, 29, 31, 33, 39; race and gender, 66
substance abuse, 65, 116–17. *See also* alcoholism
suicide, 53, 72, 76, 94–5, 96
Supreme Court of the American Indian Nations, 134n23
Swentzell, Rina, 134n19

Teitel, Ruti, 16
testimonial narrative, 65, 141n19
testimony, 54, 60–3, 77, 130n4, 132–3n14
Tharp, Julie, 142n2
theory and practice, relationship between, 103
Thomas, Brook, 6, 7, 86–7, 140n14, 146n15
Time Magazine, 104
Tobique Indian Reserve, 59
Tohe, Laura, 109–10
tradition, 14, 21, 23, 42, 44–6, 81, 93–4, 98, 133n15, 135n24, 137n36; of collective land tenure, 142–3n4; community, 26, 42, 132n12; cultural survival and, 130n3, 131n10; gynarchical, 109; Indigenous, 12, 14, 20, 109; Indigenous women's, 109–11; kinship, 9, 13; patriarchy and, 130n4, 131n10; stories and, 46; storytelling, 25–6, 132n12; traditionalism, 41, 44, 46; tribal, 14, 20, 22, 27–8, 81, 94; tribally specific literary, 106
traditional knowledge, 23, 25–6, 37, 89, 94. *See also* knowledge

transitional justice, 14–15, 51, 53, 55, 61–5, 71, 74–5, 78, 135n26, 138n3, 140n15. *See also* justice
transitional justice feminism, 14, 51, 63–4, 78
transnational Indigenous studies, 124
transnationalism, 15, 129n14; comparative transnational framework, 137–8n1; discourse, 141n19; oppositional framework, 99
trauma, 53, 58, 60
treaties, 81, 89, 114–16, 120, 136n29, 142–3n4, 145–6n12, 146n13, 147n21
trials, legal, 51, 60–2
tribal authority, 79–80, 131–2n11
tribal community, 27, 29, 31, 80–1, 131n10, 134n19, 142–3n4. *See also* Indigenous community
tribal constitutions, 23, 129–30n1
tribal courts, 79–81
tribal government, 47–8
tribal identity: colonial regulation and, 82, 84, 103–4, 107, 112, 144n6, 146n17; as "frozen in time," 9; Indigenous women and, 18, 21, 90, 111; normative male, 103; political, 131–2n11
tribal jurisdiction, 8, 19, 79–81, 134n23, 142n1
tribal land, 10, 12, 79–80, 142–3n4, 146n17; loss of, 89; protection of, 123; removal of Indigenous women from, 90; taxation of, 146n17. *See also* Indigenous land
tribal liberation, 48
tribal membership, 12, 14, 23, 29–32, 109, 123; gender discrimination and, 18, 20, 22, 26, 41, 124, 134n19; illegitimate children and, 23,